Stardust Monuments

INTERFACES
Studies in Visual Culture
Mark J. Williams & Adrian W. B. Randolph, *editors*
Dartmouth College

This series, sponsored by Dartmouth College Press, develops and promotes the study of visual culture from a variety of critical and methodological perspectives. Its impetus derives from the increasing importance of visual signs in everyday life, and from the rapid expansion of what are termed "new media." The broad cultural and social dynamics attendant to these developments present new challenges and opportunities across and within the disciplines. These have resulted in a transdisciplinary fascination with all things visual, from "high" to "low," and from esoteric to popular. This series brings together approaches to visual culture—broadly conceived—that assess these dynamics critically and that break new ground in understanding their effects and implications.

For a complete list of books that are available in the series, visit www.upne.com.

Nancy Anderson and Michael R. Dietrich, eds.,
The Educated Eye: Visual Culture and Pedagogy in the Life Sciences

Shannon Scott Clute and Richard L. Edwards,
The Maltese Touch of Evil: Film Noir and Potential Criticism

Alison Trope, *Stardust Monuments: The Saving and Selling of Hollywood*

Steve F. Anderson, *Technologies of History: Visual Media and the Eccentricity of the Past*

Dorothée Brill, *Shock and the Senseless in Dada and Fluxus*

Janine Mileaf, Please Touch: *Dada and Surrealist Objects after the Readymade*

J. Hoberman, *Bridge of Light: Yiddish Film between Two Worlds,*
updated and expanded edition

Erina Duganne, *The Self in Black and White:*
Race and Subjectivity in Postwar American Photography

Eric Gordon, *The Urban Spectator: American Concept-Cities from Kodak to Google*

Barbara Larson and Fae Brauer, eds., *The Art of Evolution:*
Darwin, Darwinisms, and Visual Culture

Stardust Monuments
The Saving and Selling of Hollywood

· A L I S O N   T R O P E ·

Dartmouth College Press · Hanover, New Hampshire

DARTMOUTH COLLEGE PRESS

An imprint of University Press of New England

www.upne.com

© 2011 Trustees of Dartmouth College

All rights reserved

Manufactured in the United States of America

Designed by Eric M. Brooks

Typeset in Albertina Pro and Verlag

by Integrated Publishing Solutions

University Press of New England is a member of the
Green Press Initiative. The paper used in this book meets
their minimum requirement for recycled paper.

For permission to reproduce any of the material in this book,
contact Permissions, University Press of New England, One Court
Street, Suite 250, Lebanon NH 03766; or visit www.upne.com

Library of Congress Cataloging-in-Publication Data

Trope, Alison.

Stardust monuments: the saving and selling of Hollywood / Alison Trope.

p. cm. — (Interfaces: studies in visual culture)

Includes bibliographical references and index.

ISBN 978-1-61168-045-4 (cloth: alk. paper) —

ISBN 978-1-61168-046-1 (pbk.: alk. paper) —

ISBN 978-1-61168-195-6 (ebook)

1. Motion picture industry—California—Los Angeles—History. 2. Hollywood
(Los Angeles, Calif.)—Description and travel. 3. Hollywood (Los Angeles, Calif.)—
History. 4. Popular culture—California—Los Angeles—History. I. Title.

PN1993.5.U65T68   2012

384'.80979494—dc23   2011040628

5 4 3 2 1

For my father

· S O R R E L L ·

• Contents •

Spotlight Hollywood

The Power of Place

In 1950, anthropologist Hortense Powdermaker published *Hollywood, the Dream Factory: An Anthropologist Looks at the Movie-Makers*, the result of a one-year field study surveying the inner workings, power dynamics, and social system that fueled Hollywood's film industry in the postwar period. In it, she observes, "Hollywood is a unique American phenomenon with a symbolism not limited to this country. It means many things to many people.... Rarely is it just a community where movies are made."[1]

Around the same time as Powdermaker published her anthropological survey, the Hollywood Chamber of Commerce produced a tourist brochure claiming, "Hollywood is . . . an entity which cannot be contained by street boundaries; for, in the fullest sense, Hollywood's boundaries are the world."[2]

Some forty years later, Michael Eisner, then chairman of Walt Disney Studios, commented on the allure of his corporation's latest venture—a Hollywood theme park called Disney-MGM Studios. For Eisner, the theme park represented "the Hollywood that never was and always will be."[3]

Anthropologist. Tourist guide. Industry heavyweight.

All offer remarkably similar descriptions of Hollywood, yet none concretely define it. Instead, all of them capture what it is not—a neighborhood and industry hub—while hovering around Hollywood's more symbolic and ineffable qualities. Hollywood is placeless, timeless, and emblematic, and if as Powdermaker suggests, "it means many things to many people," then Hollywood is also multifarious, if not contested.

Given the disjunction between Hollywood the geographic site and Hollywood the symbol, it remains difficult to articulate what Hollywood *really* is and means. Clearly, Hollywood is synonymous with Los Angeles, the American film industry, and its products. As far back as the late 1910s and 1920s, the Hollywood film industry surpassed the output of other national industries and was recognized widely as a powerful and global force that, to this day, both spurs competition and inspires imitators. While films historically constituted the primary product of Hollywood's industry, another kind of material presence simultaneously developed around the films — stars, and the Hollywood studios that produced them. Landmarks and tourist destinations, fan magazines and souvenirs, costumes and props, and box office figures and industry gossip also came to signify Hollywood and offered the opportunity for the public to see, consume, and memorialize the industry and its history.

In addition to the films, then, these concrete material artifacts played (and continue to play) a key role in shaping what Hollywood is and what it means. Indeed, they transform Hollywood as industry and material into an idea or narrative that, while potent and pervasive, often elides specificity. Hollywood operates as a brand; it becomes a name that stands in for and connotes a range of other experiences and symbols, many of which are subjective and ever changing.[4] Hollywood can embody the movies themselves, the experience of watching movies, the feelings tied up in the movies, the memories and nostalgia stirred by the movies, as well as the promise of success and personal fulfillment that can come from breaking into the movies.

As historian Robert Sklar argues in *Movie-Made America*, the name "Hollywood" historically described "a place, a people, and a state of mind."[5] Like Sklar, other writers have frequently discussed Hollywood's role in fabricating and forging cultural myths and stories about not only America but also its power to unveil a more all-encompassing, though hard to pinpoint, idea, dream, and consciousness. If Hollywood embodies a state of mind, it might also be characterized as a "feeling"—one that not only generates and perpetuates a mythology but also reconstitutes the geographical site and industry as a powerful cultural monument. The movies themselves—and the experiences and feelings they elicit—therefore play a central role in creating and maintaining a Hollywood "state of mind." These "feelings" operate by summoning both personal memories as well as prescribed and standardized associations: the gala premiere, the movie star, the "movie-struck girl," the "discovery" at Schwab's drugstore. Hollywood, in turn, comes to stand for glamour, celebrity, opportunity, fame and fortune, fantasy, magic, spectacle, and a love of being "at the movies."

Hollywood has a potent exchange value, therefore, that has symbolic and economic implications, both ripe for exploitation. Despite, or perhaps because of, Hollywood's intangible identity, there have been marked attempts throughout the past century to exploit this exchange value by concretizing the state of mind, dream, phenomenon, and feeling that it conjures. This book sheds light on the impulses that drive and breed Hollywood's monumentality, the various agendas and objects employed by those invested in it, and the contested terrain in which these ventures often unfold. Even as Hollywood's meanings and signifiers might be universally understood and recognized, Hollywood's exchange value also shifts in historical and site-specific contexts, whether nonprofit or for-profit, amateur or professional, and fan or consumer driven.

Individuals and institutions have wrestled with constructing, narrating, and visualizing Hollywood's story, facilitating the development of and often profiting from a Hollywood aura. The sites and products I discuss in the following chapters historicize and immortalize individuals, films, and institutions but, more broadly, sustain Hollywood as a cultural icon and symbol. In turn, many of the sites and products serve as monuments to Hollywood, authenticating it, fetishizing it, memorializing its past, and perpetuating its myths, aura, and mystique. The site-specific examples throughout this book not only tell Hollywood stories and histories; they communicate what Hollywood means, cultivate the "feeling" and "state of mind" around Hollywood, and secure what is fundamental to Hollywood's monumentality—its cultural hold and resonance.

The line between the personal experiences of Hollywood and those prescribed from the outside suggests a fundamental tension historically wrapped up in Hollywood's cultural identity. A Hollywood "state of mind" hovers uneasily between personal, subjective experiences and institutionally constructed messages. The feelings of individuals and the meanings generated by institutions are often indistinguishable and interchangeable so that a Hollywood "state of mind" inexorably reflects the sanctioned meanings constructed and circulated by the industry itself as well as its offshoots in both for-profit and nonprofit arenas. Such sanctioned meanings do not exist in a vacuum, nor are they always identical from one institution to the next.

Among the examples that follow, Hollywood often gets volleyed about within a complex network of cultural and corporate exhibition conventions and priorities, in-house rhetoric, public relations missions, and a volatile landscape of financial and political backing. A number of factors play a role, therefore, in the way different sites in different historical periods define Hollywood and articulate its cultural significance. Each institution uses its cultural authority and economic and political clout to construct potentially divergent, though often similar, views of Hollywood and its history. Each chapter charts the institutional and often personal motives behind these Hollywood monuments, exploring the intertwining and conflicting interests of founders, trustees, cultural elites, philanthropists, collectors, archivists, corporations, executives, and industry professionals, as well as audiences, fans, and cinephiles. Both cultural and corporate entities rely on these varied interests to sometimes collectively, and most often subjectively, define what is valuable. While some of the institutions discussed in this book are decidedly nonprofit, their need to fundraise, to exist alongside the for-profit world, and to exhibit or tell the story of an industrial medium necessarily implicates them in an economic system. Therefore, cultural and commercial values intertwine in the institutional dynamics of both nonprofit and for-profit institutions, each of which has a stake, implicitly or explicitly, in tying its identity to Hollywood.

The cultural-commercial overlap, evoked by monikers such as "the dream factory," necessarily complicates the concrete realization and representation of Hollywood and its history. The evocation of dreams and magic has tangible roots in the history of cinema—particularly in its ability to project and represent life on screen. At the same time, this magic roots itself more specifically in the self-generating and self-perpetuating spectacle attached to the Hollywood industry, and embodied in its promotion of stars, lavish lifestyles, and consumer desire. Much of the storytelling and mythmaking around Hollywood centers on the spectacle and monumental, often leaving its industrial and institutional politics to the margins. Rather than narrating and representing the full scope of Hollywood's social and political stories, many of these monuments center on fetishizing a commonly accepted vision, perpetuating Hollywood's symbolic power and influence.

While there is clearly not one vision, image, or meaning attached to Hollywood, it nonetheless can and has been easily encapsulated by what have become iconographic symbols. Since the early twentieth century, and coinciding with the growing recognition of Hollywood as a film industry capital, industry leaders as well as fringe figures trying to make their mark in Hollywood developed a set of highly visible Hollywood signs and stories to evoke, commemorate, and commercially promote Hollywood and its history. The most literal and famed sign, erected in 1923, was designed to draw attention to a new property development in the hills above Hollywood. The "Hollywoodland" sign, shortened to "Hollywood" in 1949, represents a key universal symbol of Hollywood, the place. Over the years, the sign, now a state landmark, has stood at the center of several heated campaigns to permanently safeguard the iconic white letters and the land surrounding it.[6]

Other signs of Hollywood also surfaced during this early period with the common goal of concretizing the Hollywood feeling in some tangible form or experience. In 1915, Carl Laemmle began offering a modest tour of his studio for twenty-five cents that included a behind-the-scenes look at a film in production. Sid Grauman proposed the building of a Hollywood wax museum backed by the industry in 1924, and while this project fell through due to lack of industry support, his Chinese theater and sidewalk of star hand and footprints opened in 1927 with great success. Grauman's chauffeur, Bud Delp, followed in his employer's footsteps and capitalized on his association with the stars by establishing Star Line Tours in 1935. Through the years, Grauman's Chinese Theatre, the Hollywood sign, Star Line Tours, and later the Hollywood "Walk of Fame" have maintained their symbolic significance as Hollywood signs, many of which have penetrated a global imagination. Thus, the mythological status of Hollywood has long-standing roots that have historically depended on the movie capital's international repute and ability to transcend time and space. While Hollywood represents a specific site and culture, its meaning also travels well beyond geographic boundaries, equally embodying Benedict Anderson's historical account of nationhood as "imagined community" and Marshall McLuhan's technological unification in the "global village." As I discuss in later chapters, many of these physical monuments and sites have been subsequently rearticulated in the televisual and digital realm, broadening their scope and allowing, for example, twenty-four-hour access to the Hollywood sign by way of Internet webcam (courtesy of and branded by Panasonic).

These enduring signs illustrate that watching movies embodies only one kind of Hollywood experience and only one breeding ground for its cultural worth. In what follows, I examine other signs and sites including museums, theme parks, retail stores, restaurants, classic movie cable channels, DVDs, and the Internet. On their own and in concert with one another, these sites serve historiographical functions. They write Hollywood's history, shedding light on its myriad and often contested identities as art, artifact, entertainment, social document, educational tool, memorabilia, merchandise, and object of cultural memory and history, while accentuating its cultural and historical value. These sites frame Hollywood as alternately pristine celluloid and coveted material artifact; they invoke an untouchable mystique while revealing the secrets of its backstage regions; they educate and elucidate while strategically engrossing the public in their brands; and they satisfy fans, connoisseurs, and consumers, while securing the corporate bottom line. In turn, this array of approaches offers insight into the politics of knowledge production within and between these institutions that write Hollywood's story.

The examination of such Hollywood sites is particularly topical at the beginning of the twenty-first century, given the technological developments in digital media and declining box office (as well as DVD) profits that have garnered news headlines and precipitated sweeping changes in continually fragmenting media landscapes. Along with the history that precedes them, such changes necessitate a careful consideration of the role ancillary arenas and markets can serve as monuments to Hollywood. The changes further attest to a continually transforming set of institutions and players engaged with and invested in Hollywood's monumentality.

The questions I raise in this book regarding the relationships between institutions and the objects they house stem to a large degree from museum studies, an academic field that arose alongside new historicist and poststructural debates in the 1980s. These modes of inquiry emphasize the constructed nature of exhibition and display, as well as the choices, valuation, and stories told alongside the agenda and politics of those who tell them. Just as the study of museums requires us to think about presentation, what we see, and how it came to be, this study poses similar questions about Hollywood. Cinema and media studies more recently tackled issues of exhibition in the 1990s and 2000s with general historical overviews such as Douglas Gomery's *Shared Pleasures*; microhistories that shed light on the business practices of small town exhibitors (such as by Gregory Waller and Kathryn Fuller); studies of niche exhibition arenas catering to art and avant-garde cinemas (such as by Barbara Wilinsky, David E. James, Haidee Wasson, and Peter Decherney); and analyses of the increasingly significant impact of home viewing on traditional theatrical exhibition (such as by Barbara Klinger and William Boddy).[7]

This book is different from those that have preceded it in two primary ways. First, it looks at Hollywood outside the confines of traditional theatrical distribution. Second, it takes on a wider range of sites from the high culture arena of the museum to the commercial realm of retail, theme parks, home entertainment, and the Internet. This book is both a work of historiography and a study of sites and products that perform history. The site-specific and historical assemblage I engage in the chapters that follow underscores the way each example, in its own way, has crafted a vision and story of Hollywood that is both distinct and universal. The broad terrain and historical scope reflects not only a changing exhibition landscape but, more importantly, a rethinking of Hollywood's symbolic and economic value in popular culture at large.

As I've already suggested, one of the key questions driving this project revolves around a need to concretize Hollywood's appeal and cultural significance. What does Hollywood mean to us? Why are such a broad range of players, including nonprofits and for-profits, amateurs and professionals, and fans and consumers, invested in it? What does it offer us? And how can we capture it, harness it, and preserve it, making it both monument and part of everyday life and experience? In many ways, Hollywood symbolically functions as a nation-state, instilling ideologies, even feelings, among its followers. As museum scholars such as Carol Duncan have noted, nations have used the state museum since the late eighteenth century as a site to train their citizens. Through artifacts and narratives laced with transparent visual symbols, values, cultural memories, and historical truths, the state museum rhetorically and powerfully communicates a communal bond among its citizenry.[8] In turn, the museum serves the nation-state by encouraging citizens to consume or "buy into" a particular national ideology.[9] Outside of the museum setting, Hollywood similarly constructs a sense of collective memory and ideological unity through its cultural output. Therefore, Hollywood potentially plays a role akin to the nation-state, providing images, stirring feelings, and relating stories that convey and ensure a sense of unity. Akin to the state museum, the sites examined through this book train and instruct Hollywood citizen-consumers.

While Hollywood channels a kind of national ideology, it also functions, as I've suggested, on a broader, more universal scale. In order to capture and concretize Hollywood's broad scope, the sites I examine throughout this book "anchor" Hollywood, as Spencer Crew and James Sims suggest, in "a usable past."[10] Movies, themselves, can serve as anchors, but they typically do not frame Hollywood as part of a larger or "usable" story. The museums, themed environments, home entertainment products, and Internet sites featured throughout the following chapters more readily serve as anchors in the construction of a "usable" Hollywood past as they harness key stories, images, and ideas of Hollywood and its history, often in a pedagogical context. These sites essentially train visitors and consumers, instructing them to revere a sanctioned Hollywood image and story, to adopt its long-standing mythos, to accept it as monument. The past carved out by these sites proves usable, then, in their breeding of emotional connections and memories bound to Hollywood. So, the sites serve as "backtellers," a label Tony Bennett applies to the museum, suggesting that the institution possesses a prophetic power or hindsight to frame visitors' experiences in such a way that they witness an otherwise inaccessible past.[11] For Bennett, the power of "backtelling" underlies the "narrative machinery" of the museum, immersing visitors in history and cultural memories.

This book explores both museums and commercial entities that commonly employ the above strategies to tell stories, frame histories, and propagate ideologies and myths about Hollywood. In telling Hollywood's story, many of the sites I discuss have faced and continue to face obstacles. If Hollywood embodies both ephemeral dreams and industrial pragmatism, then its story and image necessarily underscore a central tension. In the chapters that follow, each site faces a similar negotiation—a need to come to terms with the great divide between art and entertainment, culture and commerce, and elusive myths and tangible industrial goals and profits. The suggestion of a great divide, however simplistic, serves as a rhetorical subtext to this book and Hollywood history more broadly, manifesting itself in early debates about cinema's status as an art and attempts to legitimate the mass medium as something of cultural as well as commercial value.

The divide further manifests itself in various institutional struggles I highlight throughout this book. Indeed, the art-industry divide exists alongside debates over geographic locale, mission, public service, and organizational structure. This book is loosely divided into two parts, suggestive of these ideological rifts, while also challenging them by examining the myriad ways they can intertwine within and between different sites. The first part of the book (chapters 1 and 2) looks at the way nonprofits, mainly museums, preserve Hollywood and its history, saving it from loss. These sites largely operate according to missions that require reconciliation of Hollywood's industrial status within the context of enclaves and donors steeped in rarefied traditions of high culture. Many of these sites limit Hollywood's story by attempting to erase or downplay its commercial status while still struggling to find the ideal way to tell Hollywood's story through the most appropriate images and artifacts, whether celluloid or other facets of Hollywood's material culture. The second part of the book more specifically explores Hollywood's commercial side, looking at sites that encour-

age Hollywood reverence and consumption by eliciting nostalgia while foster-
ing a sense of privilege through promised access to Hollywood's backstage regions. These sites paradoxically mystify and demystify Hollywood, often struggling
to negotiate conflicting priorities among consumer pleasure and corporate
profit.

While not resolutely or neatly historical, the chapters broadly suggest a trajectory. The first chapter, "Essential Hollywood: Curating Motion Picture History in the Museum," covers the establishment of the Museum of Modern Art's
(MoMA) Film Library and the Cinémathèque Française in the 1930s, framing
their representations of Hollywood as models and testing grounds for other archives and museums outside of Hollywood. The second chapter, "The Great
Whatzit? Self-Service Meets Public Service in the Hollywood Museum," exam-
ines the institutional rhetoric and detailed plans to erect a major museum in
Hollywood. Focusing primarily on a venture that spanned the 1950s and 1960s
yet never materialized, this chapter also explores other local attempts that preceded and followed it. Moving away from the focus on museums, the third
chapter, "Out of Bounds: Remapping Hollywood as Themed Experience," centers on the 1980s and 1990s in its investigation of the phenomenon of Hollywood themed and branded environments, many of which substantiated and
profited from Hollywood history. Tackling a similar period and noting a similar
branding effort, the fourth chapter, "Hollywood in a Box: Channeling Hollywood through Home Entertainment," centers on home entertainment in the
form of classic cable movie channels and DVDs, while the fifth chapter, "Hand-
held Hollywood," takes the book from the 1990s to the present, contemplating
Hollywood's migration and notable presence in the digital arena. The loose historical narrative outlined in these chapters serves my general argument but
may also detract from it. While I can point to various institutions that have
worked to concretize Hollywood at given historical moments over the course
of the past century, it would be problematic to interpret the flow of chapters
from museum to the Internet as an evolutionary narrative from the physical to
the virtual. Instead, I see these institutional endeavors working in tandem as
Hollywood's history and mythology continue to hold cultural value, not to
mention profit potential.

Clearly, as the breadth of my study suggests, Hollywood cannot be tied to a
single practice, institution, or site; it has become, as Andreas Huyssen claims
with regard to the contemporary museum, a "key paradigm of contemporary
cultural activities."[12] Playing multiple social roles, the museum increasingly

acts as a surrogate for a variety of everyday public spaces including the classroom, retail store, restaurant, theme park or playground, tourist venue, meeting place, and party place, not to mention cinema exhibition place.[13] Hollywood similarly plays multiple roles and takes on different meanings and values in the range of sites explored in what follows. The ideas and stories told about Hollywood continue to fluctuate, particularly as the types of sites discussed throughout this book continue to open, close, remodel, and transform in both physical as well as virtual arenas.

Essential Hollywood

Curating Motion Picture History
in the Museum

In 1939, *March of Time* producer Louis de Rochemont set out to make a special installment of the newsreel series entitled "The Movies March On." The newsreel, which screened in over eight thousand theaters, centered on Hollywood history, the future of the motion picture, and the role of the Museum of Modern Art's (MoMA) Film Library in preserving the medium's past. As the *Motion Picture Herald* noted, this installment granted the motion picture the same weight as *The March of Time*'s typical subjects: domestic and international politics and unemployment.[1] Citing cinema as "not only an industry, but an art—the only art that man has developed since the ancient Greeks," "The Movies March On" efficiently echoed the Film Library's institutional rhetoric highlighting the motion picture's aesthetic value.[2]

While ostensibly focused on the Film Library, its mission, and preservation of "the full scope of the movies," "The Movies March On" more pointedly narrated a history of cinema that specifically focused on Hollywood films, stars, and behind-the-scenes players, detailing the industry's unique and significant role in the development and evolution of the art form. The newsreel quite literally portrayed Hollywood as a "dream factory," framing it as both "a community whose name alone is a magic word throughout the world" and an industrial and global powerhouse that produced 65 percent of the world's films with a capital investment of three billion dollars; employed thirty thousand workers in three hundred different trades and professions; and attended to the "ever changing tastes of . . . an army of 250 million moviegoers."[3] Calling each studio a veritable museum, based on the amassed collections of props, sets, and costumes, "The Movies March On" implicitly asked its audience to appreciate Hollywood for both its material labor and its artistic output.

The newsreel celebrated multiple facets of Hollywood: its historical and aesthetic contributions, its stars and entertainment value, and its industrial import. Tracing the chronological history of film from its so-called primitive roots to its standing as a sophisticated and serious work of art, "The Movies March On" began with sideshow curiosities and simple stories such as the Edison company's famed *May Irwin-John C. Rice Kiss* (1896) and *The Great Train Robbery* (1903). Scenes from other early silents including *The New York Hat* (1912), *The Fugitive* (1914), *Tillie's Punctured Romance* (1914), *A Night Out* (1915), *The Birth of a Nation* (1915), *A Fool There Was* (1915), and *Thais* (1917) illustrated the development of narrative storytelling and the first feature-length films. With the 1920s, the newsreel highlighted spectacles and genre films such as *The Four Horsemen of the Apocalypse* (1921), *Robin Hood* (1922), *The Covered Wagon* (1923), *The Big Parade* (1925), and *The Flesh and the Devil* (1926), as well as experiments in early sound with *The Jazz Singer* (1927) and *Steamboat Willie* (1928) and research tests from the Bell Laboratories and RCA. *All Quiet on the Western Front* (1930) and *The Life of Emil Zola* (1937) characterized a political turn in 1930s filmmaking, while scenes from the anticipated *Gone with the Wind*, due for release later in 1939, showcased the epic capabilities of the industry's most current productions. Catering to fans and the fantasies of the general public, the newsreel deliberately highlighted the star turns of popular historical Hollywood players such as Mary Pickford, Lionel Barrymore, Marie Dressler, Douglas Fairbanks Sr., Charlie Chaplin, Buster Keaton, Will Rogers, Theda Bara, Mack Sennett, Paul Muni, Al Jolson, and Rudolph Valentino. In its historical overview, "The Movies March On" also showed the inner workings of the Hollywood studios, with behind-the-scenes shots of industry executives at work behind their oversized desks, including William Fox, Jesse Lasky, Irving Thalberg, Samuel Goldwyn, Jack and Harry Warner, and Carl Laemmle, among others.

It seems fitting that *The March of Time*'s historical commemoration of motion pictures was released in 1939. Seen both in contemporary Hollywood and in retrospect as a golden year (annus mirabilis), 1939 saw the release of the aforementioned *Gone with the Wind* as well as several other films now considered Hollywood classics, including *The Wizard of Oz*, *Stagecoach*, *Mr. Smith Goes to Washington*, and *Wuthering Heights*. At this time of prolific and quality production by the Hollywood industry, the newsreel legitimated Hollywood in a different context—as art and historical artifact. The newsreel itself performed history, framing Hollywood's contemporary artistic and box office successes in a historical context, taking stock of Hollywood's past achievements, and implicitly making a teleological argument about motion picture evolution. The evolutionary narrative largely reflected what David Bordwell has called "the basic story."[4] Established as early as the 1910s and 1920s in periodicals and film societies, the basic story, according to Bordwell, was disseminated by MoMA's Film Library and remains commonplace in film curricula and textbooks. As evidenced in "The Movies March On," the "basic story" establishes a clear linear development of narrative film.

However, the pivotal and singular role Hollywood plays in *The March of Time*'s version of the "basic story" is revealing. "The Movies March On" narrates one history, a "basic" one perhaps, but certainly not the only one. It catered to a particular audience—American moviegoers—tapping into their weekly ritual of going to the pictures and their familiarity with and love of Hollywood movies and their stars. The starring role Hollywood plays in the "basic story" remains central to its own relevance as an industrial and cultural symbol in profit and nonprofit realms alike. The omission of other national cinemas in the newsreel's Hollywood-centric history captures an underlying tension in motion picture historiography and canon formation. Hollywood clearly plays a central role in the history of cinema writ large, yet Hollywood also proves a complicated object in the institutional writing of that history—especially outside the geographic borders of Hollywood and Los Angeles.

This chapter looks at a range of museums outside of Los Angeles that negotiate and attempt to reconcile Hollywood's place, meaning, and value in their own stories of cinema and its history. None of the institutions discussed in this chapter, including MoMA's Film Library, adhere to "The Movies March On" narrative in its unilateral and overt focus on Hollywood. Yet, they nonetheless grapple with Hollywood's relative significance in crafting respective narratives that situate Hollywood as a crucial component in larger stories about art, technology, national identity, social history, and media literacy. Depending on their missions, these institutions reflect different visions and mandates as they each tell their own version of the "basic" story, working in varying degrees to fulfill their founders' dreams, satisfy their donors tastes, and appeal to fans and tourists.

These institutions, in turn, not only construct a canon of films, deeming which ones merit preservation and exhibition; they also fundamentally engage in a kind of historiography. In developing their canons and stories of cinema, each institution strategically crafts its inclusion of Hollywood, befitting its own agenda and identity. The examples that follow employ overlapping approaches to narrating Hollywood's story, one centered on celluloid and the programming of Hollywood films and the other on the display of Hollywood artifacts and material culture. The relationship between these approaches and the choices a given institution makes about its writing of Hollywood history raise fundamental questions about the institutional production of knowledge and history. Both of these approaches fetishize select objects of Hollywood history and therefore share a preservationist ethos. However, they vary in the choice of Hollywood objects, display strategies, and storytelling style. These approaches therefore reflect different mandates that offer insight about support and sources of funding, location, and the proclivities and biases of those in positions of power.

In the mid-1930s, two institutions established themselves as cultural training grounds and institutional models for communicating Hollywood's history. MoMA's Film Library along with its French contemporary, the Cinémathèque Française, spawned prominent legacies in the United States and Europe as evidenced by the other examples detailed in this chapter and throughout this book. Even if other archives and museums did not directly follow their lead, MoMA's Film Library and the cinémathèque's inclusion of Hollywood became a facet of the story that others had to reckon with. By the 1930s and certainly into the 1940s, the story of cinema's history (and Hollywood's place in it) had essentially been set. These two sites therefore serve as significant points of departure to consider how other institutions and corporations follow suit or diverge from them in dealing with the politics of integrating Hollywood into the larger story and history of cinema. Their founding, programming activities, and in some cases, display of artifacts not only proved that Hollywood had meaning and value outside traditional, commercial theatrical exhibition but also showed how a particular venue, a museum or cinémathèque, under the tutelage of compelling and persuasive personalities, could play a key role in determining Hollywood's value and writing its history.

Hollywood, the High-Low Debate, and the Museum of Modern Art

The subtext of the "basic story," as told by MoMA's Film Library, revolved around a desire to legitimate film that dates back to the 1910s, when, as film historian Miriam Hansen suggests, "the cinema became a site of a struggle over cultural authority."[5] Hansen argues that the industry succeeded in the process of gentrification, in part, by "borrowing the cultural facade of a bourgeois public sphere," thereby instilling a class and cultural distinction otherwise compromised by cinema's status as mass leisure entertainment.[6] Some twenty years later, MoMA carried on this legitimation process by inculcating all types of cinema within the walls of an established and decidedly elite public sphere. The museum's powerful pedigree and philanthropic ties helped its Film Library secure and influence a new perception of film in America and, equally significant, a new perception of Hollywood both behind studio gates and around the world. The Film Library first and foremost identified film, including the products of Hollywood, as an art form. In her comprehensive account of the development of MoMA's Film Library, Haidee Wasson argues that the establishment of the Film Library signaled a more formal institutional acceptance of cinema and a clear articulation of not only the institution's cultural authority but the medium's as well.[7] As Wasson documents, the Film Library was entrusted with a two-part mandate: to collect and preserve the motion picture as an art form and to educate the public through a self-sustaining circulation system. "Saving films as valuable pieces of a lost history," she contends, "became the most common and general public explanation of the library's purpose."[8]

MoMA's first director, Alfred Barr, strategically worked to ensconce motion pictures in the museum by validating the medium's artistry within a modernist canon. The inclusion of Hollywood films proved problematic, however, requiring special vetting among divergent interests within the art world, academic circles, East Coast philanthropists, New York power brokers, and Hollywood's elite. It was hard enough to convince the trustees to include European film in the museum's hallowed halls, but Hollywood was particularly anathema to their elitist visions of art. Barr himself largely viewed Hollywood films as unimportant, vulgar, and trivial.[9] His views on modern art, in turn, spawned a rhetoric and methodology laden with contradiction.

On the one hand, Barr accepted and exhibited commercial and popular arts—finding beauty amidst the most divergent products on the assembly-line floor—a ball bearing, a vacuum cleaner, a doorknob, a Dictaphone machine, and so forth—as evidenced by his famed Machine Art Show of 1934. He extolled the merits of commercial culture, but not all of it, and struggled to find aesthetic value in the average Hollywood studio product. While such a Eurocentric stance placated some of MoMA's prickly and conservative board members, it clearly revealed a bias that not only marginalized an entire industry but also essentially nullified potential works of art simply based on the site of their production.[10]

Film librarian Iris Barry played a key role in changing what were often narrow and elitist perceptions of Hollywood within MoMA's ideologically conflicting spheres of art, entertainment, and business, thereby solving many of the problems that left Barr in an intellectual quagmire. In effect, Barry worked to erase an otherwise prevailing contradiction and mediated an impasse between two visions of film, two geographical regions, two demographics, and two taste cultures. She ingeniously reframed a traditionally hierarchical relationship between high and low culture, and East and West Coasts, as a symbiotic one. The Film Library offered Hollywood the symbolic values of class, cultural capital, and a sense of history, while Hollywood ostensibly provided the material basis and foundation of the library's identity and collection.

Barry's pivotal role in the library's early canon formation and historiography significantly impacted the way a range of nonprofit institutions and even corporate entities continue to classify, value, and narrate the history of the film medium and Hollywood's place in it. Indeed, Barry's inclusions and exclusions influenced not only film studies curricula but also more broadly the very nomenclature that has come to popularly encapsulate Hollywood's history — the Hollywood "classic."[11] As I discuss in later chapters, an array of institutions and products including Hollywood studios, niche cable channels, DVDs, and Internet sites (both fan generated and corporate) have harnessed the "classic" label as a sign of historical worth and legitimacy (not to mention profit).

When Barry first came to MoMA in 1932, after serving as film critic and cofounder of the London Film Society, she operated both within and against the aesthetic parameters set up by Barr and the museum's board. In keeping with Barr's approach to the museum at large, Barry, along with John Abbott, the library's first director (and her husband), adhered to the museum's aesthetic criteria and taste culture. Deviating from Barr, however, she and Abbott deliberately affected a balance between culture and commerce that not only included but also memorialized Hollywood.

Unlike Barr, therefore, Barry and Abbott proffered a more genuinely inclusive and decidedly heterogeneous vision of cinema and the Film Library's public. While Barr's canon consistently excluded American directors and films, Barry understood the need to create a cohesive argument about film's artistic status that aligned Hollywood with European and avant-garde cinema.[12] She specifically called attention to Hollywood's own "consciousness," claiming that the Hollywood industry was not only aware of but also frequently borrowed from the avant-garde and Europe:

> Moguls of moviedom and their minions, all of them ardent film fans, see most of the "avant-garde" and foreign pictures long before the students and amateurs of London and New York. They then continue to produce movies according to their own specifications, confident that these will and that the others would not please the great public.[13]

Here, Barry situated Hollywood in a double bind of sorts. On the one hand, the moguls and their minions were film fans, students, and even connoisseurs. On the other hand, they remained entertainers and businessmen with a narrow view, even ignorance, of their own audience. This description reveals not only Hollywood's double bind but also MoMA's and Barry's as well. Ensconcing Hollywood within the museum certainly secured its artistic stature, but what of its allure as entertainment? Barry carefully constructed an approach and historical narrative designed to allay the contradiction, appeasing the East Coast elite, many of whom were benefactors, and stroking the egos of Hollywood's filmmakers, while still reaching the general public. This approach not only reflected Barry's personal balance of her roles as professional librarian and self-proclaimed film fan; it marked her achievement as a curator and her finesse as an institutional power broker.

Early on, Barry understood Hollywood's symbolic and commercial value and established a rationale for its historical preservation. She was not ashamed to celebrate Hollywood and, according to MoMA trustee Eddie Warburg, "delighted in unstuffing the self-important and the pompous."[14] Well before her tenure at MoMA, in her book, *Let's Go to the Pictures* (1925), Barry pointed out that you don't "have to put on your best clothing to see Harold Lloyd fall off a skyscraper." In a *Vogue* review of *Stella Dallas* (1925), Barry later claimed, "The fact that it is above no one's head is a merit."[15] Barry's reviews spoke to a general public that, as Warburg suggested, "was pleasantly surprised to learn that their secret sin of having for so many years, sneaked off to go to the movies now was being dignified as a 'cultural experience.'"[16] Recognizing Barry's singular contributions and inimitable appreciation specifically for Hollywood, Arthur Knight commented years later,

> At a time when it was fashionable to admire a foreign film like Ekk's *Road to Life*, she preferred (and rightly) William Wellman's *Wild Boys of the*

Road—and added it to the Museum's collection. She felt (and rightly) that John Ford's *The Informer* was too self-consciously "artistic"; she preferred his "programmers," like *The Lost Patrol, The Prisoner of Shark Island,* and *Stagecoach.* She loved the early Disneys, the Astaire-Rogers musicals, the Jimmy Cagney gangsters, and anything with Garbo. [She] championed "difficult" films like Lang's *You Only Live Once* (and somewhat later) Nicholas Ray's *They Live By Night.*[17]

In validating commercially successful Hollywood films and filmmakers as well as the audience's experience, Barry promoted a decidedly populist brand of film appreciation, even fandom, that tapped into the pleasure and cultural memories associated with going to the movies.

Adhering to this populist approach, Barry consistently highlighted the motion picture's American roots. In 1934, she framed the medium's uniqueness in relation to its American origins: "First, it is the one medium of expression in which America has influenced the rest of the world. Second, it has a marked influence on contemporary life. And third, it is such a young art that we can study it first hand from its beginnings."[18] Barry stressed the significance of Hollywood and America, and the important role film had not only as art but also as a sociological and historical document. Such rhetoric certainly validated the inclusion of Hollywood film, but Barry and Abbott nonetheless still felt stymied. In their 1935 report funded by trustee and Hollywood producer John Hay Whitney, as well as the Rockefeller Foundation, Barry and Abbott asserted, "Makers of films and audiences alike should be enabled to formulate a constructively critical point of view, and to discriminate between what is valid and what is shoddy and corrupt." Barry and Abbott went on to offer a veiled critique of forces that impeded this approach: "There is a repressive influence exercised by censorship and by organizations critical of or even hostile to the current film; there is no constructive criticism and small opportunity for a well-grounded knowledge or a well-grounded judgment of film at its best."[19] Reading between the lines, Barry and Abbott justified the Film Library's inclusion of Hollywood film as a response to this "repressive influence." Barry and Abbott specifically cited the "disproportionate respect" given to foreign films by most film societies and the common "tendency to disregard or underestimate the domestic product." According to Abbott, "The idea seemed to have become prevalent that foreign films were art, but hardly the domestic film."[20]

Hollywood producer and Museum of Modern Art trustee John Hay Whitney (*seated*)
with other signatories at the founding of the Film Library (1935); *left to right*: John Abbott,
Iris Barry, A. Conger Goodyear, and Nelson Rockefeller. Courtesy of the Museum of
Modern Art Film Stills Collection.

In order to concretize their mission and inclusion of domestic films, Barry
and Abbott's report listed inaccessible film materials they hoped to acquire for
the library.[21] In framing these films as "inaccessible," the list underscored the
scarcity of these titles, thereby sanctioning the significance of the library's collection, preservation, and programming efforts. With this list, Barry and Abbott attached institutional worth to a particular set of films, inculcating them in
the library's burgeoning canon and, in the case of the American films, rehabili-
tating them as historical and artistic artifacts.[22]

Barry tested the efficacy of this canon in two cities at opposite ends of the
country during the months before and after the official opening of the library in
June 1935. Despite being on opposite coasts, both Hartford, Connecticut, and
Hollywood uniquely served as testing grounds for the library. Pinpointing
Hartford and Hollywood allowed Barry to target two extremes and two taste
cultures within American culture, one that lingered in the previous century's

emulation of European civilization and the other that followed its manifest destiny into the American frontier. The Hartford trip established what "counted" in the art world of East Coast collectors and philanthropists, while the Hollywood trip articulated both what counted in the popular American imagination and what Barry counted on in film donations.

In the fall of 1934, Barry organized her first public film series at the oldest public museum in the United States — Hartford's Wadsworth Atheneum. Her film choices for the Atheneum program overtly diverged from the Wadsworth's historic Eurocentric leanings, showing an allegiance to Hollywood film and a shared spotlight for Americans and Europeans alike. Barry included a substantial portion of Hollywood films such as *Way Down East* (1921), *Foolish Wives* (1921), *The Gold Rush* (1925), and Disney's Silly Symphony, *King Neptune* (1932), while her program notes set up what have since become well-worn conventions, framing the film medium according to national schools and genres. In addition, and in the tradition of the art museum and the celebration of the individual artist, she designed a few of her programs to feature the work of individual and specifically Hollywood director-artists such as D. W. Griffith, Charlie Chaplin, and Erich von Stroheim. In turn, these categories shaped the way the public, other institutions, and, as I discuss in later chapters, studios and corporations came to understand (and even sell) film history and Hollywood's place in it.

While the Hartford screening attested to the library's legitimacy and viability, the library desperately needed to acquire a sizable film collection in order to establish a permanent programming archive. During the library's first few months, Barry and other staff members hunted down and purchased a substantial amount of film previously deemed commercially valueless. The library not only conferred cultural, historical, and archival value on these films; by saving films from irreparable loss, the library also served the cause of history and tactically embedded itself in that history.

The hunt for film material necessarily took Barry and Abbott to film's commercial capital — Hollywood. Barry not only understood that Hollywood was central to film history on both a popular and critical level but also shrewdly saw in Hollywood a potentially vital ally for the Film Library. In the summer of 1935, at the urging of Whitney, Pickford, who had previously agreed to serve on the Film Library's advisory board, opened her famed Pickfair estate in order to solicit aid from Hollywood's major power brokers. As someone who worked both inside and outside Hollywood, Whitney played a key role in mediating between Hollywood and the museum. At the Pickfair event, Barry and Abbott spoke on behalf of the library, and at the close of the program, Pickford addressed her peers followed by remarks from industry insider and Motion Picture Producers and Distributors of America (MPPDA) president Will H. Hays.

It was the Film Library's focus on America, and film's "peculiarly American contribution to the arts," that likely swayed Hays to help the museum in its mission as well as its efforts to obtain films and exhibition rights. This initial goodwill between the industry and the Film Library was crucial. The industry needed assurance that the Film Library's exhibition activities would not interfere or compete in any way with its own for-profit operations. This alliance further satisfied Hays's role as goodwill ambassador for the industry and his mission to improve Hollywood's public image. As Barry and Abbott noted in the 1935 report, "A proper appreciation of this peculiarly native expression and a proper understanding of and pride in it on the part of intelligent movie-goers would ultimately influence the quality of films to be produced."[23]

At the same time, MPPDA correspondence and internal memos suggest that the Hollywood community still had misgivings in associating itself with "art." One internal document made the distinction clear: "It should be noted that Hollywood is properly touchy about the promotion of 'artiness' on the screen in which the critics' 'raves' are all for bizarre effects." In a more direct response to critical acclaim for European film, the memo continued, "too many examples already exist of the school of supercilious film criticism which sees the only evidence of progress in foreign films, the only glint of genius in foreign directors and producers."[24] The fact that Barry, in particular, celebrated a canon inclusive of, if not steeped in, Hollywood film necessarily eased the MPPDA's concerns. In response, Hays willingly and successfully mediated between the industry and the museum, thereby confirming the museum's (and the industry's) educational and cultural mission.

According to Barry, the Hollywood trip at first seemed to be a "wild goose chase." The Hollywood elite greeted the idea of film art and the need for preservation with skepticism and distrust. Corroborating the internal memos of the MPPDA, a 1935 *Washington Post* article astutely summed up the Hollywood bias: "It has long been a contention of producers that 'arty' pictures do not show up well in box office receipts. Exhibitors are fond of saying that you can lead movie audiences to a better picture, but you cannot make them like it."[25] As Barry confirmed years later about her trip, "No one there cared a button about 'old' films, not even his own last-but-one, but was solely concerned with his new film now in prospect."[26] Apparently, the Hollywood players could not get beyond film's commodity status. As Wasson suggests, "old films" were viewed as "objects of oddity, charity, or get-rich-quick schemes."[27]

Like their Eastern counterparts, therefore, the Hollywood crowd also needed to be convinced that film was art, or at least history on the verge of loss and therefore worth preserving. Unlike their Eastern counterparts, however, they needed to understand the difference between "arty" pictures and the library's expansive definition of film as art. Further, they needed to understand that this so-called racket known as a Film Library would not impinge on their reputations as entertainers or, more importantly, their box office receipts. In order to make these conceptual leaps, Hollywood stars and producers needed a skilled diplomat like Barry and a savvy ex–Wall Street businessman like Abbott who could "talk turkey" and make the library appear as friend not foe.[28]

The Pickfair reception included a program of films shown in the drawing room entitled "Motion Pictures of Yesterday and Today" and was reportedly attended by Hollywood elite, including Harold Lloyd, Walter Wanger, Jesse Lasky, Mervyn LeRoy, Merian C. Cooper, Mack Sennett, Ernst Lubitsch, Walt Disney, Samuel Goldwyn, Sol Lesser, and Harry Cohn, among others.[29] Barry's chronological film selection represented a short survey of American film history with many of the same titles that later appeared in "The Movies March On." The program pronounced its aim "to make known the work of the newly established Museum of Modern Art Film Library." However, Barry chose only selected work of the library. For obvious reasons, she deliberately excluded European films as well as American experimental films made outside the walls of the Hollywood studios. She sought to make her guests feel important, to make their films stand out as historical documents and reflections of American society and culture. "The Film Library was sold," according to Wasson, "as an enduring monument to industry accomplishment, a shrine to its preeminence, and a promise of its enduring position."[30]

In order to drive these points home, Barry gave a speech that began by stressing the library's commitment to quality film presentation and preservation. Barry's speech provided assurance that the library would not show films as "entertainment, but strictly as classroom and extra-curriculum courses under the auspices of universities, colleges and museums." She maintained, "They will be presented seriously, as part of the regular education in the history and appreciation of art."[31] Barry recognized the semantic value of the term "art appreciation," playing up its connection to education while downplaying its association with "artiness" and snobbery.

Barry further shrewdly, yet sincerely, appealed to industry leaders' consciences. Identifying herself as a fan, and distancing herself from the elitist tinge associated with the museum, she persuasively addressed the Hollywood crowd at Pickfair: "I know that many of you have felt a reluctance about permitting your older films to be seen again, because they represented only stages toward your present achievement . . . many of you feel that if those older films are shown again, people will laugh at them." Barry acknowledged their concerns but also pointed to the popular appeal of both old and new films. Framing herself as "one of the oldest fans in existence," she explained, "if there *is* laughter when the old films are shown as *we* plan to show them, it is and will be affectionate and understanding laughter, not derision—as indeed we here tonight have laughed and chuckled in affection."[32] In this speech, Barry presented the industry elite with two basic motives for supporting the Film Library. First, she charged the industry with a serious obligation to the public and to history writ large. At the same time, Barry pleaded for the individual members of the audience, the fans, who treasure the American films, finding in them a sense of nostalgia and pleasure.

Whether Barry's sales pitch to the industry that night succeeded in allaying Hollywood's fears and concerns remains unclear. In positioning herself as fan above critic, she surely stroked many egos. More importantly, however, Barry led her Hollywood audience to feel part of something larger, something more important than the movie business. Barry positioned these potential Hollywood donors as a part of American history, the American art scene, and even the American educational system. She also assured them that the Film Library would help ensure their place and stature in America's future through exhibition and preservation.[33]

Despite the well-attended gathering at Pickfair, the warm greetings and genuine interest shown by some of the guests, and the positive press coverage in Louella Parsons's column in the *Los Angeles Times*, Barry and Abbott never succeeded in meeting with Louis B. Mayer, considered at the time according to Barry "as *the* big shot of the business." Indeed, after wining and dining with various stars, directors, and producers during a six-week stay, and returning to New York reportedly with over one million feet of film, Barry later admitted that, despite formal letters of introduction from Whitney, she and Abbot "had not succeeded in putting our case to a single one of the heads of the big producer-distributor companies."[34] So, while several local and trade papers reported that MoMA's Hollywood acquisitions, including some of Mary Pickford,

Film Library reception at Pickfair (1935); *left to right*: Mrs. Samuel Goldwyn, John Abbott, Samuel Goldwyn, Mary Pickford, Jesse Lasky, Harold Lloyd, and Iris Barry. Courtesy of the Museum of Modern Art Film Stills Collection.

Thomas Ince, and Harold Lloyd's private collections amounted to the most film "ever to leave Hollywood at one time," it was far from what Barry and Abbott hoped for or expected. The interest was there, it seemed, but the control over copyright was not always clear.[35]

Eventually, Barry and Abbott learned that their cocktail party finessing with stars and directors was not enough. As Barry conceded after the fact, "We also had had to realize that the way into open water lay not through Hollywood, but through New York, where real control of the industry resided in the big corporations, the lawyers, the banks."[36] The question remained: would these corporate entities see the commercial value in Hollywood's history and the need for its preservation? With the help of Will Hays and the MPPDA, the Film Library leaders negotiated a formal agreement regarding duplication and exhibition rights in October 1935 that was signed by most of the major Hollywood companies. The agreement permitted the library to reprint negatives at its own expense and exhibit them for strictly educational and noncommercial purposes.

Meanwhile, the studios maintained full control over their products, reserving the right to withdraw them from the library's collection at any time (generally for commercial reissue or remake), while stipulating that exhibition must not compete with local theaters or screenings for the general public. Years later, Mary Lee Bandy framed this agreement as a milestone achievement for the library, noting, "It was a brilliant step, ensuring that the study of film history could be independent of commercial exploitation. For the first time, Hollywood producers would allow their films to be seen without charging a fee."[37]

By the end of 1935, the library had acquired films from many studios and former producers and stars. Aside from the support of Whitney, however, no cash donations ever came from Hollywood during the library's formative early years, a sobering fact that subsequently affected the establishment of film museums in Los Angeles as discussed in the following chapter.[38] While the Film Library successfully put Hollywood product on a cultural pedestal and relieved the industry of the literal burdens and expenses of preserving its own history, the industry did not monetarily show its appreciation for the Film Library. Without clear financial incentive, it proved difficult to convince Hollywood leaders of the value of direct monetary contributions. Over time, in fact, Barry redefined her earlier unerring respect for Hollywood and the generosity of its players. She began a 1946 article in *Hollywood Quarterly* with a blatant critique of Hollywood's narrow-mindedness: "Since the cobbler's children are always the worse shod, it is natural enough that Hollywood should be almost the last place in the world where the films of the past are esteemed seriously." Despite Bandy's praise of the agreement between studios and the library, the library clearly got the short end of the stick. Per the agreement, the library accrued all expenses in copying prints and preserving them. In effect, Hollywood donations were in name only. As Barry reported in 1946, "No gift money has ever been made, nor has even one $1,000 life membership ever been subscribed by anyone in films, and in ten years only two contributions have been received from any organization."[39]

Despite the lack of direct monetary support, the Hollywood industry officially recognized the Film Library's public service activities by granting it a Special Award for Distinctive Achievement during the 1938 Academy Awards ceremony. Cecil B. DeMille presented the certificate to gossip columnist Parsons, who accepted on behalf of the museum as its "Honorary Vice President." The academy, in particular, praised the library's "significant work in collecting films dating from 1895 to the present, and for the first time making available to the public the means of studying the historical and aesthetic development of the motion picture as one of the major arts."[40] This award and Parsons's role in accepting it publicly recognized the museum's mark on Hollywood and its legacy in other American institutions such as the George Eastman House and the Library of Congress as well as the plethora of film societies, art houses, and repertory theaters that infused a prominent postwar cinephile culture. The award further, and perhaps more importantly, called attention to the nascent symbiosis between the Film Library and Hollywood, underscoring the library's role in erecting a lasting memorial to Hollywood and its history.

The Cinémathèque Française and Europe's Liaison with Hollywood

The Film Library's relationship with Hollywood was not lost on those abroad, particularly the three other major film archives that opened in Berlin, London, and Paris from 1935 to 1936.[41] Comparing MoMA's Film Library to its 1930s European contemporaries, Henri Langlois, founder of the Cinémathèque Française, astutely surmised in 1936, "The Film Library leaves the German, English and Russian cinémathèques far behind," in large part because it "is officially recognized and supported by the firms of Hollywood."[42] While Langlois clearly oversimplifies this vision of easy money and Hollywood largesse, his sentiments nonetheless tap into the way in which Hollywood loomed large as a site that was consistently valued among the European archive community — for its role in history as well as its vaults of films.

European interest in Hollywood product and cultural cachet stems no doubt from Hollywood's industrial dominance beginning in the teens and the resultant impact its films continued to have on European audiences and filmmakers alike through the first half of the twentieth century.[43] Many historians have expounded upon the impact of Hollywood film on Europe. And Hollywood clearly plays a key role in the history of world cinema, whether the story is told from the point of view of an American institution such as MoMA or its European counterparts. It would be misleading and simplistic, however, to argue that all European institutions identically internalized this impact and told the same "basic story." Framing Hollywood in a story about styles, themes, and the international character of the film medium, some national archives have marginalized or even omitted Hollywood in an insular and often strategic focus on homegrown product and a desire to stake claim on cinema's origins or stylistic innovations. Still others, and the majority perhaps, have embraced the ci-némathèque model, working to negotiate and reconcile Hollywood's role in larger stories about cinema history and national identity.

Hollywood potentially presents a dilemma for national institutions invested in and charged with monumentalizing their own localized cinemas. These institutions must reckon with not only Hollywood's significant industrial role in the history of cinema but also the still potent attraction Hollywood's stars and films have for audiences across the world. For many cultural institutions, especially those that struggle with financing, Hollywood's inclusion often proves crucial because its symbolic power still attracts tourists, and therefore income, even well outside the geographical boundaries of Los Angeles. Indeed, over time, many European institutions have learned, like the Hollywood studios, that there is commercial value to be mined by exploiting Hollywood's symbolic value.

In the case of the cinémathèque, French films have historically worked in tandem with the international scope of its collection and the institution's framing of film history. Like Iris Barry, cinémathèque founder Henri Langlois was an avid film fan and could be a persuasive cultural diplomat. Unlike Barry, however, Langlois adhered to a different collection strategy, embracing all genres, styles, and national cinemas, collecting any film he could find, and refusing Barry's careful selection and molding of the Film Library canon.[44] Langlois further avoided (as much as possible) a common proclivity among many film archivists and budding institutions such as MoMA's Film Library to privilege the celluloid object. In his quest to amass a decidedly international and inclusive collection, Langlois crafted a mandate that included the preservation and exhibition of films as well as other materials related to the filmmaking process—scripts, posters, costumes, stills, equipment, set designs, and contracts.

Langlois envisioned a dual-purpose institution. On the one hand, he sought to establish an internationally reputable archive and public programming venue like MoMA's Film Library. At the same time, Langlois planned to erect a museum that would permanently exhibit cinema's material culture. Langlois's hybrid approach paired two modes of display: the viewing of films and the viewing of the material objects that contributed to their production. In turn, this approach reflected not only a rethinking of the relationship among films, directors, styles, and nations the world over but also a remapping of the bounds and objects of film's canon. For Langlois, celluloid alone did not constitute the cinema. As he stated in 1986, "Qu'on ne vienne pas nous dire que Cinémathèque et

Musée sont deux choses différentes" (One cannot say that the cinémathèque and the museum are two different things).[45] Watching a film provided merely one kind of experience. The material artifacts offered another—one that promised potential proximity to stars and filmmakers who were otherwise inaccessible. These objects could therefore satisfy both the fetishist-collector, whose love of film extended to tactile artifacts one could hold, and the outsider who yearned for a glimpse of the goings-on backstage, behind studio gates. For Langlois, who valued film as both art and historical artifact, only an eclectic array of films and other artifacts could fully capture the magic and complexity of the cinematic experience.

First and foremost, Langlois was a cinephile, and Hollywood featured prominently as an object of his affection. As biographer Richard Roud argues, Langlois's interest in Hollywood was "pioneering."[46] Early on, he acquired D. W. Griffith's *Intolerance* and *Way Down East*; the films of William S. Hart and Rex Ingram; and Erich von Stroheim's *Greed*. Langlois also championed many American films and filmmakers that had otherwise been neglected, most notably Howard Hawks. Aligning himself with Barry, he set up exchanges with the Film Library as early as 1936, and by 1938, exchanges among other archives in Great Britain, Germany, and Italy were formally established with the foundation of the International Federation of Film Archives (FIAF). The onset of World War II and the German occupation of Paris necessarily impeded the work of the cinémathèque and compromised the international exchange of films. However, by war's end, Langlois had saved many films, including hundreds of Hollywood prints, from being seized or destroyed by the Nazis. Roud claims that Langlois returned the films to the Hollywood film companies, and his good deed, according to legend, was rewarded in kind, with the Hollywood studios permitting the cinémathèque to screen their films without incurring fees.[47]

Following the war, the cinémathèque's public screenings resumed with great fanfare. Langlois's regular screenings at the Avenue de Messine during this period typically featured a range of films from different periods, nations, and genres, juxtaposing works by Hollywood filmmakers such as Erich von Stroheim, Raoul Walsh, and Alfred Hitchcock alongside the likes of Jean Renoir, Sergei Eisenstein, and Kenji Mizoguchi. Through such juxtapositions, Langlois created his own thematic and stylistic connections and historical narratives, which he shared with a growing cohort throughout the late 1940s and 1950s. At this time, the cinémathèque served as a well-documented meeting ground and site of inspiration for writers of the burgeoning *Cahiers du Cinéma* as well as filmmakers later associated with the "New Wave." His programs, particularly the historical retrospectives of American directors, not only offered lessons in film history but also led its audience to understand the significance of Hollywood's history, studio system, and stylistic conventions. The writers and filmmakers who attended the screenings during this period, sometimes three in one night, further buoyed Hollywood cinema in their writings and commentaries, marking its international influence and elevating even its most seemingly generic and derivative films.[48]

In the 1960s, with a move to a new location at the Palais de Chaillot and an increase in government support, Langlois continued to pay homage to classical Hollywood directors, films, and the studios themselves. Between 1964 and 1967 and with assistance of the Motion Picture Export Association of America, the cinémathèque commemorated the work of five key studios: Columbia Pictures, Warner Bros., MGM, Paramount, and Twentieth Century Fox. According to Glenn Myrent, the studios appreciated the honor, loaning Langlois prints "whenever he wanted them," often "leaving them on deposit" indefinitely.[49]

Hollywood also featured prominently in Langlois's exhibition of artifacts. Making it one of his lifetime goals to erect a permanent museum space to display his artifacts, Langlois began to collect publicity photos of stars, movie posters, film reels, magazines, and movie cameras when he was a young boy in the 1920s. He continued collecting through his teens, raiding editing rooms for outtakes and flea markets for discarded objects.[50] When the time came to officially establish the Cinémathèque Française, Langlois did not lose sight of this interest in collecting all things cinematic.

By 1948, at the Avenue de Messine, Langlois carved out an artifactual history of cinema on three floors of the nineteenth-century Parisian mansion. He used artifacts collected over more than two decades (some of which had been part of earlier temporary exhibits) to construct what many considered a revolutionary and fantastical exhibit space that allowed visitors to travel back to the birth of cinema.[51] Visits by Hollywood luminaries to the cinémathèque and some of its temporary artifact exhibits through the 1950s and 1960s helped legitimate Langlois's collection and exhibition efforts among the Hollywood community despite lingering rumors that he sought to monopolize film loans and acquisitions.[52]

During this same period, Langlois drew up plans for other sites where he could construct a more expansive and comprehensive exhibit and continue to program public screenings. In the early 1960s, Langlois outlined plans for a permanent museum space that he deliberately framed as an "international museum . . . not a museum of French cinema alone."[53] In 1972, Langlois succeeded in opening a permanent museum at the Palais de Chaillot with an exhibition entitled "Three-Quarters of a Century of World Cinema." This exhibit, with its epic narrative structure, became the model for the permanent installation and significantly influenced the Musée du Cinéma's successors in Germany, England, Italy, and the United States.

Like his film programs, Langlois's displays reflected the passion and pleasure of a fan more than the rigor of a traditional curator or the drive of a corporation banking on admissions fees. While the titles of his exhibitions suggested epic chronologies, he firmly worked against an encyclopedic rendering of cinema's history, interested instead in immersing visitors in themes and ideas. Langlois began his story of cinema well before the medium's recognized origins, rooting it in a fundamental human desire to visually capture and represent the world. This humanist perspective (paired with his goal of immersion) nullified to a large extent the penchant among traditional museums and archives to organize works according to national schools and styles. Indeed, Langlois often used his exhibits to foreground the similarities of cinemas across time and geographic space.

Myrent, who worked closely with Langlois as a tour guide at the musée, suggests that the site's exhibition design promoted a kind of cross-pollination, wherein "stylistic influences ricochet from one country to another."[54] Langlois was well known for his idiosyncratic style of mixing themes, time periods, and national cinemas, hanging a photo from Sergei Eisenstein's *Que Viva Mexico* beside Jeannette MacDonald's dress from *The Merry Widow*, for example.[55] Such idiosyncrasies fueled criticism by those who found his juxtapositions nonsensical, elitist, and needing textual explanation and exposition. As François Truffaut commented, "putting a Garbo costume next to the skull from *Psycho* was a gimmick for tourists."[56] Truffaut's criticism rejects Langlois's spiritual claims about the interconnectedness of cinema artifacts and history, and instead views Langlois's juxtaposition as not only personally but perhaps also economically motivated. Clearly Truffaut and other critics distinguished between an acceptable fetishism attached to celluloid while rejecting one tied to a costume or prop. Meanwhile, supporters contended that these exhibitions of artifacts attracted a wide audience and, in turn, encouraged the growth of film culture, which was reflected in attendance at the cinémathèque's daily alternative and historical screenings. It is difficult to determine which objects drew visitors and whether or not visitors made such distinctions between films and other objects. Still today, however, celluloid arguably still retains a privileged place within the context of museums and cinémathèques, even as the material artifacts possess an undeniable symbolic and economic value, particularly in the context of the memorabilia marketplace and popular culture.

Langlois's permanent exhibition of artifacts began with Chinese shadow puppets, and moved into their seventeenth- and eighteenth-century incarnations (théâtre optique, magic lanterns, and illuminated pantomimes). Roughly half of the museum established what has become a conventional narrative of precinema history. The other half of the museum explored the 1920s through the present and therefore more directly engaged Hollywood and its history. Langlois actively sought and received material donations from Walt Disney, King Vidor, Dudley Nichols, and Cecil B. DeMille; he also sought the original script for *Sunrise* as well as numerous costumes worn by the likes of Vivien Leigh, Douglas Fairbanks, Rudolph Valentino, and Mae West from Hollywood's Western Costume Company. Through the 1960s and early 1970s, in preparation for the opening of a permanent museum, Langlois and Lotte Eisner traveled numerous times to Hollywood.[57] They contacted many of Hollywood's famed directors, including Joseph Mankiewicz, Elia Kazan, Otto Preminger, Stanley Donen, John Ford, William Wyler, Clarence Brown, Nicholas Ray, Vincent Minnelli, John Cassavetes, Arthur Penn, Raoul Walsh, and Mervyn LeRoy in order to solicit donations or loans. It was also in May of this year that MGM's holdings were put on the auction block. In his absence, Langlois entrusted director Curtis Harrington to bid on behalf of the cinémathèque. Despite fierce competition from Debbie Reynolds (also seeking artifacts for her own museum), Harrington came away with several prized objects including costumes worn by Katharine Hepburn, Robert Taylor, Marilyn Monroe, Leslie Caron, Ingrid Bergman, Elizabeth Taylor, Greta Garbo, and Marlene Dietrich.[58]

The attention to Hollywood was notable and essential to the museum's story, even though the majority of exhibits, not surprisingly, focused on French cinema in great detail. The Hollywood artifacts offered a unique fetish or cult value, particularly in French culture. While the museum included other, primarily European, national cinemas (early Scandinavian cinema; German expressionist cinema; early talkies in Germany, the Soviet Union, and England; British wartime cinema; Italian neorealism; and Soviet postwar cinema) in its story, Hollywood remained second only to France in Langlois's narrative.[59] The museum's permanent exhibit featured Hollywood cinema in mul-

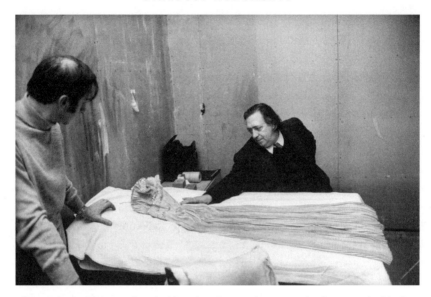

Cinémathèque Française founder Henri Langlois gently inspects the dress worn by Marilyn Monroe in 1960's *Let's Make Love*. Originally published in *Life* magazine, December 10, 1971. Photo by Enrico Sarsini. Courtesy of Time & Life Pictures/Getty Images.

tiple contexts, demonstrating both Hollywood's global reach as well as Langlois's clear devotion to the industry and its products. Langlois included posters, costumes, sketches, publicity materials, contracts, set designs, and photographs from hundreds of Hollywood films in extensive exhibits, some devoted specifically to or heavily featuring Hollywood (early American cinema, silent masterpieces, early talkies, animation, and the golden age of Hollywood) and others exploring the influence of other national cinemas and industries on Hollywood (German expressionism) as well as Hollywood's influence on the international scene (French New Wave). Hollywood demonstrated its appreciation of Langlois's inclusion and interest when it awarded him an honorary Oscar in 1974.

In many respects, Langlois deserved the Academy Award, for he represented a unique persona and held a prominent place in the history of national archives. While his uncompromising and broad embrace of Hollywood did not necessarily suit the missions and institutional mandates of all of his archival peers, Langlois's vision, like Barry's, served as a model that other archives took notice of and often took into account. Indeed, the programs at MoMA's Film Library and the Cinémathèque Française served (and continue to serve) as a template for archives and cinémathèques across the world, particularly in Europe and North America. European institutions established after the ciné-mathèque such as the Royal Film Archive in Brussels, the Nederlands Filmmu-seum, and the Munich Filmmuseum have adhered closely to its programming models.

In the case of museums that exhibit artifacts and cinemabilia (in addition to or in lieu of celluloid), many also follow the model established by Langlois, cel-ebrating the medium's historically sweeping and international scope, and prominently featuring Hollywood's role in that history. At the same time, Lan-glois's desire to build a museum proved more difficult for many institutions to emulate. Still today, the exhibition of material culture requires a more expan-sive (and therefore costly) exhibition space, and the objects themselves—if they have not been discarded, fallen into the hands of personal collectors, or become part of the display in commercial venues, like Planet Hollywood—often remain packed away in storage facilities. Given the choice, many institutions also opt to program films because celluloid widely remains culturally prized over other objects tied to film production.

Some institutions negotiated Hollywood's place with greater difficulty than others. While the French, and particularly the filmmakers associated with the French New Wave, idolized Hollywood, those associated with the New German Cinema were more cautious, if not suspicious of America's cultural influence and impact.[60] The famed line from Wim Wenders's film *American Friend*—"The Yanks have colonized our subconscious"—captures this sentiment. Working against a tide of cultural imperialism and in an attempt to stimulate national film production and cultural heritage after the war, individual state govern-ments in Germany subsidized many institutions dedicated to German film his-tory and the development of a localized industry.[61] Museums like those in Dus-seldorf and Potsdam used Hollywood specifically as a foil to examine the crossover and mutual influence on German cinema. These museums illustrate the influence of German filmmaking styles and émigrés (namely, Alfred Hitch-cock, Firtz Lang, Marlene Dietrich, and Michael Curtiz) on American cinema, while more implicitly making a statement about Hollywood's symbolic value in a global marketplace.[62]

In England, meanwhile, David Francis (who had formerly served as curator of the British Film Institute's [BFI] National Film Archive) and Leslie Hardcastle (former controller of the BFI's National Film Theatre) drafted more ambitious plans for a museum. Francis and Hardcastle's museum idea had the BFI's name and support behind it as well as the institution's fundraising know-how but was nevertheless conceived as a privately funded and self-supporting museum. Thanks to donations from private philanthropic sources outside the film and television industries, particularly J. Paul Getty Jr. and Hong Kong shipping magnate Sir Yue Kong Pau as well as Robert Stigwood and Garfield Weston, the museum's planners were able to raise the twelve million pounds for the building, research, and museum contents, and open the Museum of the Moving Image (MOMI) in 1988. Without any initial government subsidy, founders Francis and Hardcastle, like Langlois, likely had more creative leeway in their design and exhibition choices.

The museum, which the BFI closed in 1999 in a low-key announcement buried in a press release on another subject, offers another interesting case study of a national cinema's negotiation with Hollywood.[63] In MOMI's case, Hollywood not only played a key role in the story of cinema but also was strategically harnessed, especially in publicity materials, as a cultural icon that could attract prospective visitors. Francis and Hardcastle envisioned the three-thousand-square-meter space to "tell the whole story, technical, social and artistic, of the evolution of moving images."[64] MOMI's story was not quite as expansive or epic as proposed, skewing to focus on precinema and cinema history predating World War II. As a storyteller, MOMI, on the one hand, offered a fairly traditional chronological historical narrative. At the same time, however, the museum challenged traditional display conventions in order to bring history to life with re-created historical scenes and actors dressed in period costume. Employing strategies derived from mass leisure spaces, these re-creations revealed the influence of theme parks on MOMI's design and storytelling, and a desire (or need) to entertain visitors.

Publicity for the museum further highlighted its entertaining qualities. While press releases during the planning stage argued for an emphasis on British films and filmmakers (with the qualifier that "the overall vision of the cinema will be international"), the publicity materials designed for the public clearly highlighted Hollywood's significance.[65] Brochures from the 1990s featured iconic imagery from several Hollywood films including *Some Like It Hot*, *The Wizard of Oz*, *Top Hat*, *King Kong*, *The Bride of Frankenstein*, *Mary Poppins*, *Casablanca*, *City Lights*, *Raiders of the Lost Ark*, and *Star Wars*, while mentioning other Hollywood films (*Superman*, *Gremlins*, *Intolerance*, *The Jazz Singer*, and *Easy Rider*) and directors (Alfred Hitchcock, Charlie Chaplin, etc.) in the text. British and other European films took a backseat with limited references such as Georges

Brochure for London's now closed Museum of the Moving Image. The theme park–style Hollywood set puts you in the middle of a shootout at the Ramirez Saloon. Author's collection.

Méliès *A Trip to the Moon*; *The Third Man*; *Metropolis*; *Help*; *Howards End*; and Nick Park's *Wallace and Gromit* series. One brochure focuses on Hollywood specifically by exclusively highlighting two of the museum's re-created set pieces: a 1930s movie palace with marquee advertising for John Wayne and Claire Trevor in Walter Wanger's *Stagecoach* and the Hollywood soundstage, highlighting a section where visitors could pretend to audition for a film role.

MOMI's planners, or more likely the marketing team at the BFI, viewed Hollywood as not only historically relevant but also, and more importantly perhaps, a clear tourist draw. Hollywood appeared prominently in key areas of the museum, and as the *Hollywood Reporter* claimed, the exhibitions leaned "heavily on Hollywood's past and present."[66] The "Birth of Hollywood" celebrated the Los Angeles film capital, while sections on the "Silent Cinema" and "Chaplin" focused heavily on iconic stars and the origin of the star system. The "Coming of Sound" and "Animation" meanwhile featured iconic American studio successes in Warner Bros.' *Jazz Singer* and Disney's Mickey Mouse respectively. A tour of Hollywood's golden age stood out, however, as one of the largest and most elaborate exhibit areas in the entire three-floor museum space. A replica of the Paramount studio gate ushered visitors into a re-created Hollywood studio soundstage whereupon visitors encountered an enormous crane used by Hitchcock in his 1949 film *Under Capricorn*. The exhibit, which in many respects simulated a backlot studio tour, underscored the museum's ties to theme park attractions. The visitor gained access behind the scenes of a typical Hollywood studio production. Cameras, large studio lights, boom microphones, and scaffolding bordered a re-created Western saloon facade. On the outer edges of the room, more conventional museum displays further depicted the various roles and behind-the-scenes departments within Hollywood's studio system. Each department—costume, camera, art, casting, script, makeup, production, editing, publicity, and special effects—represented by a small display, re-created its original 1930s context and function through various artifacts, stills, and publicity materials. Encouraged to be a part of the fantasy experience, the visitor could play star by sitting in the dressing room makeup chair. In place of the mirror, the visitor could watch a video featuring the work of some of Hollywood's makeup artists. Rather than critically or historically examining Hollywood's universal popularity, MOMI's re-creation and seamless insertion of the visitor into the backstage arena largely upheld many of the assumptions and myths associated with celebrities and moviemaking.

Soon after MOMI closed, The Museo Nazionale del Cinema (MNC) opened in 2000 in the historic Mole Antonelliana monument in Torino, Italy. Like many other European institutions, the MNC similarly works to balance its largely Italian and European collection with Hollywood. The brainchild of Maria Adriana Prolo, a contemporary of Henri Langlois, the museum previously existed in many temporary incarnations as early as the 1940s. Prolo similarly worked throughout her life collecting films and artifacts with the goal of creating a museum of cinema. Like Langlois, Prolo also paid great attention to Hollywood cinema and stars in the museum's programming, particularly from the 1960s through the 1970s when, as Rinella Cere argues, Italians looked beyond their national borders in order to embrace the cosmopolitanism embodied by a growing international landscape. Cere frames this cosmopolitanism as a "passage," "reflective moment," or shift in Italian cinema that marked a move away from a more insular postwar phase.[67]

In balancing Prolo's renowned collection of early Italian cinema artifacts alongside a significant nod to Hollywood's global and symbolic presence, the current MNC in many ways exemplifies both sides of this passage—the homegrown Italian and the internationalism embodied by Hollywood. François Confino, a trained architect who specializes in museum exhibition as well as theme park design, conceived the entire design of the new museum.[68] Like the Musée du Cinéma, the MNC integrates an epic narrative history of cinema with a thematic approach. Confino used the Mole Antonelliana's central area to create "The Temple Hall," or a "temple of cinema," a space designated for cinema "worship." Branching out from the central Temple Hall, Confino chose themes that he considered emblematic of cinema history. Each elusive theme or cinematic style ("mirrors," "the absurd," "horror and the fantastic," "love and death," "animation," "experimental cinema," and "truth and falsehood") occupies one chapel surrounding the Temple Hall and features examples from a range of national cinemas, with a good portion representing Hollywood. Some 40 percent of the films exhibited in the chapels of the Temple Hall are, in fact, American productions, while the section of the museum focusing on the industry, "Cinema Machine," features nearly 60 percent Hollywood films.[69] The films are grouped in sections such as genres, studios, stars, makeup and special effects, production, editing, movement, sound, actors and casting, directors, lighting and photography, the script, the storyboard, and costumes. These sections largely function to break down the production process and its industrial structure.

Given Confino's background in theme parks, set design, and contemporary museum design, it is not surprising to see such Hollywood-dominant exhibits.

Humphrey Bogart and Ingrid Bergman in the famous farewell scene from *Casablanca*.
Exhibition at Museo Nazionale del Cinema, Torino, Italy. Author's collection.

Like many of the other sections of the museum, these exhibits reflect a deliberate and often seamless integration of the medium's artistic and commercial
sides. Unlike MoMA's Film Library, which tried to downplay Hollywood's commercial and industrial roots, many contemporary museums and programming
archives have embraced Hollywood's industrial side, eliding those historical
distinctions between industry and art. As the art-industry divide that so plagued
MoMA wanes, more pressing needs arise for cultural institutions to attract a
wide range of visitors and to make themselves relevant in the context of contemporary society. In the last two decades, museums have increasingly relied
on interactive displays and themed design (borrowed from theme parks and
expos) in order to make history "come to life." In telling their stories, museums
such as London's former MOMI and the MNC were designed not only to focus
on their extensive collection of precinematic and early cinematic artifacts but
also to strategically include sections devoted to industrial production (often
synonymous with Hollywood), promising visitors the potential to learn firsthand about "producing" media through hands-on interactive exhibits.

America's Museum of the Moving Image,
Hollywood, and Media Literacy

Such trends in interactive exhibits have similarly defined New York's Museum of the Moving Image (formerly the American Museum of the Moving Image) since its original opening in 1988, the same year as the London museum of the same name. These institutions both embraced the umbrella nomenclature "moving image" to describe an array of objects and so-called screen culture that could encompass both past and present and include film, television, and digital media. In its expansiveness, the term also necessarily reflects a purposeful ambiguity; it denies not only medium and temporal specificity but also site specificity.

In the case of New York's Museum of the Moving Image, the lack of specificity in nomenclature parallels the museum's broadly defined cultural mission to advance "the public understanding and appreciation of the art, history, technique, and technology of film, television, and digital media."[70] Over more than twenty years, the museum has integrated industry and art, history and the present, and Hollywood and international cinemas through exhibitions, screenings, and educational programs. The museum draws visitors and funders alike with two fundamentally related, though potentially contradictory, areas of focus—a behind-the-scenes interactive tour of the inner workings of the industry and a commitment to understanding that industry's content through media literacy. On both fronts, the museum, which has undergone two major renovations in less than twenty-five years, has tasked itself with maintaining cultural and technological currency.

The museum's founding stemmed from a desire among city planners in the 1970s to save the original Famous Players Lasky (later Paramount) Astoria studio complex built in 1920 as its East Coast facility. City planners and preservationists drove the project, with a great interest in developing a cultural attraction. While Hollywood history plays a key role in the museum's historical site as well as the story it tells of the moving image, initial plans centered more broadly on municipal politics and public service than resurrecting Hollywood history. Given its New York location, much of the museum's publicity materials tended to avoid directly citing Hollywood as a place or an industry, even though the institution depends on Hollywood for acquisitions, funds, and its primary story.[71] Understanding the film and television industries as well as the collaborative work of hundreds of artists and technicians necessitates unearthing the most powerful industry in the world, which to this day remains Hollywood. Therefore, the museum's attention to media industries and their behind-the-scenes activities reflect a substantial focus on Hollywood (or at least, Hollywood-driven industries).

In fact, the museum's exhibitions promote Hollywood adulation as much as they attempt to edify visitors of its production processes. Such adulation is not surprising, given the historical connection to Paramount, the makeup of its officers and board of trustees, and its sources of funding and acquisitions derived from Hollywood executives and families of Hollywood lineage.[72] At the same time, like many of its European counterparts, the museum needs to balance and reconcile its focus on Hollywood with its symbolic role as a municipal and national cultural institution, one that proudly claims status as "America's only museum of screen culture."

However implicit, the museum's engagement with media literacy debates helps to substantiate its national stature, civic engagement, and associated cultural legitimacy. Though the term "media literacy" does not appear in any of the museum's promotional materials, the institution's educational mission and curriculum-based activities are necessarily informed by contemporary debates on this subject and a desire to foster critical viewing. Unlike its predecessors, largely carved out of individual collections and personal passions, the New York museum therefore fits more squarely within a tradition of the public museum, whose mandate centers on social reform.[73] In fact, its social value largely hinges on its ability to educate—to reach the public and convey something useful about the history, meaning, and making of moving images. With its most recent renovation, the museum can now play host to sixty thousand students per year.[74] The museum promises to unearth the moving image's social impact and, in turn, perform a social function, training the public, especially children, how to read and decipher media images.

Focusing on the social significance of "moving images" writ large and on its national role allows the museum to legitimate itself while potentially downplaying its institutional fetishism and its focus on the commercial side of Hollywood, which remains the dominant focus of the museum's collections. The museum strategically frames the behind-the-scenes, "how-to" story as a tool that can help visitors read and understand media content. The museum thereby underscores its public service as an educational institution, a cultural institution, and a national landmark. Through the museum's public service rhetoric,

Hollywood history and the museum's industrial focus play a decidedly less significant role, despite the fact that Hollywood and the promise of learning about the inner workings of the industry undoubtedly remain a key attraction for visitors. The promise of education must be seen in conjunction with the promises of Hollywood access. Indeed, the term moving image arguably serves as a stand-in for "Hollywood," particularly as it gets explored in the core exhibit space of the museum.

The fifteen-thousand-square-foot core exhibition, "Behind the Screen," tells the institution's fundamental how-to story. Detailing the processes of media production, exhibition, and promotion, the exhibit features a range of exhibits including interactive displays as well as technology, costumes, posters, merchandise, and production design in order to outline the roles and responsibilities of industry professionals. Individual interactive stations dedicated to recording and editing image and sound allow visitors to explore the industry's use of light, color, and sound in moving image production, inscribing them in specific behind-the-scenes roles. Visitors learn how to loop lines of dialogue from actual film and television shows as if they were actors in an ADR (automated dialogue replacement) studio; they are invited to generate Foley sound effects and to insert chosen sound effects or scores to excerpts from well-known films such as Hitchcock's *Vertigo*. The special effects section illustrates industrial progress made in the shift from models, miniatures, and mattes to computer-generated imagery. Visitors are invited to stand in front of a blue screen backdrop, directly interact with a constructed environment, and further manipulate its foreground, middle ground, and background. Visitors can also see how a live baseball game is broadcast and instantaneously edited with feeds from twelve on-field cameras.

After these interactive exhibits were introduced following a 1996 renovation, the museum's director, Rochelle Slovin, pointed out, "We decided that we already lived in a world of simulations—at Disneyland, Universal Studios Tour, Sony Wonder Lab, and elsewhere—so it would be superfluous for us to recreate and romanticize. Our job is to interpret and to present the historical record as accurately as possible, using the actual objects wherever we can."[75] While it does not directly re-create historical periods in the vein of London's MOMI, New York's Museum of the Moving Image's interactive exhibits nevertheless manifest a theme park sensibility and influence that arguably does more to instigate play than to uphold historical records or educate visitors. Indeed, the gamelike approach in these interactive exhibits parallels activities found in con-

Teaching media literacy with interactivity at New York's Museum of the Moving Image.
Visitors to the museum's core exhibition "Behind the Screen" take turns dubbing their voices
into a famous film clip in the ADR (automated dialogue replacement) booth, an interactive
experience that re-creates how actors record their voices in postproduction.
Photo © Peter Aaron, http://www.esto.com/. Courtesy of Museum of the Moving Image.

temporary science centers and children's museums as well as theme park attractions and DVDs discussed in later chapters. With its focus on stars, popular
films, and television shows, and the memorabilia associated with them, the museum further reclaims the mystery and allure attached to Hollywood. The apparent contradiction here reflects the museum's struggle over its role as a moving image museum — one that must balance Hollywood spectacle with visitor
edification. In turn, the institution's struggle for balance reveals the complexity
in capturing such ephemeral media in a museum setting alongside a need to
reach audiences by wedding education and entertainment.

Each of the institutions discussed throughout this chapter faces a similar
struggle for balance. As I've argued, Hollywood plays a fundamental role in the
story of cinema and moving image media more generally; however, in telling
their stories, each site I've discussed has had to grapple with Hollywood's meaning in relation to the larger missions of their respective institutions and the pub-
lics they serve. Thus, the writing of the story requires mapping out Hollywood's

meaning in a broader frame that takes into account Hollywood's historical and symbolic significance as well as the stigmas associated with it, particularly as they relate to commercialism and global dominance. As seen through the eyes of these institutions, therefore, Hollywood embodies a vital, enticing, yet potentially fraught symbol that has had to be reconciled with each institution's own mandated values (and the cultural authorities that prescribe them). Whether the mission centers on art, nationhood, or education, Hollywood must be reframed and adapted. The Hollywood story, while "basic" in terms of content has therefore not always been simple to write.

The mid-1930s establishment of MoMA's Film Library and the Cinémathèque Française marked a significant historical turning point for the institutionalization of Hollywood outside of Los Angeles. Both sites' treatment of Hollywood served as models for other museums, programming venues, and cultural institutions that told stories of cinema while negotiating Hollywood's place in it. Hence, Hollywood took on different roles, depending on an institution's geographical location, historical founding, and internal politics. While it may seem that juggling Hollywood's role in the story of cinema would be easier in Hollywood during the heyday of the studio system, as I argue in the following chapter, even in Hollywood the place, Hollywood the symbol proves difficult to wrangle.

The Great Whatzit?
Self-Service Meets Public Service in the Hollywood Museum

On October 21, 1963, as many as seven thousand Los Angeles residents, fans, reporters, and celebrities gathered on a four-and-one-half-acre land parcel on Highland Boulevard across the street from the Hollywood Bowl. The festivities announced the official groundbreaking of the Hollywood Museum, a project that had been germinating since the mid-1950s. Rosalind Russell, presiding over the ceremony, opened by reading a congratulatory telegram sent by President Kennedy:

> Through the motion picture, television, radio and other recording media, modern technology has added a totally new and exciting dimension to the creative arts. The unique characteristics of these new art forms require special institutions. The new Hollywood Museum can make a major contribution to the educational and cultural resources of this country, and I should like to congratulate its sponsors on undertaking this challenging task.[1]

The telegram reflected the Kennedy administration's interest in promoting the arts on a national scale as well as a more general optimism surrounding the promises of global communication in the 1960s. Aligning the Hollywood Museum's mission alongside the nation's legitimated the institution based on its potential service to a broad-based public, while also ensconcing Hollywood within a larger imaginary community. By interweaving Hollywood culture with American culture, and corporate interests with national interests, the

A DREAM NEAR REALITY
Hollywood Museum—a Start

Front-page news coverage of thousands gathered for the groundbreaking of
the never realized Los Angeles County Hollywood Museum, October, 21, 1963.
Courtesy of the Academy of Motion Picture Arts and Sciences.

groundbreaking worked to reconstitute Hollywood, its products, and the idea
of film culture as symbols of civic import.

The laden significance of this presidential dedication, in turn, signaled an
important rhetorical moment. Like the Museum of Modern Art's (MoMA) Film
Library and other American institutions devoted to motion picture history, the
Hollywood Museum steeped itself in a rhetoric of public service. Unlike MoMA,
however, the Hollywood Museum planners, largely comprised of film industry
leaders, did not exclusively view their agenda in terms of disseminating art and
cultivating art appreciation—nor did they single out film's scientific and technological history. Rather, the Hollywood Museum planners sought to prove

that their museum could do more, be more, and symbolize more than its predecessors. In fact, the museum's very legitimacy depended on proving not only
that it had a responsibility to serve the public and nation at large but also that it
could be epic in its proportions. The museum was envisioned as *more* than an
art museum, *more* than a breeding ground for cinephilia, *more* than a collection
of memorabilia, and most importantly, perhaps, *more* than a monument to the
industry, films, stars, and myths that symbolized Hollywood.

Furthermore, the museum had to serve a broad spectrum of interests that
reflected a grand, multifaceted, and not always unified vision of Hollywood.
Fundamentally, the museum had to serve both the public and the Hollywood
industry. In addition to embodying national unity, the museum had to mark
itself as an industry shrine upholding the history of Hollywood films, stars, and
practitioners; an archive to house film and material culture; a science and technology showcase to promote experimentation and innovation; a tourist venue
to serve the scores of annual visitors to Los Angeles; a cultural attraction to
offer insight into the inner workings and mystique of Hollywood artifacts; and
a storyteller to perpetuate the mythology of Hollywood glamour. In the eyes of
the museum's planners and rhetoricians, Hollywood had to embody a tangible,
site-specific identity; a commercial business entity; an imaginary, universal
symbol; and, particularly as the 1960s approached, a utopian celebration of
burgeoning communications technology. The Hollywood Museum was therefore designed to serve multiple functions, negotiate multifarious identities, and
reconstitute traditional views of both the film object as well as film culture traditionally associated with celluloid, cinephilia, and a canon steeped in discourses of high art. The task of encapsulating all of the meanings connoted by
Hollywood and its history constituted a significant challenge, as evidenced by
this museum venture as well as those that preceded and followed it.

Since Hollywood's symbolic stature often stood (and continues to stand) at
odds with the everyday concrete political and social realities in Los Angeles,
problems gradually surfaced for these museum ventures. The contradictions
faced by the Hollywood Museum planners played themselves out within not
only the Hollywood studios and power brokers but also local and national political arenas. Competing visions of Hollywood and a Hollywood museum
made it difficult for the museum's planners to sustain a precarious and complicated balance among industry, civic, and national interests. Well after the
Hollywood Museum's papers and artifacts have passed into local Los Angeles

archives and lore, questions about a Hollywood museum in Los Angeles still linger. What would such a museum exhibit? Who would back it? How would such an institution navigate its relation to the film industry? How would it fit into the larger cultural landscape of Los Angeles? As competing visions of Hollywood continue to shape the way we see, perceive, and interpret larger questions about cinema's (and Hollywood's) symbolic power and as Hollywood players often remain reluctant to fund such projects, many of these questions remain unanswered.

Collecting Hollywood • Early Signs and Symbols

The county-supported Hollywood Museum venture of the 1950s and 1960s was not the first time Hollywood came together to try to preserve itself and build a museum devoted to its history. There had been previous, if lesser, attempts to establish a "movie museum" in Hollywood as early as the 1930s and by some accounts even earlier. These early exhibitions, like the later venture, similarly negotiated commercial and civic interests, suggesting the roots of more serious attempts to preserve, historicize, and immortalize Hollywood within the walls of a public museum and within the vein of public service. However, while the city and Hollywood factions shared certain interests in tourism, public exposure, and education, their values, interests, agendas, and public relations desires often significantly diverged.

Amateur historians, collectors, and industry pioneers outside of city politics and fiscal concerns initiated early attempts to construct an actual museum dedicated to Hollywood. In 1925, ten years before the establishment of MoMA's Film Library, a member of the Society of Motion Picture Engineers (SMPE) and avid collector of film equipment and paper materials named T. K. Peters envisioned a film museum that would "preserve to posterity many things now daily being lost to history."[2] Peters's exhibition designs offered insight into the behind-the-scenes workings of an industry and the artistry it produced. In January 1930, the SMPE sponsored an exhibit at the Los Angeles Museum in Exposition Park (now the county's natural history museum) loosely based on the plans drawn up by Peters and, in December of that same year, appointed a museum committee to gather the relics of motion picture history, subsequently choosing the Los Angeles Museum as its primary depository, thereby legitimating the significance of the geographical site to cinema's history and present-day production.[3]

The committee and the Los Angeles Museum exhibit played a key role in assigning cultural value to industry and technology, and implicitly validating its own work and its own organization. Los Angeles was not the only or obvious choice for the SMPE's exhibit; however, the Los Angeles Museum administrators took the exhibit under their wing, organizing their own Motion Picture Division and naming W. Earl Theissen honorary curator.[4] The Los Angeles Museum's exhibition, maintained by the county and expanded over the course of the 1930s, was designed to be educational as well as appeal to the interest of the contemporary motion picture fan. Offering one of the first complete behind-the-scenes illustrations of the function of various studio departments in the motion picture production process, and explicitly tying itself to Hollywood and its studio system, the Los Angeles Museum exhibit revealed an early interest in positioning Hollywood as a focal point in the history of motion picture apparatus.[5]

The focus on Hollywood and its industrial structure manifested an early attempt to frame cinema history in specifically American terms. Intimately involved with the everyday workings of Hollywood, the SMPE, unlike MoMA, had no qualms about honoring Hollywood in its exhibitions. Indeed, the SMPE members and the Los Angeles Museum were not beholden to an elitist institutional mission (or board of directors) steeped in traditions of high culture and, therefore, could more readily entertain the value of film's material culture as well as the everyday, even commercial, workings of the studios. In addition to highlighting the Hollywood production process, this exhibit also served a more implicit promotional purpose. Like other attempts to erect monumental Hollywood museums as well as Hollywood-based theme parks, this exhibit had the potential to mythologize Hollywood and perpetuate a mystique and allure increasingly associated with the site, its stars, studios, and films. Other attempts to build a museum in Hollywood and *about* Hollywood during the mid-1930s, which may have complemented this Los Angeles Museum exhibit, are poorly documented.[6]

Even a well-established film institution such as the Academy of Motion Picture Arts and Sciences experienced difficulty in establishing a motion picture museum. The academy's plans paralleled previous efforts to frame cinema's material culture in terms of science and technological innovation but also distinctly revealed an early attempt to legitimate cinema and situate Hollywood in a specifically national context by affiliating the academy with other nationally recognized institutions. The academy first considered building a museum as early as 1929–1930, coincident with its involvement in the University of Southern California (USC) motion picture course.[7] Donald Gledhill, the academy's executive secretary in 1940, again brought forth a plan to its board of governors to establish a "Motion Picture Historical Museum" with the expectation that it would "fulfill for motion pictures a function similar to the Chicago Museum of Science and Industry and the Franklin Institute in Philadelphia and other graphic expositions of American achievement."[8] Plans were drawn and a site proposed at the former Trocadero nightclub on Sunset Boulevard in Hollywood. This plan did not succeed, however, nor did the academy's other attempts during the 1940s and 1950s.

Nonetheless, the plans and displays for the 1940 project were likely the most concretely conceptualized of all the early museum proposals. The exhibition was designed to explore the role of the motion picture as the "world's book of knowledge," a guide to other times and places. Similar to later museums such as Henri Langlois's Musée du Cinéma and the Museum of the Moving Image in London, this academy project aimed to evoke the experience of viewing cinema through a time travel-inspired exhibition. The academy further endeavored to create interactive exhibits, soliciting visitor participation. Like the film medium itself, the academy's museum was meant to appeal to a mass audience, "indirectly and directly emphasizing and selling the conviction that motion pictures are packed with interest and entertainment." According to the plan, the museum could serve as a tourist attraction and convey industry hospitality, thereby partially compensating for the fact that visitors to Los Angeles could not be admitted to the studios. These plans manifested what became a necessary negotiation for future Hollywood museum endeavors—one that worked to balance popular interests, community interests, and industry self-interest as a strategy of legitimation.[9]

Like the later, more ambitious attempts at creating a Hollywood museum, and like Iris Barry's efforts at MoMA to straddle art and commerce, the academy's proposed exhibition was targeted at both the "intelligent and educational interests of the public" and "the lively personal curiosity about Hollywood which most people feel."[10] Unlike MoMA's Film Library with its emphasis on celluloid, however, the academy proposal along with the earlier exhibits at the Los Angeles Museum valued film artifacts and material culture (posters, scripts and other documents, technology, props, and costumes) that could be concretely displayed and reveal a behind-the-scenes picture of Hollywood production. The academy's proposal innocently suggested a juxtaposition that later became a challenge for other Hollywood museums—one that necessitated combining earlier pedagogically grounded film appreciation models with a more populist vision of Hollywood adulation and movie love.

During the 1950s, other museum plans extended the scope of earlier industry-sponsored exhibits, setting the stage for the later Hollywood Museum venture. While the aforementioned plans first surfaced within industry circles during the so-called golden age of Hollywood in the 1930s and 1940s, these later efforts to establish a Hollywood museum became more concentrated in the 1950s, when studios were otherwise losing their grasp on not only the American imagination but also the American pocketbook. Films such as *Sunset Boulevard* (1950) and *All About Eve* (1950) cynically and self-consciously commented on the superficiality of Hollywood and its star system. The postwar decline in movie attendance and the Paramount Consent Decree of 1948, which initiated the breakup and divestiture of the major Hollywood studios, further affected Hollywood as a site and a symbol.

The instability of this period likely influenced the desire to build a Hollywood museum, to memorialize and institutionalize Hollywood and its studios. The desire for such a museum at this historical juncture indeed symbolized a concrete and unified step toward self-preservation, survival, and even immortality, with the museum serving as a site for potential redefinition and revaluation. Individuals and studios alike clamored for a museum monument that promised to save their life's work, while celebrating and legitimating their contributions to not only the entertainment industry but also American culture at large. More than theatrically projected celluloid or archived material culture, a museum seemingly offered a priceless opportunity to erect a permanent architectural site that would concretely capture Hollywood imagery and symbolism.

In the mid-1950s, industry leaders unveiled a plan for a step-by-step illustration of the filmmaking process, touted as the "world's only complete exhibition of film production."[11] While seemingly focused solely on celebrating Hollywood unity and immortalizing the industry, the efforts to erect the "Motion Picture Exposition and Hall of Fame" also clearly demonstrated an interest in aligning Hollywood with the city of Los Angeles. A competitive and often divided film industry briefly came together under the exposition umbrella to collectively and possessively preserve their culture, history, and image of Hollywood. This industrywide effort to erect a motion picture museum, though unsuccessful, precipitated the more concrete and long-lasting development of the subsequent Hollywood Museum project.

Many industry leaders and organizations rallied around the exposition cause, which offered a concrete and permanent site, where the industry could publicly value itself and its work outside of theatrical exhibition and awards shows while benefiting the Motion Picture Relief Fund (MPRF). In addition to the studios, most of the professional and talent guilds supported the exposition project, as did the city of Los Angeles. The proposed civic-industry partnership represented a significant agreement on the part of both the city and industry in the 1950s, and preceded a more successful alliance between Los Angeles arts patron Dorothy Chandler and MCA's Lew Wasserman on behalf of the Music Center later that decade. The city's goal in joining forces with the industry was twofold. On the one hand, the city sought to legitimate itself and establish Los Angeles as a viable arts and cultural center, akin to New York. Further, the city's governing body viewed the Hollywood industry elite as a potential cache of philanthropic support. In promising to draw tourism (as many as 3.5 million annual visitors) and cultural attention to the city of Los Angeles, the Motion Picture Exposition seemed to counter a complex relationship between the industry and Los Angeles civic leaders that has been characterized as "benign distance."[12]

The exposition design revolved around traditional exhibition and artifact display as well as live demonstrations in which stars, directors, producers, and industry technicians would participate, offering access to the otherwise inaccessible and exclusive studio backlot and a close-up glimpse of Hollywood glamour. Such access would revive waning enthusiasm for the studios and Hollywood by acting as the industry's goodwill spokesperson. The exposition, like the subsequent Hollywood Museum venture, but unlike MoMA, centered on disseminating interest in Hollywood as a site and symbol rather than educating the American public in or promoting the value of the motion picture exclusively as an art form. In turn, the exposition plans revealed a shift in the conceptualization of film culture, away from a focus on cinephilia and art, and toward a more populist focus on film's entertainment value that acknowledged, if not celebrated, the public's fascination with stars and filmmaking.

Despite the promise of several fundraising events at various Hollywood studios including a kickoff campaign attended by two thousand studio employees on Paramount's backlot, the exposition planners did not accrue the requisite funds to launch the project. The industry leaders expected their own (especially their behind-the-scenes studio employees) to float the exposition, while the studio brass, according to *Daily Variety*, supposedly had a "greater responsibil-

ity" to help the exposition *after* its doors were open through executive and creative manpower.[13] The division set up between craftspeople and executives
belied the image of Hollywood camaraderie generated by exposition planners.
While Paramount's Y. Frank Freeman had been quoted in the March 16, 1955,
Daily Variety saying enthusiastically, "Where there is unity, it cannot fail," the
same paper five months later cited the industry's failure to work in concert as
the project's downfall. According to *Variety*, "Jealously, inertia, and eccentric
manifestations of blind personal pride entered early into the organization of
the Motion Picture Exposition, resulting in the project being shunted into blind
alleys from which it could not extricate itself."[14] This explanation seems likely,
for as the *New York Times* astutely surmised, if all the studios (and not only the
backlot personnel) had underwritten the entire cost of the exposition, it would
have only amounted to a fraction of the money each company spends annually
for general publicity.[15]

The exposition's failure no doubt reflected poorly on Hollywood, its public
relations enterprise, and its willingness to financially endorse such a public
project, exposing a veritable "black eye" on the industry, according to one local
paper.[16] The lack of unity and the fundraising fiasco also stood in stark contrast to
the philanthropic support MoMA enjoyed from New York's elite art patrons or
that of the Music Center on its own home turf and foreshadowed similar problems for the more ambitious Hollywood Museum venture. The exposition failure
disappointed many in the industry, and Hollywood was in danger of losing philanthropic support from within its own borders. Mary Pickford publicly criticized its failure as shortsighted and shameful. She was quoted in papers from
Memphis to Michigan threatening that, unless the industry soon took steps to
establish a museum, she would change her will and leave her multimillion dollar collection to three other cities that have cinema museums.[17] Pickford as well
as numerous fans, tourists, and industry employees nevertheless remained
loyal to Hollywood and continued to call for a revival of the museum project.[18]

It was not until John Anson Ford, one of five Los Angeles County Board of
Supervisors members, offered county support that a new and more ambitious
Hollywood museum project took hold. Ford first approached Pickford regarding the possibility of erecting a county museum devoted to motion pictures in
1956.[19] Ford had apparently informally discussed the educational possibilities of
such a project with other county leaders and in a letter to Pickford suggested
constructing such a museum as an adjunct to the Hollywood Bowl. With Pickford's support, the board of supervisors formed the Los Angeles County Mo-

tion Picture Committee comprised of prominent entertainment community members including Jack Warner, Walt Disney, Y. Frank Freeman, James Cagney, Gary Cooper, Samuel Goldwyn, James Stewart, Margaret Herrick of the academy, and Pickford herself.

The county, not the industry, spearheaded this initial effort, and, at its inception, the formation of a civic-industry partnership seemed promising. Potentially subduing the personal pride that had derailed the exposition four years earlier, any divisiveness between county and Hollywood factions remained invisible in May 1959 when the museum committee submitted its initial report to the board of supervisors, and the board subsequently authorized the building and operation of a museum in Hollywood to promote the entertainment industries. The county support was crucial to the museum project, both rhetorically and practically. Early on, the board of supervisors created a commission designated to supervise the nonprofit organization that would eventually manage the museum in addition to securing donations to finance the institution's initial backing. The establishment of this county commission signaled the county's official commitment to the project and the project's foundational costs. As an official body of the county, the commission had rights of condemnation and other legal powers typically reserved for government agencies. The board of supervisors' dedication indicated that the project had secured an important political and financial ally. With this legal leeway and the legitimacy and authority it offered, the Hollywood museum planners had the power and influence to act in ways that, without the county's help, would have been impossible.

Following Anson Ford, county supervisor Ernest Debs became the project's greatest champion. Debs first approached a veteran industry exhibitor, producer, executive, and avid collector, Sol Lesser, to head the museum commission.[20] Lesser soon learned that the county's leeway and privilege came with strings attached. He was immediately saddled with stipulations, ultimatums, and potential foes, especially in relation to the museum's location. The frequently oppositional supervisor, Kenneth Hahn, gave Lesser one year to finalize the location. More than a land battle, the location choice reflected the divisiveness between county and industry over partisan interests and, further, raised questions about the influential role of individual personalities and egos on both sides. The Hollywood Chamber of Commerce, Lesser, and many industry supporters pushed for a Hollywood location, and since the county owned much of the land across from the Bowl, this site seemed the most logical and cost-efficient choice.[21]

After much debate over the site, the county issued a mandate in September 1959, indicating that the location must fall within Hollywood's borders as a condition of county support. Hollywood's geographic location clearly still held symbolic weight, as did the iconic Hollywood Bowl, adjacent to which the commission accepted a county offer of a four-and-one-half-acre land parcel. With the acceptance of this ostensibly "free" land, there was no turning back for the industry or the county. From this point forward, then, the county found itself tied to Hollywood and to the film community's promise that the museum offered a needed service to the public. Meanwhile, the industry became inextricably tied to the county and the local political scene. The county support gave the museum project needed financial backing, a legal foothold in community and county politics, and further, provided the project and industry with a significant degree of clout and an illusion of unity. From the museum commission's first progress report in October 1959, Lesser stressed the united response of many major creative entities in Hollywood including the Motion Picture Association of America (MPAA); the academy; the Screen Producer's Guild; the screen actors, writers, and directors guilds; the Alliance of Television Film Producers; and the American Federation of Labor (AFL) Film Council. In effect, the report worked to erase the contradictions and potential conflicts brewing under the surface and assumed that the county's and Hollywood's goals were the same.

The Origins of a County Museum • Celebrating Communication and Community

In the late 1950s and early 1960s, the museum planners expanded their institutional scope to include the television, radio, and recording industries under the Hollywood rubric. While this inclusion no doubt reflected fundraising motives, it nonetheless suggested a rhetorical shift in the museum's institutional mission that situated Hollywood in a broader context of science, industry, and communications technology. This shift further paralleled contemporary trends in America's social and political scene tied to the space age and utopian visions of global communication. In turn, the museum offered to contribute to these ideals by not only exhibiting communications technology but also promising to promote progress in communication media. Like Langlois's Musée du Cinéma and its successors discussed in the previous chapter, the Hollywood Museum poised itself to tell an epic story, one that enveloped Hollywood within a larger discourse on human culture and communication.

When Lesser enthusiastically praised the "joined hands" of the industry, promising that, "after many years of frustration, a truly representative and permanent museum center is on the threshold of reality," he foreshadowed a unity through communication that would become the hallmark of the museum's rhetoric.[22] In keeping with the powerful collective symbolism of Hollywood, Lesser claimed in 1959 that the museum would command worldwide attention because, to millions, Hollywood was a seventh wonder of the world. The museum therefore had both concrete and elusive goals. On the one hand, it was envisioned as a site to promote tourism in Southern California and to raise funds to support the Motion Picture Country Home. At the same time, it promised to keep Hollywood's symbolic identity alive, particularly in the face of claims that "old Hollywood" was disappearing in the wake of the studio system's decline. Lesser concluded his report by pledging to make the museum "a shrine in keeping with the worldwide stature Hollywood has so creatively achieved and sustained in this exciting century."[23]

In order to link an industry-specific interest in preservation and immortality to broader civic and even global interests, the Hollywood Museum rhetoricians cleverly tied their project to Hollywood's place in Americana. They positioned Hollywood as a key player in an international industry as well as an important component of American lore—comparable in its status to the national parks and other national monuments and treasures such as New York's Radio City Music Hall. Such comparisons functioned to legitimate both the museum and the city of Los Angeles as a worthy breeding ground for American cultural life. This same report modeled the museum project on (and quoted from the brochure of) the British Film Institute (BFI) as a like venture that both catered to the national interest and established a permanent place in Britain's institutional community.

The question remained: how could the museum differentiate itself from the BFI and the Cinémathèque Française, and, in the United States, MoMA and the George Eastman House? Curator Arthur Knight, who came on board the Hollywood Museum venture in 1961 and had previously worked with Barry as an assistant curator at MoMA, contended, "Ours is a specifically *Hollywood* museum—which to me means that we are interested primarily in the American film in all its ramifications."[24] Echoing this unique and commemorative focus on America, California senator Thomas Kuchel reported to Congress on the museum's establishment in 1961 and stressed the institution's representation of the national interest as well as its devotion to the American public.

Kuchel called the film industry "uniquely American . . . ," while praising it for doing so much "to knit the world closer together."[25] He earnestly continued, "Mr. President, the people of the United States are proud of our great motion picture industry. They are proud of what Americans have done in the field of television. As I say, these are part and parcel of Americana."[26] Kuchel's salute to the institution and California citizens who devoted time and energy to preservation and filmmaking paralleled other congressional attempts to legitimate the medium as well as Hollywood.[27]

During the early 1960s, John F. Kennedy furthered the efforts of Kuchel and others in Congress to uphold film and television as a significant part of America's national identity. The Camelot era marked a major shift in government supervision of and respect for the arts. Kennedy's 1963 telegram, read at the museum groundbreaking, represented one gesture in a more comprehensive national plan to celebrate and support the arts and, further, to position film, television, and other modern media as legitimate and noteworthy art forms in their own right. This presidential support elevated the Hollywood Museum venture as an artistic institution and a national cause. In line with the civic-minded Kennedy age, the museum planners strategically and necessarily framed institutional goals around education, public service, and the future of communications technology. Whether or not these issues shaped the museum's original mission, their inclusion at this time marked an important negotiation with both civic and national arenas that increased the project's legitimacy and fundraising potential. And, while the Hollywood Museum undoubtedly benefited from the national support it received, the project faced difficulty in living up to the president's utopian ideals.[28]

Distinguishing the proposed museum from a mausoleum of artifacts, the commission proposed (and Kennedy later reiterated) the development of a new kind of institution and a new kind of public service, one that could potentially expand and redefine the traditional museum institution as well as Hollywood's place in the future of national and global communications. A 1961 document entitled "The Scope of the Hollywood Motion Picture and Television Museum, A Live Institution" conceptualized a space that would be a "live, dynamic, public institution."[29] The document opened by differentiating the proposed museum from other institutions: "Our museum is not a storage warehouse, a college, a school or a library. It is not a theater, a concert hall, a research laboratory or a publishing house. It is not a prospector, collector or industrial developer."[30] As a "live" institution, the museum offered not only a representation of

Imagining a "live" institution with behind-the-scenes access to Hollywood sound stages.
Courtesy of the Academy of Motion Picture Arts and Sciences.

artifacts and processes but also a more interactive picture of the media's function in the context of media culture, Hollywood culture, and American culture at large.

The Hollywood Museum's plans further echoed André Malraux's theoretical conception of a *musée imaginaire* or a "museum without walls"—a phrase that since invoked in 1947 had subsequently entered popular discourse.[31] The focus on liveness and dynamism also tapped into a popular conception of contemporary media and technological developments. "Live" implied being there, and for a museum, it could also imply going behind the scenes, bringing it to the visitor as it really was (or is), and making the museum visit experiential. The Hollywood Motion Picture and Television Museum took on the connotations of "liveness" already attached to television and television aesthetics in order to distinguish it from traditional museums and further to offer the visitor a sense of being part of the film and television production process. As early as the museum commission's October 1959 report, television was hailed as the newest "electronic miracle" of the twentieth century. Implicitly celebrating radio, recording, and film as technological miracles of the past, the report functioned to unite these communication media through a utopian discourse that further bolstered the stature and activity of the entertainment industry as a whole.

In addition to these television references, the connotations of "liveness" in the early 1960s were also tied to the burgeoning space race. The museum officials did not lose sight of this connection and, in fact, exploited it on the level of design and rhetoric.[32] Comparing early museum documents to those from the mid-1960s reveals a distinct shift in tone, paralleling a simultaneous cultural and national shift in attitudes toward media and technology spurred by a number of contemporary social changes. According to one late 1964 document, the "challenges of our 'Space Age' have made it incumbent on all of us, individually and collectively, to actively support the educational and curatorial needs of the local community and of the nation."[33] Within committee and planning circles, there was much discussion of the need to position the museum in relation to the space age and, further, to take into consideration the far greater and more sweeping needs of a free society.[34]

Around this same time, Marshall McLuhan published his famed treatise, *Understanding Media: The Extensions of Man*. While there is no evidence to suggest that McLuhan's writings directly influenced the museum planners, his work suggests ideas that were circulating within popular discourse at the same historical moment.[35] When the Hollywood Museum positioned the "lively arts of sight and sound" as influential on cultures all over the world, the museum, in turn, positioned Hollywood as the conduit and promoter of a global village, instigating communication and, in the most utopian vein, social change. One document from the early 1960s further justified the museum's global significance on the level of media education:

> The human problem is primarily a problem of communication. Since the beginning of time, man has striven to find new ways to express ideas and to exchange knowledge. Through the miracle of invention, communication has been extended by four modern media — cinema, radio, television and recording. Together with the printed word they are the most universal and accessible forms of education. To advance science and learning through these four magical media, the Hollywood museum is irrevocably dedicated.[36]

McLuahn's sweeping claims about humanity and modern civilization paralleled the museum's rhetoric. The museum presented itself as a universal teacher and a communicator in its own right. Situating itself in not only an American context but also a universal, timeless, and human one, the museum planners moved further and further away from the everyday workings of Hollywood as well as its emphasis on industry promotion and preservation.

Lesser's 1962 report stressed the museum's interest in science and the future, emphasizing that the history of communications technology was an unfinished one:

> The Museum will contain dramatic evidence of the past and present, with major concentration also on the future. It is to be an exposition which will compare favorably with the great museums of science and industry throughout the world. It will have a high standard of dynamic, live presentations which, because of the nature of the industries involved, will be novel, entertaining, exciting and educational.[37]

Lesser's exposition analogy is particularly significant. Through it, he invoked a specific tradition of world expositions as venues for the display of scientific and technological innovation. Specific mention of film, television, or Hollywood for that matter is conspicuously absent. Instead, Lesser framed the media within a larger paradigm of communications technologies. Lesser further argued that the museum's portrayal of the four communication technologies acted as an audiovisual contribution to humanity and human interaction, implicitly equal to, if not more significant than, their contribution on the level of entertainment. The museum showed a definitive interest, therefore, in media as both art and technology, and linked its exhibition of communications technology to a sense of national prosperity and, in turn, supremacy. In fact, as an earlier document suggested, the museum would "aid in maintaining the universal recognition of Hollywood, Los Angeles County as the World Capitol of the Motion Picture and Television Arts and Industries."[38]

Following this all-inclusive, worldwide approach to communications technology, the museum found itself straddling multiple spheres and interests. Initially conceived as a local film and television center devoted to Hollywood trade and tourism, the "Hollywood" museum was ultimately reconceived as an international center for audiovisual media and communications technology. The museum needed to not only link a "real" site to a collective symbol but also balance a sense of permanence and immortality with a national commitment to public service, a drive for progress and a celebration of liveness.

The museum's designers and rhetoricians engaged this balancing act with different degrees of success. From the outset, and as Lesser articulated at the groundbreaking, the museum would "have something for everybody . . . for the fan, tourist, student, expert, technician, artist, child." This comprehensive targeting of audience reflects a strategic approach to tourism and museum attendance. To succeed, the Hollywood Museum needed to carve out a new demographic, construct a new kind of exhibit space, and develop a new method to attract its visitors. At the same time, the museum needed to preserve Hollywood history and serve a traditional, expositional role. Upon examination, the architectural plans and interior conceptual drawings were meant to meet this two-pronged goal—the nebulous construction and maintenance of a Hollywood aura and the more practical display and preservation of historical and contemporary artifacts. On the one hand, the museum was designed to present conventional exhibits in a linear historical frame. On the other hand, its planners sought to construct a fantasyland evocative of a world's fair or Disneyland that could stir excitement about the future and potential of global communication.

The Hollywood Museum *Concept*

The Hollywood Museum's architecture and design echoed the rhetoric of liveness and the importance of communication articulated in the planning documents. The best and clearest permanent record of these designs appears in a public relations film released fall 1964. The finished film, originally titled *Concept* (and later titled *Hollywood in Focus*), was solicited by the museum's founder members and filmed at the Walt Disney Studios with Roy and Walt Disney's full cooperation.[39] The theme of communication technology promoting a bridge toward international harmony and a temporal bridge between past, present, and future served as a constant refrain throughout the film, clearly reflecting the optimism surrounding communications media in the early 1960s.

While much of the museum's rhetoric foregrounded Hollywood and American supremacy in the field of media communications, it simultaneously emphasized the potential for international unity and a collective consciousness through the converging networks of electronic communication—a popular expectation associated with communications technology, dating back to the nineteenth century.[40] Part of the museum's difficulty in balancing visions of Hollywood immortality and communications progress similarly rested in the difficulty of balancing Hollywood as both a national and transnational symbol. From the film's focus and the museum's plans, it is apparent that the museum developers had these competing and utopian impulses in mind.

Drawing by architect William Pereira of exterior facade of the proposed Los Angeles County Hollywood Museum set to welcome three million annually. October 20, 1963, program for groundbreaking. Courtesy of the Academy of Motion Picture Arts and Sciences.

The museum commission chose William Pereira, of the local architecture firm William L. Pereira and Associates, as its official architect as early as October 1959.[41] Maureen O'Hara unveiled drawings and models to the press at the museum's first convention held at the Disneyland Hotel in September 1961. Pereira essentially conceived the four-story central building as a large structural cage with platforms that would suspend and highlight the various technologies from concrete beams. The architectural shell was the only aspect of the structure meant to have permanence, while the rest was conceived to be "live" and therefore receptive to new inventions and developments in the four media's history. The design, therefore, stressed continuity, suggesting a flow through the space and an evolution of time and history that conformed to contemporary visions of communications technology.

The public would enter the museum by way of a naturalistic outdoor setting and a platform leading to a glass rotunda. Within the transparent rotunda, the four stories of the museum would be visible overhead. This entrance area would be dominated by huge dioramas reminiscent of a natural history museum, four

Drawing of proposed first level of the interior of the Los Angeles County Hollywood
Museum with live, closed-circuit television coverage of all events within the building.
October 20, 1963, program for groundbreaking. Courtesy of the Academy of
Motion Picture Arts and Sciences.

stories high, with scenes and events from history that had been depicted in
Hollywood films. In one part of the space, visitors would find themselves in the
midst of a "structural orchard of sprouting television screens." Even the description of this exhibit evoked liveness by conflating technology with nature.[42]
These closed-circuit television sets would show all of the "living" activities in
the museum so visitors could understand the interconnectedness of media in the
exhibition space. In order to avoid a cacophonous din and show off the latest in
communications technology, visitors would be given a small portable receiving
device that would enable them to tune in and listen to select televised events. Integrating such technological innovations, Pereira's plans echoed the museum's
promotional rhetoric in its deliberate intermingling of past, present, and future.

The film *Concept* offered the Hollywood community a concrete and familiar
way to contribute to the museum project. Similar public relations tributes to
the museum appeared on radio and television throughout the early 1960s.[43]
Concept opens with a stoic Edward G. Robinson thumbing through the pages of

a book in a traditional library setting. The staid library set offers the perfect contrast to the Hollywood Museum, which Robinson subsequently introduces as one of the most exciting showplaces in the world. According to Robinson (and the scripted museum rhetoric), the museum represented a "living memorial" to the industries, inventors, developers, and creative artists of the four communications media. Through its exhibition of the four media's present influences, future advancements, and past accomplishments, the museum would, according to Robinson, "help man communicate with man." The film argued, then, that the museum, like the media it exhibited, could serve as a conduit for human communication.

The film promoted the open communication channels between industries by inviting stars from each to narrate including Dinah Shore, Gregory Peck, Bing Crosby, Gloria Swanson, Ed Wynn, Lucille Ball, Bette Davis, *Amos 'n' Andy*'s Freeman Gosden and Charles Correll, Edgar Bergen and Charlie McCarthy, Doris Day, Mickey Mouse, Bob Hope, Nat King Cole, Jack Benny, Mary Pickford, and Art Linkletter. Each of these stars was chosen for their involvement in the museum project, their American character, and their international iconic status. Each of them also symbolically represented Hollywood.

Robinson began the guided tour of the museum with an explanation of the exterior architectural model and facade. The museum plan consisted of three main parts: the four-level pavilion, the educational tower, and two sound stages. Following Robinson's introduction, each media star featured in the film walked the viewer through a series of ninety-two animated drawings of various parts of the main pavilion.[44] After the reception hall, visitors would enter a so-called Synthesis Show. Standing in a giant elevator with rear-screen projection, visitors would be "transported" back in time. In an effort to uphold the museum's value and legitimacy beyond entertainment, the public relations film foregrounded the educational role of such historical re-creation, only secondarily emphasizing the power of illusion achieved by the technical feats of art directors, special and sound effects engineers, and other craftspeople.

The museum's "international" restaurant was designed to continue this motif of historical re-creation. Sets donated by various motion picture and television companies punctuated by music and sound effects would reconstruct a given locale and time period. The museum's preliminary plans included King Arthur's court, a Parisian sidewalk café, the mysterious Casbah, and *The Sound of Music* ballroom. Another part of the restaurant was slated to re-create a historical Hollywood landmark, the Hollywood Canteen, providing the visitor

Drawing for restaurant at the proposed Los Angeles County Hollywood Museum. A precursor to Planet Hollywood, the restaurant was designed to feature a King Arthur Room with sets from actual motion pictures. October 20, 1963, program for groundbreaking. Courtesy of the Academy of Motion Picture Arts and Sciences.

with actual canteen performances through rear-screen projection. These re-creations were designed to create an alternative media experience by putting visitors into the movie set and making them feel part of the production process.

Aside from re-creating the past, the museum also invoked the future by playing on space age ideals. The "Discovery Ramp"—an exhibit equaling two city blocks—would wind through all four museum levels and include forty specially crafted theaters allowing visitors to chronologically experience the major developments of the four media industries. The ramp's design followed a fairly conventional historical trajectory—a decidedly American narrative of technological innovation, progress, and evolution, centered on American inventors, American corporations, and Hollywood studios. The film excerpts playing on individual screens throughout the ramp were designed to construct a traditional historical canon and trajectory of "firsts"—situating the discovery of communication technology and arts firmly within America, if not Hollywood. The final level of the discovery ramp would display the "most modern

Drawing of a proposed sound exhibit at the Los Angeles County Hollywood Museum.
Voices and sounds travel through a shapeless tunnel as visitors sit on individual,
nondirectional sound devices. October 20, 1963, program for groundbreaking.
Courtesy of the Academy of Motion Picture Arts and Sciences.

developments of space communications." The overall movement from the
lower levels of the museum to the highest suggested historical evolution and
scientific progress — one that was rooted in yet exceeded the boundaries of
Hollywood and entertainment media in order to celebrate the au courant technology of the space race.

In addition to these historical discoveries, the museum plans included three
experience-based "shows" designed to explain connections between technology (sound, image, and special effects) and audience reception. According to the
museum's promotional material, "Each viewing experience will transport the
spectator from his own natural point of view into the art director's and camera-
man's perspective." These exhibitions, like others tied to specific behind-the-
scenes jobs in which visitors could "meet" a craftsperson via life-size projection
or view magical media transformations in makeup and wardrobe, clearly celebrated technological and craft-based ingenuity. Like more contemporary mov-

ing image museums and science centers as well as movie theme parks, they also foregrounded the visitor's access and potential participation in the production process. The museum's intricate and moveable designs themselves mimicked the spectacle and attraction of contemporary media, supporting but also complicating the museum's utopian drive to promote universal communication. While such exhibits were intended to explain a process of communication, the museum's design seemed to cater more to entertainment than education.

In addition to these interactive showplaces, the visitor could view historical and canonical programming in one of two theaters, accessible through the facade of a re-created nickelodeon. These theaters could also serve as concert hall, theatrical venue, and audience research site. In one of the theaters, banks of television screens could be lowered, featuring closed-circuit access to different studio backlots. Live demonstrations of film and television techniques and access to an advertising conference could fulfill the museum's educational mission. In offering up its visitors as test cases in many of these exhibits, the museum elided potential conflicts between its commercial and educational aims, assuming the two could easily intermingle.

At the end of *Concept,* radio personality and daytime variety host Art Linkletter commented on the museum's philosophy of constant change and the need to keep pace with ever-transforming media. The film closes on a giant globe, representing the earth, and Linkletter pleads for the interest, ideas, and participation of all (especially donors) to help mark a great force in the development of the audiovisual arts and sciences. Like many of Lesser's museum reports, the film concludes on a humanistic note, claiming that the four communications media circle the world, partaking in a great human adventure. The film upheld the four media for their service to education, government, industry, and "all purposes of man." The final shot of the film shows an overhead view of the museum with an expansive urban backdrop. While this image visually broadened the museum's geographic context and goals, situating Hollywood and Los Angeles in a global context, Robinson's final voice-over extended the *cultural* scope of the museum, presenting it as a service for the betterment of all mankind.

Divided We Fall • Competitors, Critics, Crusaders, and Curmudgeons

Despite all of the positive feedback and promises made during the museum's planning phase—the initial 1960 financial survey; the legislative approvals and granted permits; Lesser's receipt of a Humanitarian Academy Award in 1961 for his museum activity; the significant attention and industry leaders assembled for the 1963 groundbreaking; and the supposed successful reception of *Concept* within industry circles—a confluence of factors led to the museum's eventual downfall, many of which can be traced to the museum's initial planning stages, if not earlier. By the mid-1960s, the ideological differences among civic agencies, the public, and the Hollywood industry reached a breaking point and swiftly eclipsed the museum planners' rhetoric about communication and unity.

Aside from the difficulties that lay in trying to tackle and contain so many meanings in a single institution, the venture was plagued by negative perceptions of Hollywood and the project among the county board and the public. The civic-industry partnership dissolved, and with its dissolution, no single body could sustain the museum plans. Historically, Los Angeles has been criticized for a long-divided and ineffective civic leadership. The wedding of civic interests and Hollywood values has often proved ineffective and problematic. Since the 1920s, when the entertainment industry made its mark in Los Angeles, a notable schism developed between Hollywood and the city's founding fathers—the downtown-centered corporate elite and local politicians. Resentment toward the entertainment industry, often negatively identified as Jewish, liberal, communist sympathizing and nouveau riche, played itself out in the House Un-American Activities Committee (HUAC) trials, Hollywood blacklisting, and persistent calls for censorship that lingered through the end of the 1950s and into the 1960s.[45] Most of the Hollywood Museum's problems, indeed, were rooted in this schism and played themselves out in a battle between public and private values and interests.

The county board of supervisors and the Hollywood Museum planners disputed the museum's mission and the significance of its public service role. In addition to internal skirmishes between county and museum planners, certain external factors, which could not have been foreseen, also affected the perception of the museum in the eyes of county board members and the public. During the museum's lengthy planning phase, developments in the Los Angeles tourist industry indirectly impacted the museum's prospects and the uniqueness of its exhibition plans.

In 1962, MCA, then a talent agency headed by Lew Wasserman, proposed a museum at their Revue Studios. At the time, County Supervisor Debs accused MCA of seeking to put a major roadblock in the way of industry plans for a Hollywood Museum. Wasserman steadfastly denied these plans. However, when the project was further exposed in *Daily Variety*, Wasserman abandoned it, undoubtedly seeing the political dilemma in divesting from the industry unity associated with the museum.[46] In the meantime, MCA continued to run tours of its Revue Studios.[47] While nothing ever came of MCA's proposed museum, a few months later, in May 1962, the $1.5 million Movieland Wax Museum opened in Buena Park near Disneyland and Knott's Berry Farm. Though not directly competing with the Hollywood Museum because of its location and kitsch commemoration of Hollywood history, the wax museum nevertheless profited from a built-in tourist population, not to mention its Hollywood ties. Conspicuously echoing the Hollywood Museum's origins, Mary Pickford dedicated the museum, and the proceeds from its opening gala benefited the MPRF. Reviews of the wax museum confirmed its import, similarity to the Hollywood Museum, and competitive edge in local tourism. According to *Box Office*, the museum was an "important historical exhibit as well as a new major entertainment attraction; the museum gives visitors the feeling of a Hollywood studio and at the same time, of a theatrical production."[48] Therefore, even though the wax museum could not claim the legitimate status or lofty plans of the Hollywood Museum, at a fundamental level both museums essentially shared similar goals.

While many tried to re-create the "feeling" of a studio and offer a behind-the-scenes view of Hollywood, believing this to be the primary attraction for tourists, others such as banker Bart Lytton took a more traditional exhibition approach. In June 1962, Lytton opened the one-million-dollar Lytton Center of the Visual Arts, adjacent to his Hollywood savings and loan. At the request of Sol Lesser, Lytton had purchased the Mogens Skot-Hansen collection of precinema artifacts in 1961 as a donation to the Hollywood Motion Picture and Television Museum.[49] Lytton subsequently decided to display the Skot-Hansen as his own "Bart Lytton Collection" until the Hollywood museum officially opened in 1964. In many ways, the Lytton Center proved to be a miniature version of the proposed Hollywood Museum, offering exhibitions of priceless artifacts and production processes; a theater for audiences that screened canonized works of film and television; round table discussions with Hollywood craftspeople; a library; and a photomural of films and stars. The Lytton Center opening was meant to inspire, encourage, and run parallel to the completion of the Hollywood Museum, and it received praise from Lesser, among other industry leaders and museum planners. The Lytton Center must also be viewed, however, in the context of Lytton's ambitions as a businessman and, perhaps, his failure as a screenwriter. As became apparent, Lytton harbored resentment toward the Hollywood industry and, through his public criticism of the museum, exacerbated the long-standing schism between Los Angeles' civic, corporate, and Hollywood leaders.

In addition to Lytton's exhibit, competition arose from within the Hollywood industry itself. Comprehensive tours of real studio activities and star sightings necessarily threatened the promises of a still unfinished Hollywood Museum.[50] MGM inaugurated a backlot studio tour in May 1964. Universal followed suit two months later, and the *Hollywood Reporter* described the tour as classy "à la Disneyland."[51] Well received by the public and the trades, these tours offered views of standing exterior sets, constructed lakes, sound stages, stars' dressing rooms, the studio commissary, and dailies from actual films in production. Lesser's idealistic vision of the industry's joined hands waned, and the museum planners had little recourse.

Given the museum's competition and rising costs, the museum commission also faced opposition from its supposed ally, the county board of supervisors. Many board members were not convinced of the museum's intrinsic or economic value for the county. As early as December 1960, when the board was scheduled to vote on the financing of the museum's construction and operational costs, three of the five members opposed the proposal, claiming that the entertainment industries should contribute half of the four-million-dollar cost. Seventy-five shocked industry leaders attempted to allay county concerns, while also pointing out that the county had originated the museum project. Industry insiders found the two-million-dollar request inequitable considering their support in the form of time, expertise, and artifact donations.[52] Following this initial clash between county and industry, the board reluctantly approved the financial proposal with specific stipulations.[53]

Certain county supervisors still maintained reservations about the project even after this agreement was reached.[54] Although such controversies could often be calmed, they nonetheless took a toll on the county's patience with the museum and its ever-increasing budget. In early 1961, many misunderstandings over the four-million-dollar construction cost surfaced in the public and press. Many viewed these costs as a major burden on the average taxpayer and, therefore, a far cry from serving the public. The board of supervisors supported the public outcry, often scapegoating the museum for its mismanagement of taxpayer money.

Key players on the county board were especially hostile, notably Kenneth

Hahn, a foe from the outset. As early as 1959, Hahn had his own ideas about the museum and repeatedly threatened to extricate the venture from the industry-based commission, questioning its motives and warning against commercial tie-ins that implicitly compromised a public service agenda. In August 1961, Hahn blamed the industry as a whole for the exhibition of risqué films at a Walnut Park theater, claiming,

> While this is only one theater, it is the industry itself that makes the motion pictures that are junk films. The industry can't wash its hands of this thing. We don't want censorship, but on the other hand, as one famous Supreme Court Justice said, "You can't yell fire in a crowded theater and call it freedom of speech." We will have to tell these people we won't build their motion picture museum or provide any money for it.[55]

Hahn's critique of the industry invoked the rhetoric of reformers who had rallied against cinema in the 1910s. Despite a seemingly anachronistic tone, Hahn's characterization of the industry as *these* people clearly indicated a common negative, monolithic view of Hollywood and the museum's planners. The depiction further worked to rhetorically separate the industry from the general public and its value system. Hahn's harsh words constructed the industry as a wasteland of crass commercialism—views that, unfortunately for Hollywood, many outspoken members of the public shared.

While Lesser attempted to control the public relations damage instigated by Hahn, neither he nor the county board were prepared for the next obstacle facing the museum project. In January 1962, the county supervisors ordered eleven land parcels to be condemned for the museum's use under eminent domain. Eminent domain had been applied relatively successfully with other county projects, notably Dodger Stadium and Bunker Hill, and therefore the county board and museum planners did not expect major problems with their site.[56] In this case, however, even after real estate owners showed clear unwillingness to accept the county's settlement, the board nonetheless proceeded with the condemnation. Aside from delaying the groundbreaking and overall progress, the land disputes mired the project's reputation and ostensible service role in the eyes of the public.

In February 1963, while the condemnation lawsuits were well underway, and as Pereira finalized the museum's interior design, a part-time actor and sometimes bartender at Barney's Beanery, Stephen Anthony, battled the museum commission and the county in Los Angeles Superior Court. Anthony was not

satisfied with the $11,750 court award for his half interest in one of the con-
demned land parcels. Despite court orders of immediate possession and condemnation, Anthony steadfastly refused to vacate the premises. When workers
attempted to bulldoze at the site following the October 1963 groundbreaking,
Anthony pounded on the chain-link fence, screaming and attracting media attention. Anthony's timing could not have been worse for the intended museum.

In 1964, the museum project faced especially hard times and was beginning
to lose support and legitimacy. Three months after the museum's celebratory
groundbreaking, former supporter Bart Lytton demanded that the county
board of supervisors probe the museum's finances. On the surface, Lytton and
his fellow crusaders questioned the museum's dedication to the public and its
status as a service-oriented, civic institution. Beneath the surface, bruised egos,
mean-spirited competition, and resentment largely dictated the criticism lev-
eled against the project.

Lytton publicly accused the county of negligence, citing his opposition to
the project, while the museum's other antagonists, Hahn and Anthony, were
not far behind. While the museum had, in the past, weathered potential competition and opposition, Lytton's attack, Anthony's aggression, Hahn's criticism,
the studio tours at MGM and Universal, and increasing property taxes in Los
Angeles County colluded at a particularly inauspicious time for the museum
venture.[57] In February 1964, when a Los Angeles County sheriff attempted to
evict Anthony, he barricaded himself in his house, with a shotgun cradled on
one arm and a baby in the other. Armed with a carbine rifle and three hundred
rounds of ammunition, Anthony sustained the barricade for ten weeks. During
the standoff, he was continually denied petitions for hearings and appeals but
managed to gather the support of several ex-marines, Young Republican
groups, and others who identified with his anticommunist rhetoric and name-
calling directed at the county.[58]

In early April 1964, after Anthony had moved out his wife and three children
and was living amidst comrades in arms, the police planned a Trojan Horse–
style ambush to seize the property. Strategically and fittingly, the police exe-
cuted their attack on the night of the Academy Awards, when the press corps
was conveniently occupied. Two county deputies, posing as ex-marine sympathizers, lived with Anthony for two days prior to the ambush. In the midst
of the televised ceremonies, one of the undercover sympathizers surprised Anthony and handcuffed him, while thirty police deputies crouched outside in
darkness. The next day, after Anthony was arrested and his house was being

razed, nearly two hundred angry demonstrators battled with one hundred police officers at the site.

Even after his arrest, Anthony maintained his cause célèbre status in the media—an innocent bucking the system. The *Herald Examiner* and other local papers described in detail the "guerrilla skirmishes" throughout the day between the press and officers bent on blocking coverage.[59] By the end of the day, many were arrested, while others in the crowd assaulted the police verbally, calling out, "Heil Gestapo," "Here come the Brown Coats," and "Greetings Judases." At the same time, irate citizens flooded the county sheriff's office and Hollywood Police Station with calls protesting the police's manhandling and deceitful tactics. These protests, to a certain extent, reflected a trend of anti-authoritarianism in the 1960s. They nevertheless damaged the reputation and legitimacy of the museum project in the eyes of the public as well as the county board, many of whom placed sole blame on the Hollywood industry for the museum's problems.

In the midst of the Anthony debacle, the *Los Angeles Times* called the museum project "the great whatzit?" This single phrase summed up the museum's core dilemma. What was it? And what was it meant to be? Despite the voluminous paperwork, plans, progress reports, conventions, and committee meetings, competing visions and interests plagued the museum venture, while resolution, in the form of a united front, did not appear on the horizon. These competing visions reflected a change in the nature of Hollywood and the role of media (particularly film and television) within both national and international arenas. They also marked a struggle over the museum's status as a public service institution.

As time passed and the project stalled, there was an increasing sense that the Hollywood Museum was trying to tackle too much, trying to be too much, trying to erase difference, and trying to stake out new terrain and construct an alternative institution that, in the end, went against the grain. The project's failure stemmed from differing values, perceptions, aims, expectations, and accounts of how the project should and could be envisioned. Was it a tourist venue that would bring visitors to Hollywood and satisfy the economic motives of the county and Hollywood Chamber of Commerce? Was it a public service institution that would cater to the people of Los Angeles and celebrate the arts and industry of Hollywood? Was it a memorabilia collection, a technology center, a science and industry exploratorium, or an exhibition space? Was it a world-class art museum and archive comparable to MoMA? Was it a slice of Americana, a representation of civic pride? Or was it all of these? It seemed that the intention or need was to create some kind of synthesis, a balance of high and low, art and industry, private and public, education and tourism, culture and commerce, real and imaginary, and national and transnational.

The intersection of capital and fantasy that fuels Hollywood could not sustain such a multidimensional museum enterprise. In the midst of the county-museum battle, the press labeled the museum a "Taj Mahal," a "white elephant," a "boondoggle," a "peep show," and a "tourist trap"—labels that, along with Hahn's denunciation, ideologically reverted back to the early days of cinema, framing Hollywood as foreign and its products as bad objects and vulgar entertainments.[60] Although, by the 1930s, if not before, the film medium had established itself as a legitimate form in many institutional circles, the Hollywood museum brought these old negative associations to the fore. Lambasting the Hollywood industry's action and inaction (in raising funds) for its own museum venture, reporters criticized the purported total cost of over twenty-one million dollars; the press claimed that bankruptcy threatened the project and, above all, wondered what had gone wrong.

Many began to question the museum's status as a public institution, seeing instead a vehicle for industry promotion and commerce. At a press conference soon after Anthony's arrest, and in one of many attempts to salvage the venture, museum officials witnessed firsthand the public's hostility.[61] A project that had once been nationally recognized as a monument to the future of technology and the ideals of global communication was reduced in the public's eyes to a trick and a drain on their municipal monies. Whether museum officials understood how deeply the public hostility penetrated, or how much it could affect their museum, remains unclear. Many in the public considered Anthony a sympathetic figure and, putting themselves in his shoes, would not have wanted their property or family treated in the same manner. Seemingly unable to grasp this widespread public sympathy and the symbolic weight of the Anthony incident within a greater international context of social unrest, Warner Bros.' Edmund DePatie characterized Anthony's sympathizers as a "fringe group which has lost respect for law and order." DePatie continued, "They are people who could be easily inspired by Communists. It was a ready-made situation for Communist groups to exploit."[62]

DePatie and other museum planners did not realize that the public saw a different side of the Anthony incident rooted in civil rights. The Communist name-calling seemed naively misplaced. DePatie and many museum committee members attempted to move forward with business as usual, and they hoped the public would forgive and forget the Anthony incident. Unfortunately for the museum supporters, however, Anthony would not forgive or forget and neither would the press or the public. After losing his second appeal to the U.S. Supreme Court in May, Anthony's attorney filed a suit, directed against the county and Lesser personally, claiming that state law prohibited the financing of such an institution without submitting the matter to public ballot. The suit's focus on the ballot issue highlighted what many viewed to be the museum venture's fundamental flaw. Did the public want this Hollywood museum, and how would it actually serve the public? These were questions that a publicly funded project needed to adequately answer, and at this stage, the museum's rhetoric about liveness and community rang hollow.

Between fundraising hurdles and public relations debacles throughout the remainder of 1964, the county was forced to take the public's criticism seriously. The county responded with a review of the museum. Meanwhile, Hahn launched and made public his own investigation, asking for an audit and reimbursement of county money. By the end of the year, the county board had issued a moratorium on all museum spending. Chaired by a biased Lytton along with UCLA chancellor Franklin Murphy and economist Harrison Price, the review committee issued its report in March 1965, blaming Hollywood for not raising adequate private capital to finance the museum's interior; offering no cohesive plan to open the museum with the county's four- to six-million-dollar budget; not adequately realizing the museum's function as a place of study and as an educational institution; and failing to take into consideration major changes in the Los Angeles cultural and tourist arena since its initial conceptualization in 1959.[63]

According to the report, the project was at an impasse and needed to be restructured by a newly constituted administration directed by civic rather than Hollywood industry leadership. Unless such action was taken, the report concluded that the museum should be abandoned as a community and county effort.[64] The report signaled a direct attack on the Hollywood industry, particularly its leadership and unity. The animosity between civic and Hollywood industry leaders escalated, with civic leaders chastising the industry for causing public problems rather than offering public service. Lytton and the review committee dwelled on a perception of the industry's responsibility and stake in the project that did not necessarily correspond to the contractual and legal reality of the situation. As with the Motion Picture Exposition, many within the public and local government could not understand why a wealthy industry could not (or would not) financially maintain such a project.

In the end, the private commercial ventures and the often contentious local political scene fractured and overwhelmed any possibility for a monument to Hollywood and audiovisual media. The museum project also failed to strike the right working balance. Lesser understood the museum's bind and was well aware of the museum's nebulous concept and mission. In May 1965, he was quoted in the *Los Angeles Times*:

> Some people feel that the Hollywood Museum should be a showplace which presents in entertaining fashion the thrilling accomplishments of motion pictures, television, radio and recording industries. Others maintain the emphasis should be on an educational facility. There are those who insist the "glamour concept" is an absolute requirement in order to attract visitors whose admissions are expected to pay off the construction bonds. Opposed to this viewpoint are those who stress the educational and cultural potential of the museum and believe it should be paramount even if a taxpayer's subsidy becomes necessary. The County represents the viewpoint of the taxpaying public.[65]

With all of these competing viewpoints, it is not surprising that the Hollywood Museum had difficulty maintaining a consistent and workable vision.

By the fall of 1965, the county terminated its financial commitments to the museum project; in poor health, Lesser officially resigned; and, over time, even the project's most staunch supporters, such as Mary Pickford, abandoned the museum. The public and the supervisors called for the sale of the property; the press attempted to place blame and expose the project's failures; while many donors and museum planners, concerned about the welfare of their artifacts and their dreams of a monument to Hollywood, tried to salvage the venture. After abandoning the project, the county paved the proposed site, which was subsequently used for overload Hollywood Bowl parking. Meanwhile, the artifacts and films gathered dust behind chicken-wire partitions in a warehouse in downtown Los Angeles. Some collections reverted to the original owners or families when the museum did not materialize. However, most donors had signed binding agreements that gave full rights of ownership to the nonexistent museum.

While the county played a role in the museum's failure, many still insisted on putting the blame on Hollywood alone. In a letter to the *Los Angeles Times*, well after his retirement from the board of supervisors, John Anson Ford commented, "As a County supervisor, I worked to establish such a museum. Unfortunately some of the picture interests could not clearly differentiate between appropriate historical exhibitions and promotion of their own forthcoming productions, and the promising beginning turned to failure."[66] Arthur Knight echoed these sentiments in 1976. Espousing what has by now become a familiar refrain, Knight contended that Hollywood did not care about the past, showing interest and opening their pocketbooks solely for the present and the future. The Hollywood elite has been criticized consistently for its disinterest, indolence, and all-out negligence in contributing to the arts and the local community at large. Aside from Lew Wasserman's alliance with Dorothy Chandler; the more recent contributions made by David Geffen to the Geffen Playhouse and the Geffen Contemporary at the Museum of Contemporary Art; and the erection of downtown's Disney Hall, major civic responsibilities have been left in the hands of the city's established government leaders.[67]

However, the fault cannot lie exclusively with Hollywood. The often strained relationship between local industry, local politics, and established civic leaders as well as the failed alliance between the county and Hollywood Museum undoubtedly affected the industry's participation in civic projects. In the same 1976 article, Knight conceded that the museum had become a "political football," volleyed by Bart Lytton, numerous county careerists, and a growing faction of the press and public.[68] After the Hollywood Museum failure, the promise of unity on a museum project among and between civic and industry factions seemed irreparable. With or without county assistance, the factionalism that plagued the initial project persisted, infecting subsequent efforts to form a "Hollywood" museum.

A Dream Deferred • Remapping History and Memory in Commercial Redevelopment

In the wake of the museum's waning support, the county proposed a number of alternatives. Some of these alternatives relied on private interest groups and Hollywood development projects. Others, such as MCA-Universal's proposal, would have explicitly commercialized the project, making it one of the stops on its studio tour.[69] The county also proposed seeking federal aid under a new bill President Johnson had signed for arts appropriations, thereby attaching the project once again to national interests and American culture.[70] However, most of these alternatives never materialized in any public way except for a few articles in the trade papers. These planners likely experienced what other large industry groups, and the original Hollywood Museum, had: the difficulty of fundraising, locating a site, and devising a clear and united vision.

The majority of these museum projects, small and large, nonprofit and commercial, and industry driven and real estate driven, exemplify a bifurcation within the entertainment industry, the symbolism attached to Hollywood, and the Los Angeles landscape. The unity both anticipated and promised in conjunction with the original Hollywood Museum had become a pipe dream, a 1960s science-fiction fantasy. A stark reality lurked beneath the fantasy visions of Hollywood glamour, beauty, and industry unity. The reality manifested itself in power plays and egotism, in possessiveness and envy, and in profit motives and tourist dollars. In the mid-1980s, the *Los Angeles Times* labeled the drama "As the Museum Turns."[71] The soap opera cast ranged from the most successful and reputable institutions such as the Academy of Motion Picture Arts and Sciences to the most dubious and amateur collector-historians. All of these failed ventures further signaled the demise of the Hollywood Museum and a shift away from its distinguished groundbreaking in 1963.

In January 1968, the city of Los Angeles' Department of Recreation and Parks purchased the artifacts, films, and memorabilia amassed by the museum planners for a mere $22,500, a sum that covered the museum's outstanding debt. Under the city's patronage, the collection remained indefinitely in storage, with no plans for future exhibition. Within the first year of the city's title over the objects, only two items were put on local display. In 1969, however, a large collection of artifacts was taken to Berlin, attracting four hundred thousand visitors in seventeen days. It seemed that Hollywood, the image, garnered more cachet *outside* Hollywood and the purview of local politics and rivalrous Los Angeles social circles. Despite this generous European reception, the artifacts were boxed up upon their return to Los Angeles and stored in their new resting place at the abandoned Lincoln Heights Jail in downtown Los Angeles.

Attempts to recuperate the original project, or at the very least, retrieve the priceless artifacts and films from behind bars, continued to surface and circulate in the form of museum proposals and land offers throughout the late 1960s, and well into the 1970s. The proposals, like those made by the county a few years earlier, initially revealed a range of for-profit and nonprofit interests. Proposed sites included historic city landmarks such as Wattles Park and Pickfair as well as two new Hollywood area hotel developments—a Holiday Inn on Highland Avenue and an eight-story hotel complex slated to include a television soundstage, convention center, showcase theater, and museum on Sunset Boulevard. Each of these proposals came with its share of problems, and the city had little, if any, money to spend on development or improvements.

The desire to maintain the nonprofit, noncommercial purity of the original museum venture became a veritable struggle throughout the 1970s. At a certain point, however, the combination of a Hollywood museum venture with a commercial entity seemed inevitable. The Department of Recreation and Parks entered into a two-year agreement with MCA in 1972 arranging for part of the original museum collection to be displayed at the "Universal City Museum," a regular stop on its studio tour. Attempting to counteract criticism of the potential commercial implications of this agreement, the city stipulated that students and educational study groups would not be required to pay for a museum visit and that the collection would be returned immediately upon the acquisition of a permanent museum site.[72] The threat of commercial tie-ins and the city's seeming receptivity to alliances such as the hotel developments and the studio tour led certain donors to fight the city in the early 1970s, in what amounted to a vain attempt to regain their donated possessions.[73]

Film pioneer, Jesse Lasky's daughter, Betty, became a key figure in the move to preserve the museum artifacts. While her initial correspondence with Governor Ronald Reagan in 1971–1972, consultations with the American Film Institute, and plea to then Los Angeles mayor Tom Bradley in 1973 stemmed from a desire to save her father's personal artifacts, Lasky eventually became embroiled in an effort to save the entire collection from ruin, theft, and commercial exploitation. In 1974, Betty Lasky attempted to secure the support of the entire Hollywood celebrity community by exposing the conditions at the Lincoln Heights Jail and calling for action against the potential commercialization of the project.

Ironically, members of the Hollywood industry, who according to the original museum's critics were most interested in commercial gain, contested the prospect of commercializing their history, artifacts, and images. Debbie Reynolds led a VIP group of industry figures vowing to block the city's plans to lease the museum artifacts to a proposed hotel/soundstage/convention center on Sunset Boulevard.[74] James Fletcher, director of the original museum's promotional film, addressed his industry peers in the *Hollywood Reporter*, claiming that any future museum "has got to be done with class. It can't just be someone who wants a drawing card for a hotel."[75]

While anticommercial on the surface, the industry's concerns about classy and legitimate representation indicated an ongoing preoccupation with self-image over public service. It remains unclear whether this struggle reflected a schism between the commercial world and the nonprofit museum venture, or as others have claimed, a competitive, ego-driven battle between non-Hollywood real estate development brokers and entertainment industry elite. In 1975, the Hollywood Chamber of Commerce proposed the coordination of a task force to organize a new Hollywood museum effort. As an institution, the chamber regularly walks a fine line between its financial interests and civic mission. When the city of Los Angeles promised the chamber a twenty-five-year loan of the artifacts provided it could successfully establish a permanent museum space, therefore, it is not surprising that the city and chamber became targets of public criticism.[76] However, the chamber did not face such criticism alone. Studios (particularly MCA-Universal), stars, corporations, and property developers all faced obstacles in proposing plans for the museum's artifact collection—especially those with an explicit commercial tinge. While the Chamber of Commerce attempted to negotiate its stake in the Hollywood Museum narrative, Betty Lasky worked to change the story's ending. Tired of commercial entanglements, a lack of progress in acquiring a permanent museum, the flagrant disinterest of city politicians, and the poor care given to the artifacts in the jail, Lasky hired attorney Terrys Olender in 1976 to assist her cause. Lasky and Olender toured the artifacts housed at the jail and found them in a state of disarray and decay. Without plans for a museum and without a site, the collected artifacts stood as the only remnant of the Hollywood museum dream.

Beyond Hollywood the place and Hollywood the museum, these artifacts retained value solely as icons of an imaginary, symbolic Hollywood past.[77] Since the city had not come up with any viable options, and further, had been exposed for mishandling the collection, Mayor Bradley approved and signed an agreement devised by Olender and city council member Peggy Stevenson to divide the massive collection among four local institutions with vested interests in Hollywood history and preservation. The agreement drawn up by the Department of Recreation and Parks in 1981 loaned the materials to four institutions for a twenty-five-year period that was subsequently extended.[78] The institutions were the University of Southern California (USC), the University of California, Los Angeles (UCLA), the Academy of Motion Picture Arts and Sciences (AMPAS), and the American Film Institute (AFI). These institutions were chosen for their reputations as well as their willingness, interest, and ability to care for significant portions of the collection, then valued at ten million dollars. In addition, these nonprofit institutions planned to make the artifacts and materials available for educational and research purposes, thereby fulfilling a more discernible public service mission. A 1985 audit of the entire Hollywood Museum collection subsequently judged it to be "priceless." This valuation and validation likely gratified the original Hollywood Museum donors, despite the lack of a unified collection or permanent exhibition space. All of the institutions put on minor exhibits; however, barring the academy's future plans for a museum, none of the four institutions have functioned as veritable, permanent exhibition spaces.[79]

While many individuals worked to save the Hollywood Museum's original collection and place it within the hands of reputable local archives, others like Debbie Reynolds and the Hollywood Chamber of Commerce remained intent on establishing their own museums in Hollywood. Most of the splinter museum efforts of the late 1970s through the present diverged from the original Hollywood Museum mission. Scaled down and sponsored by small groups or specialty interests, these ventures abandoned the focus on communications, technology, art, and science, instead invoking highly nostalgic symbols and myths that highlighted and celebrated Hollywood's classical era.[80]

An array of institutions, memorabilia collectors, amateur historians, corporations, and entrepreneurs looking to make a profit on Hollywood's redevelopment and symbolic cachet pursued the museum dream in the context of a decidedly postclassical nostalgia industry throughout the 1980s and 1990s. Each of these projects took something from the original Hollywood Museum and experienced varying degrees of success. In 1979, the Hollywood Historic Trust procured "the Barn," a piece of Paramount's heritage used by Cecil B. DeMille, Samuel Goldwyn, and Jesse Lasky in 1913 to film the alleged first feature-length Hollywood motion picture. In 1983, the Los Angeles County Board of Supervisors donated a small portion of the site ironically designated for the original Hollywood Museum on the Hollywood Bowl parking lot, and the four-thousand-square-foot Barn reopened as the modest Hollywood Studio Museum with exhibitions devoted to the silent era.[81]

The continued interest in the establishment of a Hollywood museum is notable. It not only manifests a desire to preserve and commemorate, and thereby value, Hollywood but also reflects the ego-driven aspirations of those desiring to attach themselves to Hollywood history, and, in most cases, turn a profit. At the same time, this interest signals the gradual dissolution of the original 1960s Hollywood Museum vision as well as a general divisiveness within the entertainment industry itself. The industry's joined hands had unequivocally deteriorated, and it was every star for him- or herself. Debbie Reynolds proved particularly adamant about her role in the establishment of a Hollywood museum. In 1983, when the Academy of Motion Picture Arts and Sciences announced plans for a twenty-five-million-dollar museum, Jimmie Baker, vice president of Debbie Reynolds's nonprofit organization, asserted, "I don't know what they (the academy members) have, because we have it all."[82] The academy envisioned the so-called Cinema Center as a site that could both explain motion picture production as well as provide an archive of its history. As rival (or perhaps comparable) to the soon-to-open American Museum of the Moving Image in New York and the Museum of the Moving Image in London, the academy, an organization built on the unity of a range of industry crafts, hoped to succeed where the Hollywood Museum had failed.[83]

Most of the museum projects that abounded in the 1980s, including the academy's, failed to prosper, if they materialized at all. In 1982, a collector and former Universal Studios tour guide opened the Hollywood Memories Museum, which featured his own memorabilia collection.[84] Two years later, and coincident with the 1984 Olympic Games in Los Angeles, three other small museums, also featuring memorabilia from private collections, opened in the heart of Hollywood, with at least two others in the planning stage.[85] Echoing earlier redevelopment projects, one of the proposals featured a museum inside a larger entertainment complex, called "Hollywood, Hollywood."[86] The Max Factor (Beauty) Museum had a longer run than the rest, opening in 1984 and closing eight years later. Since 2002, the historic building has housed the Hollywood History Museum (now "The Hollywood Museum"), while most of the artifacts were donated to the now closed Hollywood Entertainment Museum.[87]

Unlike the aforementioned museum ventures, the Hollywood Entertainment Museum, originally the Hollywood Exposition, originated in the California State Senate. In 1984, state senator David Roberti pledged funding for a museum dedicated to Hollywood film and entertainment. To date (excluding the academy's plans for a future museum), this project proved to be the most extensive and costly Hollywood museum attempt since the 1960s. Like the original Hollywood Museum, this project was primarily established through a governmental agency and therefore relied heavily on the state legislature and governor's office. Unlike the Hollywood Museum, however, this project did not di-

rectly involve or rely upon the entertainment industry in conception or planning. Except for the sponsorship of the Hollywood Chamber of Commerce, in
fact, the Hollywood Entertainment Museum kept the industry at a safe (yet accessible and solicitable) distance.

Roberti and the Chamber of Commerce strategically allied themselves, instead, with the city's Community Redevelopment Agency (CRA) and its $922
million, thirty-year urban renewal plans.[88] Besides invigorating the local economy, the museum plans were celebrated for the institution's potential to revitalize the Hollywood neighborhood. The museum, Roberti claimed, would
preserve California's heritage and memorialize the historic bond between California and the entertainment industry. Following in the footsteps of the original Hollywood Museum, the Hollywood Entertainment Museum centered on
the four core entertainment industries, and in many ways, espoused a similar
rhetoric. Roberti originally justified his proposal on the basis of civic interest
and public service; celebrating the museum's potential to attract millions in annual tourist dollars, create thousands of new jobs, and bring in millions in sales
and sales-tax revenue. Some press reports even suggested that the museum's
plans for soundstages would help alleviate runaway production that had damaged the state economy.

Despite the project's pledge to the entertainment industries and its aim to
reinforce the image of Hollywood as a world entertainment capitol, many in the
industry remained skeptical, reluctant to support the project.[89] The site was a
key deterrent. The public perception of Hollywood as "a blight, an eyesore,
a haven for prostitutes, pimps, drug dealers, notorious bikers and plain old
wierdos" did not lend itself to supporting a Hollywood site.[90] However, the alliance with the CRA proved an advantageous business and political arrangement
for the museum venture. The public-private partnerships encouraged by the
CRA, unlike the model used by the county in its alliance with the original Hollywood museum, provided for tax-exempt, low-interest loans, grants, and subsi-
dies. Roberti's plans and his lobbying to secure seed money from the state's
Department of Commerce decimated the other fledgling museum competition in Hollywood.[91] Like the original Hollywood museum, this project went
through several planning phases, many of which stalled and complicated the
project's public image. In the midst of declining property values and a de-
pressed economy, major problems began to surface as the press, reputable film
historians, Roberti's political rivals, community activists, and disgruntled collectors, not to mention failed Hollywood Museum founders, regularly criti-

cized the project and its rising costs, projected to top eighty million dollars in 1989.

The museum's executive director and former Roberti aide, Phyllis Caskey, shrewdly conformed to the CRA's gentrification goals and procured great amounts of CRA and other state funding throughout the decade.[92] Aligning herself and the museum with the CRA, Caskey approved a permanent site for the museum at the Hollywood Galaxy mall on Hollywood Boulevard. A former CRA project then owned by Citicorp, the Galaxy provided the museum a dreary space in the structure's basement, previously occupied by a failed food court. Caskey justified the move as more realistic than earlier and more grandiose plans to occupy a range of historic Hollywood sites. With a multiplex theater chain then occupying the upper level, Caskey naively envisioned the Galaxy as comparable to Universal City Walk—a themed entertainment destination with commercial potential and popular appeal.

Two months after Caskey made the Galaxy announcement in 1995, the *Daily News* published a scathing exposé of the museum's financial situation, with the headline "History of Hollywood Museum Reads Like Horror Movie Script."[93] From public records and more than a dozen interviews, the reporter critiqued the museum's mismanagement of public funds. The article claimed that the museum board exaggerated its fundraising successes, overpaid Caskey as executive director, misused public funds, misrepresented its progress, and mishandled donated artifacts. Despite these criticisms, a growing disrespect for the venture, and a state audit of the museum's books, the CRA approved another two-million-dollar loan to the museum, and it successfully opened in September 1996.[94]

In addition to facing mounting debt, the museum remained a target of criticism for its paltry permanent collection, its commercial ties, and its use of public funds. Until it closed in June 2006, the museum continued to receive substantial sums from the state based on dubious public service projects that had little if anything to do with the museum's mission.[95] Indeed, political maneuvering and creative accounting were arguably the sole factors that kept the doors of the museum open for its ten-year run. While the hiring of former Eastman House and Munich Film Museum archivist Jan-Christopher Horak in 2000 greatly improved the quality and scope of its temporary exhibits, the museum never transcended its primary role as mediocre tourist venue.[96]

Before the Hollywood Entertainment Museum even opened, CRA chairman Dan Garcia forecast that its fundamental flaw lay in its political origins. Like the original Hollywood Museum, and other attempts to create civic-industry projects in Los Angeles, the Hollywood Entertainment Museum negotiated a slippery divide between politics and entertainment, nonprofit and profit, and civic pride and monumental narcissism. Some would argue that a Hollywood museum, whether established as a national-, state-, or city-financed operation, and whether dedicated exclusively to motion pictures or to all four entertainment media, needs to dialogue on some level with the industries from which it is inspired and produced. The original Hollywood Museum and its successors elucidated the problems, dilemmas, expectations, and responsibilities that can arise when crafting a social contract between an industry and its community.

Of course, the blame cannot be placed evenly on the side of industry or civic interests. A museum is an institution that needs extensive and widespread support and, in the end, must find that support wherever it can. For the many reasons enumerated throughout this chapter, the Hollywood Museum "cause" continually floundered in the face of dreams of unity, camaraderie, and support within the entertainment industries as well as the political, economic, and social landscapes of Los Angeles. Indeed, the varied terrain of these landscapes complicated the idea of constructing a common and unified landscape or culture around Hollywood—whether geographic or symbolic. In the end, Hollywood does not encompass a single vision, nor by the 1980s and 1990s, a single site. Therefore, it is not surprising that the Hollywood community could not muster the strength or united support to represent a national cause within the confines of a traditional museum institution.

Every Institution for Itself

Within the entertainment industry's ever-expanding corporate culture, niche museums devoted to Hollywood continue to surface. These Hollywood museums largely bypass civic and public interests in favor of a more profitable focus on the immortality of and nostalgia for stars and the branding of individual studios. In 1996, Warner Bros. opened a seven-thousand-square-foot museum on its Burbank studio lot that celebrates the studio's well-known films and stars, notably *Casablanca* and James Dean as well as its successful history in the field of animation.[97] Universal Studios briefly gained clout and attention within archival and academic circles in the late 1990s when it hired Jan-Christopher Horak as studio archivist for Universal's material history, with plans to open a museum on Universal City Walk by 2002, but soon thereafter dropped these plans, firing Horak.

For studios and other corporate institutions, then, the museum not only aids in historicizing and memorializing a distant past but also can serve an explicit commercial function in the delineation of a corporate brand.[98] While Universal never opened a museum, it still uses the material culture archive, founded by Horak, to support multiple branding efforts. Even the Academy of Motion Picture Arts and Sciences' reentry into the museum arena in 2004 may potentially be viewed as a branding effort. Until 2004, the academy tended to keep its museum plans behind closed doors, promoting its other more low-key efforts to historicize Hollywood through exhibits at its Wilshire Boulevard gallery, its oral history program, and other collections in the Margaret Herrick Library, as well as its expanding archival and preservation work at the Pickford Center for Motion Picture Study. The academy possesses a widely recognized, significant collection in both its library and film archive, and regularly presents historically valuable public programs. Some of its institutional activities, even those that appear to be educational and fulfilling a public service agenda, nonetheless implicitly center around promoting the academy's most prized, lucrative possession and commemorative product—its Academy Awards telecast.

The academy sponsors an annual media literacy program in conjunction with the Academy Awards telecast. The money for this ostensibly educational endeavor is derived from the awards budget, rather than the nonprofit arm of the Academy Foundation, and is overseen by the public relations committee for the telecast. While the media literacy kit, sent out to numerous schools across the nation, offers some educational information about different craft areas, it also unashamedly centers around the Academy Awards, encouraging students to view the telecast as part of their studies, and hang the enclosed, official telecast poster in their classroom. The focus on the awards, even within this pedagogical context, is not surprising. The annual telecast (and the institution's Internet component http://oscar.com/) single-handedly constitute the academy's "brand," associating the institution with a combination of high glamour, cultural authority, and the potential for future lucrative dealings with the television networks.

With $134 million accrued largely from the lucrative network broadcasting of the awards show in the late 1990s, the academy's board of governors announced in 2004 that it was the right time to build a "world-class" motion picture museum. According to then president Frank Pierson, "The time has come to make the decision to go ahead and do it before someone else does it badly."[99] The academy, seemingly ignoring unheeded advice and the other museum attempts that have gone badly, hopes to emulate the successful erection of other notable Los Angeles cultural landmarks, namely, the Getty Center and Disney Hall, claiming its museum will similarly make a "major statement." Procuring an eight-acre land parcel adjacent to its archive near Sunset and Vine in 2006, the academy chose the French architecture firm Atelier Christian de Portzamparc. Envisioned as part tourist attraction and part education center, the academy may run into some of the same problems faced by earlier museum attempts. Even with their sizeable coffers, and especially since the stock market crash of 2008, the organization admits the need for donations and potentially local government assistance—both of which plagued many of the previous ventures.[100] The specter of past museum ventures, Hollywood seediness, an overzealous purchase of property at the top of the market, and the industry's historical lack of generosity hangs over the academy's plans.[101] The museum plans seemed indefinitely postponed for several years until the fall of 2011, when the retirement of longtime academy executive director, Brue Davis, ushered in new leadership and ideas about the museum. Rather than stubbornly cling to the geographic borders of Hollywood and property hastily purchased for some $50 million, a more open-minded director, Dawn Hudson, saw the wisdom in aligning with an established museum institution, the Los Angeles County Museum of Art. It remains to be seen whether this twenty-first century county–Hollywood union will lead to a happier ending.

Certain institutional efforts to memorialize Hollywood still garner integrity and import as historical projects, yet many continue to repeat the problems and mirror the downfall of the original Hollywood Museum. When the Hollywood Museum received criticism for its fusion of entertainment and culture, profit and nonprofit, and spectacle and education, the proposed institution was labeled an indoor Disneyland, a wax museum, a world's fair, and a department store of mementos. Despite changes in the cultural and economic landscape since the 1960s, the same criticisms continue to be directed against contemporary incarnations of the original and now defunct museum venture. The growing and ever-evolving synergy of culture and commerce is at once celebrated and chastised, imitated and resented.

Many questions linger behind this multilayered response to the culture-commerce merger, especially as it gets played out in the many divergent Hollywood museum ventures. However, the pivotal question raises a larger issue of how to position the film medium, film culture, and the feelings and experiences associated with Hollywood in the context of a museum institution. In other words, is the synergy of culture and commerce the inevitable result of bringing film and entertainment media into the museum sphere? Or is this synergy more broadly a reflection of the state of contemporary museums, the contemporary economy, and contemporary film and media culture?

Unlike MoMA's Film Library, supported largely by private philanthropy, and other recent museum ventures in the United States and Europe that successfully accrued state support, Hollywood has proven a difficult site in which to negotiate cultural and commercial values while satisfying all involved. Since the original Hollywood Museum's downfall in the mid-1960s, Hollywood the "place" and Hollywood the "image" have drastically changed. As a Los Angeles city district, Hollywood and Hollywood Boulevard, in particular, faced severe economic recession dating from the 1970s and lingering into the present. A few noteworthy redevelopment ventures surfaced in the 2000s such as the beleaguered Hollywood and Highland Center, the Arclight theaters adjacent to the original CineramaDome, a W hotel at the famed intersection of Hollywood and Vine, and a slew of bars, clubs, and restaurants; however, most of these commercially driven gentrification projects do little to revitalize the historical idea of Hollywood glamour and fantasy. Instead, these shopping centers, hotels, theaters, and eateries adhere to generic gentrification trends that have become central to the revitalization of many urban American centers.

Despite some gentrification success stories, most of the city's and state's attempts at renewing and restoring Hollywood's image have failed, stalled, or remained tourist traps. Furthermore, as multinational conglomerates gradually enveloped Hollywood studios in the 1980s and 1990s, Hollywood's symbolic, historical, and nostalgic image garnered increasing cachet and economic return outside of Hollywood and the borders of Los Angeles. In some sense, all that is left of Hollywood is its imaginary status as a symbolic, historical, and nostalgic image. While many still long for the return of Hollywood Boulevard as an entertainment and fantasy epicenter, it is clear that commercial interests increasingly harness Hollywood the dream outside the confines of its complicated Los Angeles reality.[102] Indeed, as the following two chapters suggest, the digital age and the values associated with the New Hollywood increasingly question, if not eradicate, the need to situate Hollywood history in a single physical site.

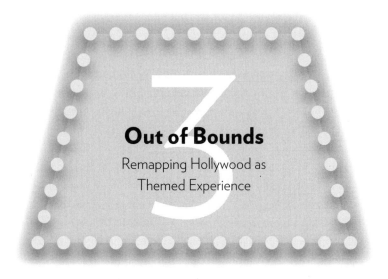

Out of Bounds

Remapping Hollywood as
Themed Experience

On April 1, 1995, Debbie Reynolds hosted a gala to inaugurate her very own Hollywood Movie Museum at her Las Vegas hotel and casino. In addition to the real guests in attendance such as Esther Williams, David Geffen, Jack Haley Jr., and the Smothers Brothers, Reynolds constructed a Hollywood wax museum to permanently populate the hotel's lobby with life-size figures of Hollywood luminaries including Frank Sinatra, Mae West, and Laurel and Hardy. After more than twenty years of trying to attach her collection to a suitable Hollywood institution, and with the dreams, plans, and artifacts of the original Hollywood Museum scattered among several institutions throughout Los Angeles, Reynolds faced the inevitable: if Hollywood wouldn't have her, she would re-create Hollywood elsewhere.

Unknowingly, perhaps, Reynolds stood at the threshold of a promising gateway—not only to a new city but also to an alternative way to memorialize Hollywood and its history, a way exploited by corporate conglomerates throughout the 1990s. These conglomerates banked on Hollywood's global and symbolic stature during an era steeped in conspicuous affluence and consumption, transforming the site and its products into portable and mutable themed environments and brands. Bent on reglorifying Hollywood and restoring its golden age in a passé traditional exhibition format a shortsighted Reynolds did not fully seize upon the opportunity offered by the ultimate themed city; in 1998, after filing for bankruptcy, she sold the complex at auction to the World Wrestling Federation.

That same year, a corporate collaboration between Hilton Hotels Corporation and Viacom's Paramount Parks Inc. opened in the style of a Hollywood premiere. Tapping into consumer trends in themed environments during the 1990s, and seizing an opportunity missed by Reynolds, the corporate conglomerate constructed a Vegas-Hollywood hybrid, Star Trek: The Experience, on a more populated and profitable section of the Las Vegas strip. This combination theme park attraction, casino, retail store, themed restaurant, museum, re-created Hollywood set, and 3-D immersive film attraction sold visitors a complete package and an experience designed to satisfy multiple entertainment functions. The themed environment Star Trek: The Experience further embraced and thrived on the kind of excess and spectacle, typical of the period, that proved unwieldy for many more traditionally conceived memorials, including the original Hollywood Museum venture, discussed in the previous chapter.

Thus, by the late 1990s, at the opposite ends of the famed Las Vegas strip, between Reynolds's now defunct Hollywood Movie Museum and Star Trek: The Experience, two related, yet divergent, monuments to Hollywood coexisted. One was consumed with self-possession, self-preservation, and immortality; the other, with amusement, attraction, branding, and consumption. One embodied nostalgia; the other was driven by the tenets of an ever-growing nostalgia industry. While Reynolds's hotel-casino-museum fiercely clung to the past, to old-fashioned glamour, and historical models steeped in traditional museum convention, Star Trek: The Experience took cues from themed environments that rose in popularity largely during the 1990s, remaking Hollywood iconography, material culture, and history into a consumable, interactive experience and an exclusive event.

Despite their notable differences, both the Reynolds and Star Trek attractions relied on Hollywood's referential, even cult, status; its power to move beyond site-specific geographical boundaries; and its ability to tap into the lure and cachet of stars, popular genres, and iconic, blockbuster films. Hollywood's powerfully influential makeover was not limited to Star Trek: The Experience or to Las Vegas as a city, for that matter. While Las Vegas is often touted as the ultimate postmodern city, particularly since the publication of Robert Venturi's seminal 1972 architectural manifesto Learning from Las Vegas, the reinterpretation, remapping, and "theming" of Hollywood proliferated within many other arenas of the postindustrial global economy at the close of the twentieth century, indicating a clear shift in the agendas and protocols tied to the writing and understanding of Hollywood and its history.

Indeed, the proliferation of Hollywood-specific themed environments represented a key moment in the 1980s and 1990s that paralleled the rapid expansion and heavy spending of multimedia conglomerates. These sites imbued Hollywood's history and the artifacts that materially signified it with a new-found symbolic cachet as well as a very real economic value. Hollywood studios seemed to discover an untapped and vested interest in films and other collectibles otherwise languishing in their vaults and, in turn, seized on and largely drove the market value of their histories.

While themed entertainments are not entirely new to Hollywood, by the 1980s and 1990s, the Hollywood-specific "theming" took on more direct roles tied to trends in marketing, the rise of the blockbuster, an explosion in the Hollywood memorabilia market, and the increasing presence of conglomerates running the studios. Even as the marketing and distribution of Hollywood film products and stars has long depended on Hollywood's universal recognition, a global economy increasingly capitalizes on Hollywood's ability to travel outside the theater, as well as outside its geographical and historical bounds.[1] Studios and other corporate entities have uncovered new ways to mediate Hollywood's symbolic stature in both national and international markets. Since the 1980s and 1990s, in fact, with the increased role of marketing as a central force driving the film industry, Hollywood has expanded upon and exploited its global status and power, banking not only on the international recognition of certain stars and the distribution of current film releases in foreign markets but also, in many cases, on a well-developed and carefully crafted nostalgia for Hollywood.[2] Even as the fast-paced nature of this expansion started to slow by the end of the decade, such sites precipitated the rise of other spaces and practices that supplemented, if not supplanted, the role of theatrical film exhibition in public life and cultural memory. In many cases, such ancillary products and experiences continue to play a key role in economically sustaining Hollywood conglomerates, often outperforming lackluster film releases, and serving as a central component of the corporate revenue stream and bottom line.

Finding meaningful roles in a range of public institutions and corporate spheres, the sites explored in this chapter, then, represented a significant synergistic model that allowed Hollywood to migrate beyond the silver screen and in many cases beyond the geographic locale. Like their successors in the realm of home entertainment and the digital realm discussed in the following chapters, these themed environments reconstituted Hollywood (often synonymous with a generic body of entertainment media, including television and music) as part of an ever-evolving arena of ancillary products, brands, sites, and everyday ritu-als.[3] Hollywood and, in some cases, its history took on an exchange value that held definitive profit potential for media conglomerates.

The earlier star, studio, real estate, and corporate-driven projects and insti-tutions that attempted to memorialize Hollywood through optimistic dreams of industry unity gave way to a redirected focus on the values and more overt economic interests of a global marketplace. In this global context, Hollywood the site, the feeling, and the idea was reframed as brand—an approach that lent itself less to museum display or site-specific exhibition and more to the profit-ability and bountiful extension of Hollywood-inspired products and corporate identities. Branding in the context of a well-honed global economy, in fact, be-came a key driving force in conceptualizing those sites that could exhibit, con-cretize, and commodify Hollywood and its history. While the contemporary home entertainment and digital landscapes discussed in the following chapters adhere to a different economic model with far less outlay, seemingly less risk, and at their height, a more stable revenue stream, the foundational principles guiding themed entertainment as well as home and digital entertainment re-main relatively similar. Indeed, the themed environments of the 1990s laid the groundwork for continued experiments in the re-creation and reworking of Hollywood-inspired themes and references, interactive and edutainment com-ponents, and corporate branding. Such branding efforts reflect a working sym-biosis of economic strategy and Hollywood memorialization.

Setting the Stage

The themed environment is a modern phenomenon, dating to the industrial era by some accounts, but gathering a different kind of momentum in the latter half of the twentieth century. Many of the historical precedents of today's themed environments, including the aristocratic garden, the exposition, the de-partment store, and even the museum in some cases, offered landscapes and exhibits designed to visually and symbolically capture an expansive arena or concept through familiar references and innuendoes, making it concrete and tangible for mass audiences.[4] These displays relied on an amalgamation, juxta-position, and hybridization of objects, taste cultures, and audiences. Such counterparts to the contemporary theme park produced a liminal space be-tween high and low, and between cultural and commercial consumption—one that was simultaneously praised and shunned.

While highbrow critics regularly attacked these historical approaches, finding fault with their embrace of a mass sensibility, cultural institutions over time have increasingly had to reckon with the rise and competition from mass leisure and so-called cheap amusements.[5] As early as the 1910s and 1920s, museum curators, in particular, found that their mission was "not to chronicle art as a fact but to enact it as an event and to dramatize its function," viewing their role less as custodian and more as entertainer.[6] The inclination (even the need) to enact art and culture as events continued to evolve in the second half of the twentieth century, prompted both by constantly transforming and competing leisure forms as well as the increasingly meaningful place of entertainment and technology in everyday life and consumption. Many contemporary cultural institutions, not unlike their predecessors in the early twentieth century, have had to interface with, if not exploit, the tenets of spectacle, attraction, entertainment, and commodity. In essence, these institutions must negotiate directly with influential contemporary realms of leisure and consumption outside of more traditional repositories of high culture.[7]

The history of theming changes in the mid-twentieth century when, according to Mark Gottdiener, "more frequent use of symbols and motifs characterizes the spaces of everyday life in both the city and the suburb."[8] From this time onward, Gottdiener suggests, designers, architects, city planners, and corporations regularly began to use these generally familiar or easily recognizable symbols and motifs (often synonymous with brands) to engage a broad public and create a bond among its members. Reflecting little about shared convictions and values, such communal bonds often reveal more about shared cultural and historical references as well as a collective nostalgia.

Nostalgia proves to be a common theme in a number of historical and contemporary themed environments.[9] The evolution of a nostalgia industry and the concept of the nostalgic tourist site have proven instrumental in pioneering a more commercial approach to history and historical merchandising.[10] In the last few decades in particular, nostalgia and a nostalgia industry have engendered the foundation of heritage centers, eco-museums, and a variety of redevelopment and gentrification projects in historical urban districts. Nostalgia as an industry also increasingly encroaches on everyday life through retail sales and mass media. These by-products of the nostalgia industry bring history and historical memory to life, positioning them as concrete and consumable entities or experiences of a living, though highly sanctioned, history.[11] Personal and collective identification with history—its images, artifacts, and stories — further elicits pleasure among those engaged by a nostalgia industry.

In addition to the shared references and cultural memories proffered by this industry, themed environments engage visitors through an amalgamation of highly formulated activities including shopping, dining, and other entertainment-oriented leisure. They further employ principles associated with "experience design," in crafting highly regulated and reproducible encounters that are strategically designed to be compelling and memorable.[12] Despite their generic qualities, the creation of such "total" or amalgamated environments potentially adds value, both real and symbolic, to a core experience or theme. Indeed, as one contemporary amusement park designer suggests, "Theming is about adding value."[13] The notion of adding value implies that the whole or total environment is more than the sum of its parts. In the context of marketing and branding, "value added" can convey a need to diversify, disperse, or exceed a single product or venue's functional value, thereby broadening the base of its appeal and cultural impact. In the contemporary global marketplace and specifically as it relates to Hollywood products, "theming" manifests itself in logos and branding but also in the creation of highly mediated experiences designed to associate the brand or product with a shared feeling or idea about Hollywood. Therefore, the Hollywood themed environments commodify generically constructed Hollywood themes, images, and personae, attempting to concretize them for visitors. In turn, Hollywood's otherwise ephemeral and symbolic values get marketed and transformed into economic value.

The representation and exhibition of Hollywood, and more broadly film or media history, in themed environments of the 1990s signaled a shift in conceptualizing Hollywood as an institution. In the 1980s, as studios increasingly profited from a film's life outside of its theatrical exhibition, they took greater advantage of ancillary markets, particularly home video and recording, as well as licensing opportunities. The multinational conglomerates spawned from the heavy merger and acquisition activities of the 1980s further stressed the value of positioning film (and even film history) as one part of a larger entertainment and leisure arena. As historian Stephen Prince argues with regard to the amplified role of movie tie-ins and corporate synergy, "This fusion would operate like a brand label, unifying as products with a common corporate identity the film and its music and music video spin-offs. Each product would thereby reinforce in the consumer's mind the arch-image and identity of the franchise."[14] The marketing and branding strategies of the 1980s signaled an economic drive to create a single, all-encompassing Hollywood image or brand around a specific product that would reflect on the studio brand at large. In many instances, the fusion Prince discusses also manifested itself in specific sites—theme parks, themed retail, and other "urban entertainment destinations," which sell licensed merchandise and thereby expand a studio's ancillary sites and identity.[15] While the economic value of such strategies no doubt remains the key incentive for individual studios, the themed sites served another important function in fueling and perpetuating the symbolic value attached to Hollywood.

In order to brand and sell a Hollywood mythology and nostalgia, the themed environments discussed below tend to use two complementary approaches. First, they design and market highly customized products, inculcating them within orchestrated, immersive experiences. The union of product and experience reconstitutes the media product as a new and valued artifact—one that the visitor can be inserted into or take home. Here, "theming" typically revolves around creating an experience of privilege and access, letting consumers in on a secret, and bringing them behind the scenes so they feel close to an otherwise remote world of glamour, celebrity, spectacle, and movie "magic."

Second, these sites use memorabilia and nostalgia-imbued displays of Hollywood glamour and history in order to promote and memorialize a generic image of a Hollywood past. Hollywood's products—films, television, stars, studios, fashion, and music—regularly produce cultural memory and serve as conduits for nostalgia. They can therefore evoke a mood and a yearning for an ephemeral past, one that is little known, general, and even vague but nonetheless easy to fabricate.[16] Hollywood corporations and institutions regularly seize on nostalgia in order to package and market their history, selling it to a mass audience. However, like the history of much popular culture, Hollywood history does not always neatly fit within the rubric of traditional historical discourse. The Hollywood nostalgia industry, like the themed environments that engender it, reduces history to icons, fetish objects, and ultimately commodities.

The juxtaposition of these two Hollywood visions potentially manifests a contradiction. These sites simultaneously demystify Hollywood through promises of behind-the-scenes access while mystifying it through stories of unattainable glamour and excess. They sell Hollywood through attraction and physical sensation, while also promoting its history and cultural import. The themed environments discussed below negotiate and even elide these potential divides by unifying visions of Hollywood as both leisure experiences and commodities. Tapping into Hollywood's hybrid identity as geographic site, industry, and symbol of money, power, glamour, celebrity, spectacle, and dreams of success, these themed environments offer an additional and valuable dimension to the corporate brand.

Relying on themes to anchor and unify a disparate group of consumers, as well as a disparate collection of icons, symbols, and events into single and totalizing narratives or experiences, these sites have catered to a wide range of consumers through a plethora of leisure and entertainment-oriented activities.[17] While purists, historians, collectors, and fetishists may eschew this generic vision of Hollywood and its history, it has tactically served a contemporary economic climate and at the same time reflected a need to renegotiate Hollywood's boundaries at the end of the twentieth century. In essence, these sites offer perspective on the changing and significant role Hollywood can play in everyday public spaces and popular leisure, one that necessarily also penetrates and influences the current home entertainment arena as well as the Internet.

The Movie-Themed Theme Park

The opening of Disneyland in 1955 manifested an incorporation of earlier approaches to mass entertainment as well as a pointed attempt at synergy. Some of the early public relations materials for the theme park crafted it as an all-inclusive or total environment, one that would be "something of a fair, an exhibition, a playground, a community center, a museum of living facts, and a showplace of beauty and the supernatural."[18] Disney's juxtaposition of the museum and community center alongside the fair, playground, and showplace reveals a desire to be comprehensive and all inclusive, to attract a wide audience, capturing the fusion Stephen Prince attributes to the 1980s. At the same time, like one of his predecessors, P. T. Barnum, the Disney rhetoric revealed a conscious desire to blur the lines between high and low culture, to actively seek some cultural value alongside the commercial profits. Disney's first theme park would ostensibly serve multiple purposes, yet all of these purposes would serve the greater good of targeting the widest audience possible, while promoting the main theme: the Disney brand. The park further promoted the Disney brand by serving as a launching pad to synergistically sponsor Disney's television shows, feature films, and stock characters.[19]

Attracting mass audiences has always been the goal of the mainstream Hollywood film industry. In the 1980s and 1990s, however, the Hollywood studios more clearly channeled Disney's vision in creating themed entertainment that functioned in a synergistic model. In 1989, at the opening of the 110-acre Disney-MGM Studios, when Walt Disney chairman Michael Eisner called the themed environment "the Hollywood that never was and always will be," his comment neatly summarized the way in which movie-themed spaces such as Disney-MGM conjure up an idealized vision of Hollywood that exists largely within a collective imagination.[20] In its distinctive focus on Hollywood history and iconography, this park set the stage for other Disney re-creations such as the Hollywood Pictures Backlot section of Disney California Adventure, which opened in Anaheim in 2001, and the Walt Disney Studios Park, adjacent to Disneyland Europe, which opened in 2002. Like a film print that is reproduced and distributed to theaters across the globe, these parks similarly reproduce rides, characters, settings, and overall design, adhering to a mold that is hardly unique. The parks subscribe to the aforementioned approaches found in other themed environments. They create alternative experiences of media by framing the original film, television show, and popular characters in the context of a ride or attraction, while also perpetuating fantasies about the inner workings of contemporary Hollywood. Such parks further exploit a studio's brand name, economic clout, and history in order to instill nostalgia in their visitors.

In addition to the more standard theme park fare such as stage shows and rides, Disney theme parks appropriate Hollywood landmarks and icons in order to reimagine the geographic site in a variety of themed experiences. Following in the footsteps of Disneyland and Universal Studios, many contemporary movie-themed theme parks play on two kinds of value. They celebrate sensory stimulation in the form of rides (many of which are based on blockbuster film properties and popular television shows) and simultaneously frame the park experience as a process of discovery afforded by access to backstage regions. In framing Hollywood (and the theme park, even) as a place of magic and secrets while simultaneously divulging the contents of those secrets and the essence of this magic, these parks function both to mystify and to demystify Hollywood. The parks negotiate this apparent contradiction by engaging visitors' interests in Hollywood's symbolic stature as well as their desire to understand the practical inner workings of the production process.

When Universal opened its backlot tour in 1964, the park offered visitors a tram tour with displays illustrating various special effects, makeup techniques, and movie props, as well as access to sets, sound stages, dressing rooms, and most importantly, the studio commissary, where one could potentially "run into" a star. The promise of a star sighting largely fueled the tours and sparked visitor fantasies. John Wayne would supposedly eat hot dogs at the tour's Entertainment Center, which featured live shows.[21] Even stars like Cary Grant, who wanted to maintain their privacy, understood the value of their own and other star's symbolic power. At the opening of Universal's tour, Grant wryly commented to legendary *Daily Variety* columnist, Army Archerd, "I know if I paid to get inside a studio, I'd want to see Rock Hudson."[22] The studio tour offered the *potential* to see Rock Hudson (whether or not it would ever actually happen) as a way to concretize Hollywood and, as fan magazines had done for decades, make the otherwise glamorous, untouchable star a regular, accessible person. The potential star sighting further perpetuated a mythology about the studio backlot as a place of stars, secrets, and movie magic.

Such backstage access was not entirely novel in 1964. As early as 1915, Carl Laemmle saw the benefit and profit potential of showing the public what went on behind the scenes at his chicken ranch turned burgeoning Universal Studios, with tours for twenty-five cents. The Hollywood Museum and other local ventures discussed in chapter 2 attempted to mimic Universal's success, which in large part was based on a consumable image and a highly constructed experience of Hollywood. These images, objects, and experiences, whether in a theme park or museum setting, promised to satisfy visitors through a tangible and concrete experience invoked by a studio backlot, star's costume, recognizable prop, or re-created set.

The 1990s, the age of conglomerates, corporatization, and franchising, exploded with theme parks that replicated and reinterpreted this interest in backstage Hollywood access as well as the fantasy and magic generically tied to Hollywood and its history. Clearly motivated to exploit the theme parks as a site of branding, contemporary multimedia corporations shunned the rhetoric of scarcity tendered by earlier institutions seeking to preserve Hollywood's past. Relinquishing the coveted uniqueness of their artifacts and studio identity through licensing arrangements, many corporations allowed even their competitors to use and profit from certain popular properties, particularly animated ones. The fact that Dora the Explorer and Shrek, for example, appear at multiple theme parks across the globe reveals their economic and symbolic power, not to a single studio, but rather to a more basic corporate goal of conjuring Hollywood.

While many themed ventures failed or were sold off by conglomerates by the early 2000s, their sheer number and international presence through the 1990s attest to the fact that Hollywood, as a symbol and commodity, can travel

Dreams come true. A staged exchange, disguised as chance encounter, between John Wayne and tourists on the Universal Studios Tour, 1964. Courtesy of the Academy of Motion Picture Arts and Sciences.

and garner meaning in sites outside of the theater as well as its own geographic boundaries. Universal Studios Hollywood, the park closest to the real geographic site, has retained and revamped its backlot studio tour and still claims to be the "world's largest movie studio and theme park," encompassing "the best of both worlds: a complete theme park and a unique, authentic Hollywood tourist attraction all underneath one experience."[23] The park, therefore, promises a total experience in an environment that offers both attractions and the more intangible, though legitimated, connection to Hollywood.

Positioning itself as an immersive and interactive environment, Universal Studios sells the park's behind-the-scenes access as exclusive. The park claims to put "you so close, you can hear the cameras rolling." Touting the proximity afforded by the studio tour, the park promotions assert, "You can't get any closer to the real Hollywood!" The promotional rhetoric further calls on the visitor to get immersed "in the movie action with pulse pounding rides and full sensory attractions."[24] Harkening back to cinema's early days, the promotional material for the park echoes the medium's roots as a cheap (though now, not so cheap) amusement and attraction. At the same time, however, the theme park also to some degree frames cinema and Hollywood as historical, classic, and "legendary," harkening back to a decidedly rarefied interpretation of its past.

In reinterpreting Hollywood and cinema as a ride, Universal Studios, like its successors, implicitly touts immersion and interactivity as supplemental, if not superior, to the theatrical film and home-viewing experiences. The attractions supersede the film or television program by offering, even promoting, a highly visceral and pleasurable interaction. The park's website presents a slide show depicting a Universal Tours tram bus driving through harrowing movie sets: a careening helicopter in flames, a flooded Western town, a shark attack, a devastated cityscape from *War of the Worlds*, and an exploding car crash from the *Fast and the Furious* franchise. Other promotional photos show the tour bus driving beneath a production crew using a crane shot to capture action on a supposedly real set. These images work in conjunction with text, which promises to situate visitors "deep behind the scenes" and "in blockbuster thrills."[25] Based on promotional photos of startled, frightened, and excited visitors, Universal attests to the immersive potential of these attractions, however simulated they may be. And the attractions serve as both ancillary boosts to Universal film products (past and present) and stand-alone entertainment, offering the studio commercial value in perfect synergy.

The theme park's promotional materials reflect an economic incentive to reinvent, repackage, and remarket a film (or, to a lesser degree, television) title. Universal framed its Terminator 2: 3D attraction, which opened in 1999, as a bigger (shot on 65 mm film at 30 frames per second) and more physically engaging *sequel* to the original film.[26] Meanwhile, the park touts its 2010 King Kong 360–3D attraction, based on Peter Jackson's 2005 remake, as the "world's largest, most intense 3D experience." Celebrating the sixteen ultrahigh definition projectors that can display at a rate of sixty frames per second, the attraction promises to surpass the theatrical film's twenty-four frames per second rate and create "an incredibly fluid sense of reality."

In addition to constructing attractions as a supplement to or improvements on the original film, the studio further foregrounds its ability to envelop visitors in the film itself. Fast and the Furious: Extreme Close-Up is designed to "thrust guests into close-up range of the pulse-pounding, rubber-burning underground world of street-racing." Terminator 2: 3D similarly "thrusts [you] right into the heart of a 3-D cyber adventure"; Waterworld "brings the movie surging to life!"; Jurassic Park: The Ride brings the visitor "face-to-face" with "living" dinosaurs; Shrek 4-D "puts you in the action with hair-raising, eye-popping, and butt-busting effects so real, all your senses will be on ogre-time"; and Spider-Man Rocks! permits the visitor to "witness" Peter Parker's transformation. This "you are there" or "in your face" framing also reflects a cultural desire to experience firsthand and up close the spectacle and fantasy associated with the Hollywood filmmaking process, to be inserted into the action of these largely science-fiction, fantasy, horror, action-adventure, and disaster-themed movie rides.[27]

Aside from the focus on spectacle, Universal Studios Hollywood also foregrounds the potential for more "intimate exposure," revealing Hollywood secrets and "magic." In offering visitors inside information, the promise of a potential star sighting ("you never know who you will spot or bump into, so don't forget your camera!"; "keep your eyes peeled for stars!"), and the secrets behind movie illusions ("catch an inside glimpse of films and television shows *currently in production*"), the theme park enhances not only the theatrical experience but also the traditional amusement park experience. The visitor's experience is structured around special access to behind-the-scenes moviemaking and special effects demonstrations. While viewing scenes from historic Universal films shot at various studio locales on a monitor installed in each tramcar, the studio tour also offers visitors a "live" ride through the sets of Universal blockbusters (*The Scorpion King, The Mummy, Jurassic Park, War of the Worlds, Spider-Man, Meet the Fockers, The Fast and the Furious,* and *King Kong*), television shows (*Desperate Housewives, CSI,* and *Crossing Jordan*), and classic fare such as *Psycho*.

The intimacy, spontaneity, and authenticity promised by Universal and other parks suggest the value of the tour experience over traditional media viewing. Even after more than forty years, the promotional rhetoric for the park continues to suggest that the visitor may glimpse (in passing) the actual production of an upcoming release. The website offers updates of films and television shows currently in production on the lot to solidify this claim. The suggested spontaneity of such an encounter or star sighting, while highly unlikely given the fixed route of the trams and scripted routines of the drivers, secures the park and the studio's authority within the context of the real backlot setting and its adjacent location to the "real" geographical Hollywood. Universal increases the value (and cost) of the tour by offering the "VIP Experience," a pricier option (fifty dollars over general admission) that allows visitors to access closed sets and additional behind-the-scenes locations beyond the regular tour.

The backstage zones at Universal Studios Hollywood have set the standard for other theme parks in the re-creation of an aura associated with Hollywood and Hollywood history. Extending the Hollywood re-creation, many of Universal's descendants offer detailed simulations of Hollywood icons and Los Angeles landmarks. The Hollywood pastiche constructed by Disney-MGM in the late 1980s migrated to several other movie-themed parks all over the world throughout the 1990s and 2000s. Like Disney-MGM and its Disney descendants, many of these parks have re-created iconic images that have been historically associated with Hollywood as both a geographical site and a cultural symbol. The Warner Bros. Movie World theme parks in Australia and, until 2004, Germany and Spain as well as some of the former Viacom-owned theme parks, namely, Paramount's Great America and Paramount's King's Island, have striven to re-create Hollywood.[28] Using rudimentary references and icons, these parks present an easily reproducible, superficial, and sanitized vision of various recognizable Hollywood and Los Angeles sites. In addition to the Disney parks, Universal Studios Florida, which opened in Orlando in 1990, as well as its Japanese counterpart, which opened in Osaka in 2001, use famed streets and historical sites such as Hollywood Boulevard, Sunset Boulevard, Rodeo Drive, Grauman's Chinese Theater, Schwab's drugstore, the Beverly Wilshire Hotel, and the Brown Derby. Paramount's King's Island replicated the famed Bronson Gates that mark the entrance to the historical studio lot in Hollywood. Palm trees also represent an often requisite Southern California symbol in these parks, which operate under the assumption that their visitors want to travel to Hollywood and be enveloped by its glamorous past and present. The theme park, branded with a Hollywood studio logo and key symbols of the actual site, positions itself as the next best thing.

In some cases, landmarks such as the Bronson Gates and Grauman's Chinese Theatre are touted as authentic replicas. Ignoring the apparent contradiction, Hollywood theme parks frequently use a rhetoric of authenticity to legitimate their simulated ties to Hollywood and its history. Most of the street sets, building replicas, and store and restaurant names therefore summon a fictionalized, yet easily accessible and highly nostalgic, image of Hollywood. Despite their varied locations and studio backing, all of these movie theme parks commonly and crudely mix a similar set of references from Hollywood's past and present in order to invoke generic cultural memories about Hollywood that, in turn, get rewritten and remapped as easily digested, nostalgic commodities. Even in such cases where the replicas and the attractions more generically recall and re-create Hollywood films, television shows, and geographic sites, most parks will nonetheless use authenticity as a selling point.

These theme parks appropriate iconic figures, images, and landmarks as stand-ins for a historical era, but more importantly, they use decidedly ahistorical symbols of glamour and star power. Disney-MGM features retail stores with names such as the Celebrity 5 & 10, Oscar's Classic Car Souvenirs & Superservice, and Sid Cahuenga's One-of-a-Kind as well as restaurants like the Hollywood Brown Derby and the ABC Commissary. Its Paris counterpart has a film street set with old-time establishments named for films like *Gunga Din* (Gunga Den) and performers like Carmen Miranda (Carmen's Veranda) as well as more general allusions to Hollywood glamour and celebrity (a 1930s-style building named Glamour Girl Cosmetics, a newsstand called the Gossip Column, and the Hep Cat Club, which pays homage to the Rat Pack). At Warner Bros. Movie World in Australia, the Star Parade features costumed classic and contemporary animated characters and previously paid tribute to historical icons such as Marilyn Monroe. While decidedly fictional, the names and re-created historical sites nonetheless support the park's legitimacy, provided they can convincingly summon a symbolic connection to Hollywood. In focusing primarily (if not paradoxically) on the classical era of Hollywood history as well as children's animated fare, these parks bank on the universality, nostalgia, and cachet tied to iconic references, while further perpetuating their place in popular culture and memory.

In order to further invoke ties to a "real" Hollywood, many of the movie theme parks modeled on Universal Studios Hollywood offer tours or attractions that ostensibly show visitors what happens behind the scenes of an actual film or television production. Some of the parks, directly emulating Universal Studios Hollywood, are affiliated, however loosely, with real working studios.[29] Universal Studios Florida boasts a tour of its Nickelodeon Studios, while the Japanese park gives visitors access to Mainichi Broadcasting System, Inc. (MBS), a working Japanese television studio. Warner Bros. Movie World in Australia is also affiliated with a working studio, Village Roadshow Movie World Studios, though the park and studio are separate entities.[30] Meanwhile, Walt Disney Studios Park in Paris offers a "Studio Tram Tour," which winds its way through props from famed European studios such as CineCitta and Pinewood, sets from Hollywood blockbusters such as *Pearl Harbor*, and craftspeople at work making costumes. In addition, this park features a tour of Walt Disney Television Studios, home to the Disney Channel France, as well as a tour of a fictional film soundstage, where a film is supposedly always in production. Whether these behind-the-scenes experiences are real or simulated re-creations, all of them are designed and promoted as genuine and unique. The visitor gets positioned as a select guest who can gain insight into Hollywood's secrets and magic.

Most of these movie theme parks tend to highlight their access to Hollywood secrets and "movie magic" through the use of special effects–based attractions. They also tend to frame these attractions as educational. The promotional rhetoric used at most of the parks claims that visitors can "learn" about these Hollywood secrets even as they are immersed in the spectacle. At the Disney parks, they can learn about animation, while Warner Bros. Movie World in Australia offers insight into blue screen and sound effects techniques. The Universal parks in Florida and Japan provide visitors with the opportunity to "learn" about makeup special effects. Paramount's Magic of the Movies Live, a former standard attraction at all five Paramount Parks, exposed visitors to the special effects "wizardry" in Paramount films such as *Titanic* and *Sleepy Hollow*. The attraction invited visitors "to learn firsthand the tricks of the trade on how movies are created" in a twenty-five-minute stage show that illustrated what was purportedly framed as the entire filmmaking process—from story conception to postproduction.[31] Even outside of the traditional Hollywood corporate superstructure, movie theme parks such as Babelsberg Studios in Germany and Futurscope in France present backstage attractions designed to divulge the mysteries and secrets of the filmmaking process. All of these theme parks tend to frame education or learning in the context of exposing secrets, as opposed to the public service mission touted by museums and other nonprofit institutions. The Hollywood production process is portrayed as untouchable and magical, on the one hand, but accessible and knowable on the other. This tension between untouchable and accessible belies the actual learning afforded by these parks, which remains limited by each site's highly regulated presentation of media production.

Certain parks, particularly Disney-MGM and Walt Disney Studios Park devote key attractions to Hollywood's history as an additional educational opportunity. For example, Disney-MGM's The Great Movie Ride, situated inside a life-size replica of Grauman's Chinese Theatre takes visitors on a tour through classical Hollywood history and contemporary production. Some fifty audio-animatronics perform scenes from classic genres and films such as the farewell scene between Rick and Ilsa from *Casablanca*. Numbers from *Footlight Parade*, *Singin' in the Rain*, *Mary Poppins*, and *The Wizard of Oz* represent the musical. The gangster film and the Western are grouped together with re-creations from *Public Enemy* and a depiction of John Wayne on horseback. Meanwhile, scenes from *Alien* and *Raiders of the Lost Ark* represent more contemporary popular productions. All of these carefully chosen, iconic, and popular film scenes from different genres are designed to conjure a unified and sanctioned vision of Hollywood, collapse the past into the present, and stimulate feelings of nostalgia for the recent and distant (even if unlived) past. Above all, the ride demonstrates how Hollywood history can be condensed and reinterpreted as an attraction and an experience distinct from traditional theatrical moviegoing.

The American Film Institute Showcase, the last stop on the Disney-MGM backstage tour, originally took a more traditional approach to Hollywood's history. In February 1997, the Los Angeles–based American Film Institute (AFI) opened this attraction at the Disney-MGM Studios, which on the surface, seemed to depart from theme park conventions. According to AFI director Jean Picker Firstenberg, the attraction was designed to illustrate AFI's work "to preserve and enhance moviemaking and to continue the great tradition of American film."[32] Despite AFI's presence and feigned complicity with the theme park environment, its cultural and national mission necessarily diverged from a theme park such as Disney-MGM. The expectation AFI placed on the Disney-MGM showcase to continue "the great tradition of American film" revealed more about the AFI. Like many nonprofits that struggle to survive in a climate not always generous to the arts, the AFI's need to self-promote and brand marks a clear collusion with commercial interests.

The showcase, modeled on conventional museum display, formerly included a behind-the-scenes interactive display on preservation. In its present incarnation, the exhibit continues to feature costumes, props, and set pieces used in contemporary and classic film as well as a section highlighting AFI's Lifetime Achievement Award recipients. Like AFI's television specials, which served as inspiration for some of the exhibits over a ten-year period beginning in 1998, the showcase undeniably functions as an AFI public relations vehicle. Disney-MGM's Academy of Television Arts and Sciences Hall of Fame Plaza similarly celebrates television history and also clearly serves as a promotional tool for the institution's annual Emmy Awards telecast.

Echoing Walt Disney's original vision for Disneyland, many of the contemporary movie theme parks attempt to create environments where they negotiate spectacle with a modicum of education. In addition to the behind-the-scenes demonstrations of film techniques, some of the parks offer museum-type exhibits of their studio properties. Disney-MGM features Walt Disney: One Man's Dream, a biographical exhibit designed to commemorate the one hundredth anniversary of Disney's birth. The exhibit includes audio interviews, archival footage, and inventions illustrating Disney's pioneering achievements and contribution to the fantasy and magic associated with animation but, in a larger sense, with Hollywood history.

Universal Studios Hollywood and Florida celebrate history through another legendary media figure in Lucy: A Tribute. This so-called interactive walk-through museum traces Lucille Ball's life and career in film and television from 1933 until her death. The exhibit, put together with the help of the Lucille Ball estate, includes artifacts such as vintage photographs and magazine covers, costume, jewelry, awards, and Ricky Ricardo's drums, as well as an interactive quiz based on I Love Lucy and scenes from the television show continuously looping on monitors throughout the exhibit space. Playing on nostalgia and the long-standing popularity of the television show, the exhibit also re-creates the Ricardo apartment and a room in Ball's actual Beverly Hills home.

Both the Walt Disney and Lucy exhibits, clearly modeled on traditional museum design, stand out as anomalies in their respective theme park contexts. In particular, Universal's Lucy exhibit seems incongruous in a park that tends to recycle attractions from films as recent as the 1980s in order to make way for new ones based on more current blockbuster releases. While the Lucy tribute may seem anachronistic, on some level in its devotion to television history, it nonetheless demonstrates Lucy's sustained cultural value as a star and Hollywood symbol. In light of the constant reruns of I Love Lucy in syndication, Lucille Ball has indeed become a decidedly ahistorical figure. In choosing Lucy, Universal selects history that retains commercial viability in the present day. Yet, despite the staying power and cultural resonance of Lucille Ball, Universal's promotional materials tend to downplay this and other historical properties that have a presence on the studio tram tour, such as Psycho and The Sting. Universal may frame these attractions as rare, solidifying the privilege afforded by backstage access to Hollywood history, but the park clearly targets their demographic, highlighting the more recent and spectacle-driven films and television shows.

Other exhibits at Universal Studios Hollywood and Warner Bros. Movie World also feature contemporary films in museumlike exhibitions. Universal offers re-created set pieces and authentic props from films such as Van Helsing as part of a mazelike entryway for the attraction. Warner Bros. Movie World in Australia touts its Official Matrix Exhibit as a "walk-through experience" of sets, props, and costumes from the film. The experiential value of such an exhibit remains limited by the regulated designs of the typical theme park. While the park clearly places value on the access to backstage zones of a film production, in many cases the opportunity to "walk through" suggests a more conventional exhibition style than a truly immersive or interactive one.

In Germany, the former Warner Bros. park offered an even more traditional exhibition that included a museum of German film history with film posters, cameras, projectors, and scripts, tracing the development of film from 1900 to 1980. Again, the museumlike exhibits played upon the legitimacy and authenticity attached to artifacts and sets from actual films. They traded on the symbolic power attached to Hollywood and its backstage arena while simultaneously marketing a particular studio's intellectual property. And, while they remained largely motionless, these exhibits traded on the "liveness" attached to surrounding theme park attractions by framing the exhibits as "living experiences" of the original film. Similar to the rhetoric tied to earlier Hollywood museum ventures discussed in the previous chapter, the rhetoric of "liveness" indicates a desire to reconstitute the exhibition of static artifacts as well as an attempt to legitimate an exhibition site beyond the theater.

When Planet Hollywood opened its doors in 1991, it similarly promised a "living" alternative to the original film in the form of potential star sightings. As movie theme parks, largely modeling themselves on Universal Studios' original tour, sprouted from 1989 through the mid-2000s, so did other movie-themed environments in comparable business sectors, namely, food and retail. Planet Hollywood similarly evoked museum and gallery exhibition in its design and display practices and, like the theme parks, tied its cachet value to Hollywood history, glamour, and stars. Like these theme parks, Planet Hollywood also translated the symbolic power of Hollywood into a consumable experience that could be easily transported across the globe.

Planet Hollywood • Building a Global Dream-Theme Factory

In September 1995, at the opening of the Beverly Hills Planet Hollywood, the *Los Angeles Times* called the themed restaurant "the closest thing to a movie museum in [the] film capital."[33] Keith Barish, who in addition to cofounding Planet Hollywood, produced such films as *Sophie's Choice*, *Nine ½ Weeks*, and *The Fugitive*, echoed the sentiments of Michael Eisner in his remarks about Disney-MGM, claiming the themed restaurant also filled a void and restored an often overlooked disjunction between Hollywood the place and Hollywood the image. According to Barish,

> There's no Hollywood. You come here and you see the Paramount gates and the footprints at Mann's Theatre (formerly Grauman's Chinese Theatre), and that's it. "Hollywood" is still working, but there isn't much to look at. People still make an emotional connection with movie memorabilia that's incredibly powerful, though, and to bring these treasures back to the movies' hometown is very important to us.[34]

In bringing objects "home" to Los Angeles, or by placing them in spaces and displays that recalled this Hollywood "home," the Beverly Hills Planet Hollywood, long closed, exploited the emotional connection that Barish described and embodied the mission of many 1990s themed environments. At the same time, in emulating museum display, the restaurant chain followed the catchall approach to attract visitors popularized by Barnum and Disney.

After first opening its doors in New York City in 1991, the restaurant chain and corporation expanded throughout the decade, consolidating and cornering a global market that, along with the Hard Rock Café chain, paved the way for and made a trend out of the theme restaurant business.[35] In the late 1990s, the Beverly Hills location, among others, closed amid the company's money woes and two separate declarations of bankruptcy. The previously publicly traded Planet Hollywood International subsequently scaled back its global reach of ninety-five restaurants in thirty-one countries with locations as diverse as Las Vegas and Jakarta to a more modest, yet still significant, sixteen restaurants, mostly outside of the United States.[36] Arguably a dated symbol of the 1990s, Planet Hollywood nonetheless continues to reinvent itself by exploiting its connection (in name, millions' worth of memorabilia holdings and star affiliation) to Hollywood, particularly in international markets and tourist destinations, and further by appropriating and negotiating Hollywood and its history as commodities.[37] The corporation's more recent endeavor in a Las Vegas hotel and casino reworks the original theme. Rather than focus exclusively on Hollywood and its film culture, Planet Hollywood, as evidenced by its Times Square site in New York, has tapped into a more generic and broad-based interest in celebrity culture.

Despite all of its corporate shuffling, Planet Hollywood adheres to a fundamental agenda. It strategically targets a global audience and a global marketplace, indiscriminately tapping multiple tastes, classes, educational backgrounds, and national identities by treating everyone generically as potential Hollywood consumers. Though not necessarily its aim, Planet Hollywood links itself foremost, by name and logo, to a notion of global or cultural imperialism. The chain evokes the concept of "planet" as a vehicle to construct a coherent universe that offers consumers a myth of unity and totality surrounding an equally vague vision of Hollywood. Since the mid-1980s, the Hollywood industry has fairly consistently grossed more from overseas markets than domestic, and many of its major stars, who often participate in advertising campaigns outside the United States, arguably garner more attention abroad than in America.[38] In its heyday, Planet Hollywood emulated the industry's global reach, expanding on this imperialist tradition by conquering the international market through another leisure space—the restaurant—and another more literal form of consumption—eating.

Planet Hollywood exemplifies one of the ways in which contemporary cultural institutions and corporate entities solidified and profited from the cult status of Hollywood by incorporating it into everyday commodities and rituals. In many ways, Planet Hollywood identifies and markets itself as a purely traditional tourist site. At the same time and like the Hollywood theme parks, Planet Hollywood expands on typical tourist conventions by transferring and translating a single vision of "Hollywood" within multiple venues. While most tourist sites thrive on the uniqueness tied to their provenance, Planet Hollywood remakes a geographic site and universal symbol into a highly constructed and easily replicated environment.

The Planet Hollywood experience depends in large part on sensory and memory stimulation. Remembering (or at least recognizing) films, television shows, stars, and the objects associated with them becomes an act of ritual consumption at Planet Hollywood, comparable to the ritual of eating meals with family and friends, the ritual of watching films or television, and the ritual of shopping. More than mere media consumers, or media connoisseurs for that matter, Planet Hollywood assumes its visitors share an interest in all things Hollywood. Therefore, the restaurant displays an eclectic, if not random, array of cultural artifacts that, when united under one restaurant's roof, are devised to channel a vision of Hollywood, increasingly associated with all aspects of stardom and entertainment instead of just films. The pleasure at Planet Hollywood can operate as a simple identification game. Looking at iconic memorabilia, watching film excerpts with popular stars, and listening to familiar music

Diorama featuring an ahistorical mixture of film and television history references at Planet Hollywood Beverly Hills, circa 1997. Author's collection.

can provide a context through which different consumers can quickly and easily identify a film product. Pleasure can therefore come in the form of cultural capital, in the knowledge and ability to name a film or song title. Similarly, pleasure can come from identifying stars and seeing their costumes as well as making sense of a genre or theme constructed by a particular display. Reading against the grain, others could find enjoyment in their own personal camp readings of the artifacts and their display contexts. Regardless of the object, pleasure at Planet Hollywood is tied to a shared acknowledgment and fetishization of Hollywood's past and present.

Planet Hollywood summons its customers to consume authorized memories and mythologies about Hollywood stardom and glamour, thereby buying into a unified, generic, and largely ahistorical Hollywood narrative. A film or television clip, a costume, a musical score, or prop can conjure memories (even recent ones) of the original viewing of a particular film or television program, of a given era, or of personal memories otherwise elicited by artifacts on display. Thus, elements of collective memory and personal memory operate within both the Planet Hollywood context and the popular mythologies that circulate around Hollywood in general. Likewise, the cultural and commercial value of the objects at Planet Hollywood depends on a confluence of factors: the corporation's reputation and popularity, the display strategies, and finally, the visitor's reception.

At the height of the chain's popularity, the Beverly Hills location held the largest collection of memorabilia out of over ninety restaurants. Even with all of the corporate changes and restaurant closures, the focus on memorabilia and seemingly random display conventions at Planet Hollywood remains fairly consistent. Some artifact and costume juxtapositions seem to make an explicit connection, tying the present to the past with a display of Charles Laughton's uniform from *Mutiny on the Bounty* beside Tom Cruise's from *Top Gun*, or Marilyn Monroe's dress from *The Prince and the Showgirl* paired with Robin Williams's fat suit and dress worn in *Mrs. Doubtfire*. Interestingly, most of the noteworthy items (to "mediaphiles" and collectors) at Planet Hollywood are not foregrounded in the main exhibition spaces. Artifacts such as Charlie Chaplin's jacket from *The Great Dictator* and Gregory Peck's suit from *The Gentleman's Agreement*, among other classical Hollywood memorabilia at the Beverly Hills location got placed in less prominent positions.[39] The same remains true for the current locations. The New York Planet Hollywood displays James Cagney's suit from *Yankee Doodle Dandy* and Steve McQueen's from *The Getaway* on a stairwell.

It remains unclear from the museum-inspired placards which of Planet Hollywood's diverse artifacts have been purchased and which are on loan and, in the case of star handprints reminiscent of Grauman's Chinese Theatre, which are real and which are facsimiles. The actual authenticity of objects is irrelevant, however, as long as they can conjure Hollywood and maintain a guise of authority. Planet Hollywood cultivates a symbiotic relationship with studios, and more recently, record companies and sports teams, in order to reaffirm its industrial authority.[40] In the 1990s, the Beverly Hills entryway featured a shrine-like display with a video monitor and other studio public relations materials, drawing attention to a designated film slated for release that week. When the video monitors throughout the restaurant were not playing custom-designed Planet Hollywood videos, they ran trailers of upcoming releases or music from

Costumes and props from the 1997 blockbuster *Titanic* encased in glass beside restaurant seating. Planet Hollywood, Times Square, New York. Author's collection.

a wide array of film soundtracks. While the current Planet Hollywood locations tend to focus less on direct studio promotion and more on music video and sports programming, the studio connection remains operational, especially at Disney's Orlando and Paris theme park sites. Unlike the symbiotic relationship between the studios and traditional museums such as MoMA and the failed Hollywood Museum venture discussed in previous chapters, the media conglomerates' relationship with Planet Hollywood is more indirect, especially with the declining role of its original star owners, Bruce Willis, Demi Moore, Arnold Schwarzenegger, and Sylvester Stallone. Nevertheless, Planet Hollywood operates as an ancillary market in other ways, serving as a promotional site for the Hollywood brand in a wide range of markets.

The restaurant chain retains a promotional foothold in the entertainment industry, hosting premiere and launch parties for films and, increasingly, television shows and albums. Such events and the popular entertainment press that surround them lend credence to the impression that stars frequent or drop by the themed restaurant chain. This belief is furthered by a visit to the Planet Hollywood website, which features photos of celebrity sightings as well as interviews with stars in recently released films. The chance meeting with a star is central to Planet Hollywood's corporately constructed fantasy of Hollywood and the Hollywood encounter. It is also literally inscribed in the corporate strategy; each restaurant is required to have six star (ambiguously defined) appearances per year.[41]

The ubiquitous focus on contemporary stars at Planet Hollywood complicates the restaurant's representation of Hollywood history. Like a backlot studio tour, the in-person chance star encounter functions as a behind-the-scenes enticement for Planet Hollywood customers. In the absence of real Hollywood stars and encounters, Planet Hollywood substitutes costumes, props, video excerpts, star look-alikes, and other artifacts as stand-ins. On their own, the memorabilia and artifacts featured at various Planet Hollywood locations might not garner much attention or satisfy a visitor's desired proximity to Hollywood. However, a popular star's image, name, and body can transform the object, giving it a meaningful context and a fetish value. When Demi Moore wore Rita Hayworth's dress from *Gilda* to the Beverly Hills opening of Planet Hollywood, for example, Moore's persona potentially augmented (or diminished depending on one's perspective) the cultural value of the original artifact and star.

Playing up the possibility of a real star sighting, the New York restaurant entrance in the heart of a tourist-filled Times Square features a wall devoted to photos of contemporary celebrities who have visited the location. On the opposing wall, the restaurant entrance features a photo collage of classical-era paparazzi. This collage comes to life as blinking lights, whistling, and cheering (emanating from speakers) position Planet Hollywood visitors themselves as stars. In constructing the red carpet experience of a premiere or awards show, Planet Hollywood offers its visitors an experience framed around privilege and access to Hollywood's exclusive backstage regions. The display of live-cam images from Times Square further situates the restaurant customer in a privileged viewing position. Visitors do not merely dine at Planet Hollywood; they mingle with stars, act like stars, and in viewing these live images, imagine themselves behind the scenes, if not behind the camera.

In order to remain commercially viable and regain a waning popularity since declaring bankruptcy and closing many locations, the remaining Planet Hollywood restaurants have cast a wider net, incorporating other themes aside from Hollywood. Many of the restaurants, such as the New York location in Times Square, feature a sports bar component. The New York location thereby plays up its local affiliation with sports teams and stars, commodifying and memorializing them as part of a Hollywood-esque celebrity culture. The focus on contemporary sports culture parallels an emphasis on contemporary memorabilia from box office hits, popular genres, and easily recognizable stars. This display strategy reflects Planet Hollywood's assessment and targeting of a specific audience, as well as the ahistorical bias enforced by its backers and display designers. Through their display choices and juxtaposition of artifacts, Planet Hollywood constructs its own popular Hollywood canon, one tied historically to a greatest hits tradition reflecting less on classic films and stars and more on contemporary box office receipts and celebrity culture.

Planet Hollywood clearly serves its own brand first and foremost through its restaurant but, additionally, through the retail store attached to each location. Emulating a theme park, the New York location welcomes visitors with iconic historical stars and characters, such as Marilyn Monroe and Batman, who pose for pictures at the entrance of the gift shop. Many Planet Hollywood sites further highlight the gift shop by featuring a separate street entrance for the store or forcing patrons to enter the restaurant by first walking through the store. The store encourages visitors to take a piece of (Planet) Hollywood home with them. The retail store also allows the restaurant to reap more substantial profits than it could otherwise garner purely from food and beverage revenue. In the late 1990s, Planet Hollywood expanded its retail presence, opening superstores in carefully selected target tourist zones. These stores initially existed independently of Planet Hollywood restaurants and food consumption, assuming a pure retail function. Some of these stores opened in high-traffic arenas such as airports (Singapore Airport and Gatwick), while others remain tied to tourist areas such as Las Vegas, Myrtle Beach, and Orlando as well as theme parks (Disney-MGM Studios). In these examples, Planet Hollywood as a corporation expanded its own sales activities and took cues from the retail industry. Merchandise offered customers direct contact and connection to Hollywood. A T-shirt can, to some, be more significant than a glimpse of the 35 mm camera Jimmy Stewart used in *Rear Window*. At the same time, the T-shirt, like the memorabilia, can mobilize new memories for consumers, tying Planet Hollywood, its artifacts, and its star power more concretely, albeit superficially, to the history and cult status of Hollywood.

Corporate Synergy and Themed Retailing

The international success of movie-themed retail environments such as the Disney Store and the Warner Bros. Studio Store in the late 1980s and 1990s paralleled the meteoric rise of Planet Hollywood and marked a significant historical moment in the consumer retail arena. While the Walt Disney corporation has sold products and merchandise at its theme parks since the 1950s and Warner Bros. has long operated a merchandise kiosk on its lot, these retail stores greatly expanded both company's brand-name recognition and global presence, making the studios and their properties part of everyday consumption.

For Warner Bros. and Disney, the retail store therefore served as a direct conduit between the studio, the corporation, and the consumer and, like their theme parks, and now the Internet, offered a much desired branding opportunity and ancillary revenue stream.

At their height, each chain boasted an extensive global presence. Disney, which first opened a store in Glendale, California, in 1987, had over seven hundred locations in 1999, while the Warner Bros. Studio Store, which first opened in 1991 in Los Angeles' Beverly Center mall, had 180 stores. It was at the end of 1999, the same year that Planet Hollywood first declared bankruptcy, when both chains also began to experience financial woes similar to those of the themed restaurant chain. Both Disney and Time Warner elected to scale back their global retail ventures by early 2000, and by the end of 2001, all of U.S.-based Warner Bros. Studio Stores had closed. Warner Bros. still has a retail presence in Europe, but the relationship between the studio and the stores is structured purely as licensing and franchise agreements.[42]

Meanwhile, Disney successfully sold off some of its foreign locations, and in 2004, sold most of the remaining 313 U.S. locations to a successful children's retailer that retained the Disney format and name under a long-term license agreement. The Walt Disney Company kept the stores on its Burbank lot as well as a remodeled Fifth Avenue store in Manhattan (called "The World of Disney Store" and operated under Disney's resort division). In 2008, the corporation repurchased over two hundred of the North American retail outlets and, the following year, closed the World of Disney Store while opening yet another incarnation at the end of 2010 in Manhattan's Times Square district. Both studios also continue to have a significant online retail presence and exploit the licensing and merchandising potential tied to their individual media properties.

Similar to the original and totalizing vision of Disneyland, the flagship locations of the Disney and Warner Bros. Studio Stores in New York's midtown represented a microcosm of the theme park, the arcade, the exploratorium, the film and television studio, the art gallery, and the global corporation. Indeed, these themed retail environments offered what the majority of stores in each company's retail chain, for the most part, did not—an experience beyond shopping and beyond each studio's popular properties. As with Planet Hollywood, consumers were bombarded by constant visual and aural stimulation. From the 1990s onward, many retail stores, particularly those owned by major corporations with indispensable budgets, increasingly introduced a kind of "retail theater" in which store design and floor plans were saturated with speakers and screens, music, and moving images. Such design-centric stores construct a highly visible brand and multisensory experience, turning retail into entertainment.[43]

The Disney Store and the Warner Bros. Studio Store stood apart from these other retail superstores such as Niketown in specifically linking the act of consumption to a generic idea of Hollywood and the images and cultural memories associated with it. With the purchase of a toy, doll, clothing article, pin, piece of jewelry, watch, picture frame, figurine, dinner plate, or even a shower curtain, the consumer supported the corporation's sales figures but, on a more symbolic level, bought into the studio's brand name and Hollywood history. Echoing the promotional rhetoric used by movie theme parks and Planet Hollywood, the Warner Bros. Studio Store contended about its clothing, the "magic of Hollywood is woven into everything."[44] The stores thus presented Hollywood magic as something even more accessible and easily consumable than the attractions offered at the theme parks. By weaving the magic into its goods, these stores implicitly promised the consumer that Hollywood could be bought and taken home—a promise furthered by the home entertainment industry later in the decade.

Throughout their histories, the Disney and Warner Bros. studios have created a legacy of classic animated characters. So, rather than focus on individual stars like Planet Hollywood, these retail stores, like many contemporary theme parks, upheld their animated characters as symbolic points of identification, central to the studio brand. Mickey Mouse, Bugs Bunny, and Donald and Daffy Duck, iconic figures in cultural history and popular memory, shared shelf space and attention with more contemporary characters that found a place in the popular memories of younger and newer audiences such as Buzz Lightyear, Ariel (aka the Little Mermaid), and the Animaniacs. These studio stores, like their theme park counterparts, employed a wide-ranging cast of characters in order to tap into past memories, while at the same time, creating new merchandise and new points of identification. Strategically focusing on the old as well as the new, like the previously discussed themed environments, allowed the stores to solicit new consumers while catering to their long-standing followers and collectors. Having significant cultural resonance, the studio's copyrighted characters offered coveted branding opportunities.

Both the Disney and Warner Bros. flagship stores sold similar product lines and employed similar display strategies and conventions. The entryways at each store featured the most eye-catching (especially for children) and mass-market merchandise—toys, dolls, and clothing, typically highlighting cultural icons of animation history. The characters' original and singular roles in a film narrative remained secondary as the corporations worked to distinguish the value of their copyrighted property in the retail arena. Indeed, their status as consumable and easily modified pieces of merchandise (T-shirts, key chains, backpacks, bubble blowers, board games, etc.) more prominently signaled their value to the brand and assured their own cultural capital and longevity.

The desire to consume not only applied to traditional merchandise: the toys, clothing, bath and kitchen accessories, and picture frames; it also applied to the collectibles. Both stores devoted entire sections to commemorative and collectible items. In this way, the brand's history became a crucial component in its value, not to mention its legitimacy, especially among aficionados and collectors. In their flagship locations, Disney and Warner Bros. constructed actual gallery spaces. Both stores consciously, if not conspicuously, segregated the gallery from the rest of the store. This segregation created a level of distinction in price and target audience; it also gave the objects an authenticity and fetish value that alluded to both the gallery and museum as well as traditional, high-end Fifth Avenue retail. The prices for limited edition watches, designer jewelry, lithographs, and animation cels ranged from as little as one hundred dollars to as much as eight thousand dollars for the most coveted Mickey Mouse serigraph.[45] Through museum display aesthetics and high-ticket prices, these galleries positioned objects as historical artifacts and rarefied collectibles above the bulk merchandise in the rest of the store.

Disney's gallery was located on the top floor of the original three-story flagship store in midtown Manhattan. The gallery display markedly departed from the conventions employed in the rest of the store. While oversized architectural objects, themed icons, drawing and painting activity stations for children, and large video screens confronted the customer at every turn on the first two floors of the store, the gallery was decidedly toned down, its style geared to an adult audience of collector-connoisseurs. By entering the gallery, the customer moved from the domestic-coded spaces of the first two floors (designed to be a townhouse for Disney's classic "Fab 5" characters, Mickey, Minnie, Donald, Goofy, and Pluto) into a more formal public space. In the gallery, the bulbous and bombastic Disney theme park style that permeated the rest of the store, while still apparent, was secondary to the artifacts on display.

Framed animation cels, paintings, posters, and stamp sets hung on wood-veneered walls. Collectible platters and figurines were arranged on wooden

Larger-than-life evil witch looms over the foyer of the flagship Disney Store,
midtown Manhattan, circa 1996. Author's collection.

display stands. Expensive designer jewelry, watches, pens, and tableware were
enclosed in velvet-lined glass cases. Recessed overhead, boutique lighting individually accented all of the gallery items. Unlike the merchandise on the first
two floors, including souvenirs, clothing, and bath and body accessories, the
objects in the gallery were labeled like museum artifacts with identifying signage that indicated title, date, and, where appropriate, status within a limited
edition series. In creating this gallery and high-end merchandise, the Disney
corporation set up two expectations. Like other contemporary studios, they
wanted to move mass-market merchandise and turn a profit; at the same time,
they wanted to preserve their historical legacy and cultural legitimacy. Expanding on the cultural power of its historical characters and signature style, the
gallery offered, albeit superficially, a more legitimate conduit for cultural memory through the act of collecting.

The gallery space at the flagship Warner Bros. Studio Store similarly worked
to summon cultural memories, while also underscoring the economic and cultural cachet of Hollywood and its history. Like the Disney Store two blocks
away, the gallery in this nine-floor Warner Bros. superstore was demarcated
from the rest of the retail space. Located on the fifth floor alongside the store's

Second-floor gallery at Disney Store, midtown Manhattan, circa 1996. Author's collection.

themed restaurant, the Motion Picture Café, the Warner Bros. Studio Store gallery, featured animation cels and a range of other collectibles nearly identical to the Disney gallery. This Warner Bros. gallery differed from the Disney version, however, in consciously and more explicitly positioning the space, artifacts, and merchandise in the context of film and animation production as well as Warner Bros. studio history. In this way, the Warner Bros. gallery paralleled not only the contemporary moving image museum but also the then burgeoning home entertainment market.

Upon exiting the escalator on the fifth floor, the visitor first viewed a group portrait of three of Warner's classical-era artisans (Friz Freleng, Carl Stalling, and Bob McKimson) flanked by famed and iconic Warner Bros. characters (Sylvester, Porky the Pig, Yosemite Sam, and the Tasmanian Devil). Entering the gallery, the visitor then encountered an interactive display called "Making Art That Talks" that provided a simple seven-step illustration of the animation pro-

Group portrait of Warner Bros. classical-era artisans, Friz Freleng, Carl Stalling, and Bob
McKimson, Warner Bros. Store, midtown Manhattan, circa 1996. Author's collection.

cess. After visually moving through the various production steps, the visitor
could push a button to see how the finished animated product materialized.
This pedagogical exhibit, with signage defining the details of the production
process, including the terms involved (i.e., cel, sericel, and production cel), resembled the interactive exhibition spaces more typically found in contemporary museums (as discussed in chapter 2), exploratoriums, and science centers,
not to mention the extra feature section on many DVDs.

The rest of the space, like the Disney Store, simulated traditional art gallery
display and lighting. In fact, the Warner Bros. gallery more strictly adhered to
art gallery conventions than its Disney counterpart. Refraining from cartoon-
ish and over-the-top stylization, the Warner Bros. gallery emulated the clean
lines and trendy industrial components found in many contemporary fine art
display venues. The Warner Bros. gallery also took a broader, more crossover
approach to its merchandise and studio image. Rather than exclusively focusing on the animated Looney Tunes and Hanna-Barbera characters or DC Comic
heroes, the Warner Bros. gallery featured paintings, serigraphs, and selected
memorabilia from other Warner Bros. products and stars such as Marilyn
Monroe (from *The Prince and the Showgirl*), Audrey Hepburn (from *Sabrina*), John
Wayne (from *Hondo*), and serigraphs from 1990s Warner blockbusters including *Twister* and *Eraser*.

Gallery at flagship Warner Bros. Studio Store New York, highlighting the studio's
DC Comics properties. Author's collection.

Targeting mass consumers as well as niche audiences, the Warner Bros. Studio Store also sponsored a Collector's Guild, a members-only club and self-proclaimed "invaluable source" of information about the wide range of Warner collectibles, from animation art to Hollywood film and television memorabilia. Throughout the year, the fifty-five-dollar membership entitled members to receive advance notice of members-only collector's editions and previews of "Gallery Collection releases," as well as quarterly editions of *A.C.M.E.* ("A Collectors Magazine for Everyone") that featured behind-the-scenes information about Warner Bros. creative production as well as previews of new collections. Membership also included enticements such as a Collector's Guild keepsake folio, a cloisonné charter membership pin, and a charter membership card. The cost and coded benefits of Collector's Guild membership brought the studio another profit outlet. More importantly, in making members feel a part of something exclusive and inaccessible to the average consumer, the Collector's Guild legitimated the act of collecting while solidifying loyalty to the studio, its history, and its brand merchandise.

Like Planet Hollywood, the Warner Bros. Studio Store further capitalized on the studio's association with and production of historical as well as contemporary star power. The pedagogical display and gallery setting within the Warner Bros. Store offered an odd, but provocative, juxtaposition of education and entertainment—one that is now commonplace in many nonprofit as well as for-profit arenas and products. Notwithstanding a studio's economic agenda and branding initiatives, themed environments rely on an intermingling of culture and commerce. Thus, the gallery and educational exhibits in the Warner Bros. Studio Store manifested the studio's efforts to initiate and indoctrinate a more cultured, high-powered, and moneyed consumer who could afford to collect (and might, in turn, desire the cultural capital necessary to understand the collectibles).

For the majority of visitors, who did not see themselves as collectors in a traditional sense, however, the Warner Bros. Studio Store still diligently incorporated its studio history and historical icons into the majority of its merchandise. The act of collecting even the most banal merchandise could activate brand loyalty. The promotional rhetoric surrounding the studio's store clearly foregrounded, even promoted, this link between past and present:

> Step inside any Warner Bros. Studio Store and you're immediately transported to the sometimes glamorous, sometimes wacky, but always exciting world of Warner Bros. Entertainment past and present. Here the stage has been set for a grand statement of merchandise in true Hollywood style, from clothing and original animation art to elegant gift items and colorful home furnishings.[46]

Here, the Warner Bros. Studio Store established a simple and singular role for itself. Like Planet Hollywood, the store could transcend time and space, conjuring Hollywood in a wide range of sites and through a diverse set of artifacts. In turn, Hollywood could represent both past and present; it could be generic but was no less meaningful. In its shorthand reference to "true Hollywood," the promotion further summoned an ahistorical, yet familiar, authenticity tied to glamour and star power.

The store windows facing Fifty-Seventh Street further evoked the connection between past and present and, like the New York Planet Hollywood site, tied the public space of the store to the larger urban space of New York City. On the lower-level window, New York City icons such as the Empire State Building, yellow taxicabs, and the World Trade Center surrounded larger-than-life classic animated characters. Above this animated display, the second-floor windows more traditionally exhibited artifacts that signified the historical film production process and old Hollywood—vintage klieg lamps and cameras. In addition to these window displays and a five-story wall sculpture on the main floor that was remarkably similar to Disney's in referencing classic Looney Tunes characters ("Looney Tunes and Friends Meet New York"), other formulated tie-ins throughout the store constructed links between Warner Bros.' past, present, and future.[47] With its colorful, oversized, and over-the-top decor, the Warner Bros. Studio Store, like the Disney Store, physically resembled a theme or amusement park setting. However, the Warner Bros. Studio Store took the theme park framework beyond the surface realm of store decor. This store incorporated actual theme park activities into the shopping experience, an addition Disney later made in its remodeled World of Disney, New York.

Most of the activities at the Warner Bros. Store centered on classic Looney Tunes characters and references from the original cartoons. On weekends and during the holiday season, the Warner Bros. Store more explicitly re-created a theme park setting with life-sized classic Looney Tunes as well as more contemporary Hanna Barbera–Cartoon Network "friends" greeting visitors at the store's entrance. On all other days, the sixth floor of the Warner Bros. Store permanently featured the "Wacky ACME Interactive Area." Designed for kids, this area resembled a video arcade with games that played off the frequent "ACME" references from classic Looney Tune cartoons. The games—a Molecular Distrortinator, an Elasticity Station, a Pedal Pressure Poultry Projection, an ACME weather station, and an ACME brain—played on the fantastical and transformative potential of animation, offering consumers another way to consume and understand and enjoy Hollywood. One floor above, visitors could also experience this potential on their own at several hands-on animation stands. These sensory attractions offered an alternative to not only the typical retail experience but the film or television experience as well.

The Warner Bros. Studio Store as well as the World of Disney (which also features character visits and an interactive "media zone") simulated interactive arenas popular in many contemporary exhibition spaces: theme and amusement parks, science centers, interactive media museums, hybrid corporate-educational centers, and Internet sites and DVDs. The popularity and pleasure associated with interactive activities in contemporary public exhibition, home entertainment, and mobile devices attests to the importance of constructing a concrete, sensory, immediate, do-it-yourself experience for visitors (particularly younger visitors). The interactive element further manifests an evolution in the composition and experience offered by themed environments. Through

Retail store meets theme park with interactive stations,
Warner Bros. Studio Store, New York. Author's collection.

this kind of interaction, visitors directly engage with exhibitions and, in turn, directly participate in a range of activities, including communications experiments promoted as cutting edge, re-created historical interviews, and the fictional worlds of film and television programs. Any discussion of themed environments as arenas of interactive freedom and exploration, however, must be tempered by an awareness of the corporation's strategic masking of its own branding incentives. Focusing on the direct engagement, even personal empowerment, suggested by such do-it-yourself interactive attractions elides the corporate construction and regulation of Hollywood's image and history.

Some fifty years ago, Disney foresaw the blurred lines between corporate, commercial, and public exhibition spheres that came to dominate contemporary public spaces at the end of the twentieth century. These sites reflected an expansion of synergistic corporate relations in the global economy and urban space as well as an accompanying desire, even a necessity, to create environments that can serve multiple functions and a wide range of visitors in ways that traditional museums likely cannot. Within the global economic arena, international corporations and media conglomerates scavenge Hollywood's synchronic warehouse, finding new ways to control, manipulate, and merchandise

Hollywood as an image and brand. Even Debbie Reynolds, who once again tried to revive her movie museum at Hollywood and Highland, the highly marketed (and largely beleaguered) redevelopment epicenter of Hollywood, has since abandoned these Hollywood dreams. She later announced plans to erect a new museum in Pigeon Forge, Tennessee, adjacent to the highly themed Dollywood. On the one hand, it seemed Reynolds did learn from Las Vegas; however, in 2010, some forty years after acquiring objects from the famed MGM auction, Reynolds announced the auctioning of her own memorabilia collection, worth by some estimates fifty million dollars.[48]

Meanwhile, Las Vegas itself continues to feature prominently as a site for many corporate themed ventures. While Star Trek: The Experience closed after ten years in 2008, the city remains central to one of the more recent Planet Hollywood vehicles.[49] With the Planet Hollywood Resort and Casino, the corporation partnered with Clear Channel Entertainment in 2005 to renovate the Aladdin resort and casino, and provide the "ultimate entertainment experience" with a "real taste of Hollywood."[50] In the context of examples discussed throughout this chapter, learning from Las Vegas serves as a metaphor for the experiential and branding potential seized by a range of media-based corporations. The learning, in these cases, revolves around appropriating Hollywood imagery, history, and icons in order to rechannel them into consumable products, events, and experiences that can proliferate outside of Hollywood. Based on the failure of the Warner Bros. Studio Store and uneven past of the Disney Store as well as the waning success of Planet Hollywood in the themed restaurant arena, however, it is clear that the idea of learning from Las Vegas may not serve all corporations, all concepts, and all sites equally. As I argue in the following chapters, the idea, experience, and branding of Hollywood, while still viable in sites such as the Las Vegas strip and New York's Times Square, plays an increasingly important role in the private space of the home and the Internet. Indeed, digital sites may prove more economically and symbolically valuable than any themed entertainment site ever could.

Hollywood in a Box

Channeling Hollywood through
Home Entertainment

In 1951, Ed Sullivan began to court Hollywood studios. In order to distinguish his variety show, *Toast of the Town*, and align it with the prestige of Hollywood moviemaking, Sullivan regularly transformed his television series into a Hollywood promotional vehicle, paying homage to individual movies, studios, and power brokers such as Samuel Goldwyn and David O. Selznick. Initially unreceptive to television, Warner Bros. shunned Sullivan's invitation in 1951 to honor the release of *A Streetcar Named Desire*. By 1955, however, when it became clear that television offered a key promotional platform for all movie studios, Warner Bros. welcomed the adulation offered by an hour-long episode of *Toast of the Town*, entitled "The Warner Story." Valuing the crossover promotion potential of television, Warner Bros. subsequently set out to produce and thereby control its own television programming. As Christopher Anderson argues, "Instead of waiting for *Toast of the Town* or the *Colgate Comedy Hour* to offer an invitation, Warner Bros. could . . . orchestrate its own publicity by coordinating television exposure with a movie's larger marketing campaign."[1]

For executive Jack Warner, *Warner Bros. Presents* told "the important story of the motion pictures to the public."[2] In asserting that Hollywood not only told stories but also had its own story, Warner clearly underscored the importance of the studio, its history, and the impressive magnitude of its elaborate production process. More than the contemporary network programs such as *The Late Show, Hollywood Film Theater*, NBC's *Saturday Night at the Movies*, ABC's *Sunday Night at the Movies*, and CBS's *Night at the Movies* that screened recycled studio films, *Warner Bros. Presents* offered the studios a regulated site of influence, economic power, corporate branding, and symbolic value.

The program, which began airing on ABC in 1955, secured legitimacy for its network distributor by featuring high-quality, movie-grade production values on television. At the same time, the program offered another site and avenue to experience and appreciate the studio and its products. The program opened with a fanfare sounding over an aerial view of the Warner Bros. backlot. Following an image of the iconic studio logo, host Gig Young, a known supporting player in Hollywood, introduced the show and set the stage for the forty-five-minute "entertainment portion," which featured filmed stories based on one of the studio's former famous productions—for example, *Casablanca, King's Row, Cheyenne.* The concluding segment, touted as the "high point of each week's program," presented a six- to eight-minute overview of current studio projects and promotions. Each of the segments added value to Warner Bros. in real profits based on its contractual agreement with ABC as well as a more elusive value gained from the coveted air time. As Anderson claims, "An idealized image of Hollywood served as the imagined referent for *Warner Bros. Presents.*"[3]

The promotional segments entitled "Behind the Cameras" highlighted an idealized Hollywood image, with Young returning to give viewers an insider's perspective on what transpired behind Hollywood's closed doors. In turn, Young served as a conduit for viewers, bringing them onto the set, the location, or the studio backlot to hear from stars, crew, and executives. Like the studio tours discussed in the previous chapter, these segments were designed to make Hollywood come to life. Adhering to the rhetoric of liveness and immediacy attached to early television, Young's role transported viewers to an idealized Hollywood.[4] These segments further negotiated two seemingly contradictory Hollywood images—one that reinforced an untouchable mix of glamour and spectacle and the other that unveiled and made Hollywood tangible by detailing the inner workings of the production process. This negotiation, which served the purposes of the studio and television networks respectively, foreshadowed later home entertainment ventures that affected a similar balance, cultivating reverence for not only a film's artistry and craft but also the power and global prowess embodied by Hollywood itself.

Warner Bros. Presents regularly highlighted Hollywood's negotiation of the intangible and tangible by featuring the charisma and romance of Hollywood stars beside the more grim realities of day-to-day production. The juxtaposition implied that both facets proved crucial to the spectacle of a successful

Hollywood production. In one episode, Young interviewed up-and-coming stars James Dean and Natalie Wood on the set of *Rebel without a Cause*, while later calling attention to the "difficulties and hazards" of shooting *The Searchers* in Monument Valley. Focusing on the grandeur and epic scale in both star power and studio labor, particularly in relation to its television competition, helped the studio assert its brand and tell its story. In order to underscore this scale of production, Young asserted that Warner Bros. had enough crews to comprise a "city on wheels" and that "when Warner crews go on location, they go like the US Army, prepared to stay."[5] Emphasizing the realism valued and expertly captured by Hollywood crews, Young explained that "the grime and dust of the valley must be ground into both the costumes and the men."[6] Young went on to enumerate the heroic risks taken by camera crews, who had to film action scenes on horseback from a worm's perspective—a hole in the ground.

While enlightening the audience by making them aware of the production process, these segments necessarily blurred the lines between knowledge production and complete veneration. As marketing tools, these segments additionally served as trailers for upcoming releases, often conveying the magic of Hollywood through before-and-after shots comparing a production in process to the polished finished feature. Young concluded each segment by encouraging movie attendance in local theaters, often plugging the opportunity to see films in widescreen Vista Vision and Technicolor—two formats unavailable to television audiences. In constructing this program and aligning itself with the other major Hollywood studios in the mid-1950s, Warner Bros. ultimately aimed to keep the focus on itself and what Hollywood could uniquely offer viewers, in the theaters and in the home.

Following in the path of *Warner Bros. Presents*, contemporary home entertainment media have continued to play a role in legitimating and monumentalizing Hollywood and its history. The home, like many of the themed environments discussed in the previous chapter, serves as a key site to write Hollywood's history as well as elucidate and make accessible various aspects of its production process. In the examples that follow, studios and other home entertainment distributors have traded on Hollywood history, a well-established canon of classic films, and behind-the-scenes trade secrets over the last thirty years in order to turn a profit but also to solidify and sanction the symbolic value tied to Hollywood and its provenance. Because home entertainment media cannot rely on the spectacle or authenticity of the theatrical experience, home media distributors, like the producers of *Warner Bros. Presents*, have had to find other ways to add value. Home entertainment content, whether on classic cable movie channels or home video, typically produces or adds symbolic value by negotiating Hollywood's tangible and intangible qualities and thereby mediating an art-commerce divide that fundamentally and historically has shaped the film industry as well as the history of film culture.

Niche cable movie programming predominantly on American Movie Classics (AMC) and Turner Classic Movies (TCM) as well as the home video market (particularly on specialty DVDs) strategically tap into a historical concept of "high" film culture, soliciting viewers as cinephiles and fans.[7] This home entertainment medium largely adheres to conventions of scholarly film study and programming models established as early as the 1930s by film archives such as the Museum of Modern Art's (MoMA) Film Library and the Cinémathèque Française. In borrowing from a nonprofit arena, these media also follow earlier industry tendencies to exploit and appropriate elements from art cinema or avant-garde cinema and reframe them to appeal to mass audiences.[8] Supplementary content, such as audio commentaries, host introductions, and associated documentaries that provide historical, formal, and generic analysis, directs home viewers, like students, to understand and appreciate a film's cultural significance in a highly regulated context.

In addition to screening the films and situating them as art, home entertainment media often feature technical and production-oriented instruction through audio commentaries and behind-the-scenes featurettes. Such forms of popular pedagogy trace their roots to both contemporary professional film education and early industry training as well as the theme park attractions discussed in the previous chapter. These supplemental media similarly solicit viewers as cinephiles and fans, while acknowledging a different underlying impetus behind their interest. These viewers seek such instruction not necessarily for edification or accrual of cultural capital but to more concretely gain knowledge that may help drive their own careers and offer them the intangibles tied to Hollywood success stories.[9] Coupled with this desire to go behind the Hollywood curtain was the steady and marked proliferation of digital recorders and mobile devices, as well as the more prevalent availability of home editing systems. Moreover, the popularity of behind-the-scenes and do-it-yourself television programs further stimulated an interest in learning from Hollywood professionals.[10]

In fact, both types of home entertainment content celebrate a do-it-yourself and do-it-at-home education, suggesting a bottom-up, consumer-driven kind of learning. Whether embodying the elusive ideals or concrete realities of Hollywood production, such contemporary home entertainment media further rearticulate many of the values promoted by *Warner Bros. Presents* in the mid-1950s. Despite the decidedly different economic climate for Hollywood and its studios, the "imagined referent" of Hollywood remains fairly constant. With the passing decades, however, an expanded array of images and stories has come to constitute Hollywood's contemporary referential status. Hollywood had a history, and it, too, had a marketable and symbolic value.

Cashing in on the Classics

The proliferation of the cable and the home video markets in the 1970s and 1980s, and the more recent tide of Video on Demand, spurred Hollywood studios to seek out and maintain control of their properties in order to secure their histories, their images, and ultimately, the profits tied to them. As multinational conglomerates increasingly took over the studios in the 1980s, such studio gatekeeping and control was likely more desirable and easier to manage. Conglomerates sought to synergistically distribute branded properties across media platforms and in a range of delivery systems in order to maximize and retain profits. With such a wide reach, the conglomerates running the studios could also ideally perpetuate the exchange value of their properties as it played out in multiple products and sites.

By the mid-1980s, historical properties retained a unique value in this marketplace and confirmed the presence of a financially viable nostalgia industry in the postclassical studio era. The nostalgia industry applied a rhetoric of scarcity, historically reserved for archives and preservation, to the most banal and reproducible commodities. Promising to bring Hollywood and Hollywood history to a viewer decidedly different from the theatrical filmgoer, a select set of classic cable movie networks and home video titles offered consumers regimented access to otherwise rarely seen historical properties. In turn, these home entertainment media underscored the cultural relevance and popular resonance of Hollywood history and set the stage for that history to become a central component of the corporate brand into the next decade.[11]

At this same time, and likely playing an instigating role in these changes, a prophetic Ted Turner realized that studio profits resided in the distribution of not only current properties but historical ones as well. Turner, a relative Hollywood outsider who owned a cable news channel (CNN) and an independent superstation (WTBS), intertwined his entrepreneurial commercial interests with the cultural value he attributed to Hollywood history. In 1986, he bought MGM/UA, in large part, to secure programming or software for WTBS without having to negotiate with the major studios.[12] Boastful after closing the deal, Turner enthused, "We've got 35 percent of the great films of all time. We've got Spencer Tracy and Jimmy Cagney working for us from the grave."[13] Here, Turner clearly articulated not only the symbolic value of Hollywood history but also the certain economic value in exploiting consumer nostalgia.

Demonstrating what proved to be keen foresight, Turner strategically understood the way history and commerce could coexist in the ownership and rights of a classic and very plentiful film studio vault.[14] In December 1987, Turner accrued more films by purchasing the RKO library dating from 1930 to 1957. As historian Stephen Prince argues, these studio libraries and the ancillary markets in which they traffic can extend the revenue life of a motion picture, not to mention its owner.[15] As studio power brokers became well aware, these libraries not only produced supplemental revenue but also, more importantly perhaps, extended the life and symbolic value of the films, the stars, the studios, and the more ephemeral "idea" of Hollywood.

Fearing lost profits and missed opportunities and stimulated no doubt by Turner's voracious raiding of studio vaults, media conglomerates adjusted their historical and preservation priorities and objectives. Such a reassessment of Hollywood history further parallels and sheds light on the development, programming, and nostalgic marketing campaigns of the two most widely received classic movie cable networks, AMC and TCM. AMC, which got its start in 1984 as a showcase cable channel for classical-era Hollywood films, hit its stride a few years later in 1987. Following in the footsteps of Bravo, which was launched in 1980 as an arts and culture cable channel by AMC's parent company, Rainbow Media, AMC positioned itself as an exclusive sphere that offered audiences an elite movie experience, playing domestic surrogate to a museum or repertory screening venue.

AMC tried, in vain, to compete with Turner's purchase of MGM/UA by buying the cable rights to part of the studio's film library.[16] Meanwhile, Turner used his film library for programming on WTBS as well as Turner Network Television, another cable channel he launched in 1988, both precursors to TCM. It was not until 1994 that Turner successfully established TCM as his own commercial-free classic film channel, and a more veritable rival for AMC.[17] (Fox Movie Channel, which also launched in 1994 as fxM and showed similar classic

Home entertainment harnesses Hollywood history and sells the "classics." Turner Classic Movies' advertisement for *Mildred Pierce*, 2005. Author's collection.

fare, has never achieved the public profile or extensive cable subscription base that AMC and TCM managed to cultivate.[18])

Two years later, the megamerger of Turner Broadcasting and Time Warner indicated another major sea change in ownership but, more significantly, a struggle to regain control over lost properties and distribution outlets. In 1996, Warner Bros., under Time Warner, reacquired its pre-1948 library along with the rest of Turner's holdings. An offshoot of the merger, this reacquisition neatly coincided with the introduction of the DVD format to American consumers the following year—a distribution platform in which Time Warner, in particular, had greatly invested. Prompted by profits from the home video market during the 1980s and 1990s, media conglomerates increasingly acted on the interlinked commercial and cultural value of their vaults and used ancillary markets to their advantage. In particular, the classic cable stations embodied this crossover between culture and commerce by adopting the guise of nonprofit ideals in their commercial-free formats and promotion of elitist film fare, while still adhering to economic imperatives of the marketplace. In creating and marketing their "classic" identities, the stations employed nomenclature and devised programming that called attention to not only Hollywood history and film culture but also a need to craft a niche market and target the affiliated demographic.[19]

Finding Film Culture on Television • The Classic Cable Movie Channel Canon

In order to create a niche and secure a demographic in the crowded cable marketplace, AMC and TCM strategically and deliberately worked to obscure the apparent tension between their commercial interests and cultural agendas.[20] Like their predecessor Bravo and their independent film counterparts IFC and Sundance, these channels strike a balance by highlighting their ties to film history and highbrow public exhibition sites such as the museum, while marketing and targeting mass television audiences. They offer insightful information about a film's production history, while conveying it in a decidedly populist frame. Since initiating broadcast, both channels have stylishly marketed and promoted classic films, Hollywood history, and film appreciation in mainstream magazines such as *Premiere* and the *New Yorker* as well as through their ties to well-established public film institutions. For both of these widely recognized and marketed classic cable movie channels, therefore, the opposition between culture and commerce was never absolute.

TCM and AMC consciously developed a programming model based on a traditional film canon and designed to elicit and confirm cinephilia and nostalgia for "classic" film (even if classic, in the case of AMC, now potentially dates from the mid-1980s). At the same time, the programming conferred legitimacy on the stations, and implicitly on their viewers, by associating them with traditional sites of film culture. Programs built around well-known stars, directors, studios, genres, and themes have been routinely presented as special events, tributes, and salutes. While alluding to the museum and festival, therefore, these programs more directly catered to a mass audience. The conscious and uncritical celebration of Hollywood, its allure, its historical charm, and implicitly, its cultural power and influence reflected TCM's and AMC's bias. In this respect, both channels deployed a populist vision of film culture, which showcased history and celebrated a classical canon often in the narrow context of celebrity and trivia, a focus that seemingly continues to attract consumers to various Internet sites.

TCM's programming choices, in particular, have reflected a film canon well established by specialty repertory theaters. Since the spring of 2001, TCM screened a series of films on Sunday nights under the banner *The Essentials: Movies That Matter*. Film industry veterans, including directors Rob Reiner, Peter Bogdanovich, and Sydney Pollack, and scholar Molly Haskell, hosted the program, choosing a series of twenty-six films to "share with viewers interested in understanding more about the most popular of art forms."[21] According to Tom Karsch, TCM's former general manager and executive vice president, *The Essentials* helped the channel bring in a younger audience. He claimed that, through research, TCM found that "for younger people the whole category of classic movies is kind of intimidating and they don't know where to start. They know these are movies they should see, like great works of art and great books, but they're overwhelmed because there's just so many that they've heard about." Framing the program in a populist vein, Karsch suggested that *The Essentials* acted as "a primer for novice audiences to be able to come in and experience these movies and get a sense of why they are 'the essentials' we claim they are."[22] Continuing the tradition, TCM launched a spin-off version of the program in 2008, entitled *The Essentials Jr.*, targeted at children and families, thereby inculcating a new generation in Hollywood classicism.

According to the channel's website, the "essential" hosts were chosen for their personal contributions to and knowledge of film history; their ability to construct their own canon of the "essential," "timeless classics" and "culturally relevant 'must-sees'"; and their astute comments on them. Clearly, like *Warner Bros. Presents'* Gig Young, they also possess a kind of name recognition, even star quality, that complicates their standing as experts. Adhering to a traditional pedagogical model, TCM presented Reiner, Bogdanovich, and Pollack (and later Carrie Fisher, *Charmed* star Rose McGowan, and Alec Baldwin) in particular, as experts or teachers who possessed not only coveted, insider industry knowledge but also a highbrow understanding of culture and history that they proved willing to share with a knowledge-seeking audience. These hosts embodied a negotiated stance between commerce and culture. TCM's success depended, in large part, on such canons, whether derived from traditional high-culture venues such as the museum or from scholars such as Haskell, or produced internally by the likes of Reiner, Bogdanovich, Pollack, Fisher, or Baldwin. The canons combined cultural relevance, therefore, with economic imperative, revealing the channel's popular and populist vision of film and film history built on a persistent and exploitable nostalgia for Hollywood films, directors, and stars.[23]

Despite their current differences, AMC and TCM historically used similar rhetorical strategies to construct privileged spheres that offered "real" people, fans, and cinephiles an exclusive movie experience, distinct from the theatrical experience. Taking advantage of parallel shifts in consumer video technologies and home-viewing standards since the 1980s, both channels welcomed audiences into private home theaters, promising exclusive access to rare and hard-to-see films as well as behind-the-scenes information on stars, directors, and the movie-making process. These channels were especially adept at using promotional rhetoric to emphasize their devotion to the public. As some of TCM's early promotions conveyed, "We're open all night! No cuts! No commercials!"[24] Emphasizing access and theatrical viewing standards, both channels positioned audiences in a privileged position with access to the best seats in the house at any time of day. They therefore implicitly compared television viewing on their stations to the difficulties of going out to the movies and the dearth of classical (or even quality) film screenings in public venues. The channels, especially TCM, foregrounded their access to self-described world-class film libraries — bringing the public realms of the archive and museum into the domestic sphere of the living room.[25]

TCM continues to emulate these public exhibition sites with host Robert Osborne, longtime *Hollywood Reporter* columnist, who offers historical introductions to the films. While AMC abandoned its old guard hosts, Nick Clooney and Bob Dorian, when the channel changed its format and target audience in 1999, TCM's Osborne continues to introduce the flagship evening lineup, regularly conveying the channel's scripted public relations rhetoric.[26] Like his former AMC colleagues, Osborne was cast for his distinguished air and authoritative yet unpretentious style, thereby assuming a top-down manner with a hint of populism. Above all, Osborne situates himself as fan and cinephile, and legitimates his audience's shared passion. As he expressed in one on-air promotion, "Art aficionados might collect paintings. Connoisseurs of literature collect rare books. But if you're a film lover like me, chances are you collect movies." White-haired, professionally attired, yet suitably casual, at times even folksy in his delivery, Osborne regularly recites his scripted Hollywood history in a television setting suggestive of a stately family room, den, or library. Using anecdotes laced with historical fact, Osborne presents audiences with a behind-the-scenes perspective on stars, studio intrigue, and politics, bringing "viewers out of their living rooms and into the world of classic Hollywood," according to TCM's web page devoted to the host.[27] Like *Warner Bros. Presents* host Gig Young, therefore, Osborne's approach adheres to the values of presence and access associated with both early television and new media platforms.

Adhering to the conventions of film festival, museum, and repertory theater programming, AMC and TCM regularly scheduled monthly themed lineups or "festivals" that focused on a particular subject, individual, or film. These tributes, dedicated to celebrated classic stars and nostalgic icons such as Cary Grant, Robert Mitchum, Katharine Hepburn, and Ida Lupino, clearly emulated and borrowed legitimacy from public, high-film culture exhibition venues.[28] Both cable channels also regularly programmed film series on special topics such as AMC's salute to film noir or its Memorial Day film festival *Hollywood and the Military* as well as TCM's *Risqué Business: Sex and the Hollywood Production Code* and *Who's Who of Whodunits*.

In many cases, AMC and TCM offered similar and sometimes overlapping programs on genres, stars, and special or socially relevant topics. National events such as Black History Month regularly inspired such cable film festivals. In 1998, TCM's *A Separate Cinema* paid a month-long tribute to black independent cinema of the 1920s to 1940s, while AMC produced and aired an original documentary in 1998, *Small Steps, Big Strides: The Black Experience in Hollywood*.[29] TCM's festival represented television's first major retrospective of "race" movies. This particular program, along with others that have earned critical attention and notoriety for both of these classic cable channels, marked a significant contribution to film exhibition (on television) as well as a new forum to disseminate film history and film culture. Paralleling the expanding role of regional film festivals throughout the world since the 1970s and 1980s, these channels, like their independent film counterparts, have made accessible little-known or hard-to-see films to a broad-based audience, reframing television as a significant exhibition site for film and the niche cable movie channel as a programming film library.

Additionally, these channels have bolstered their cultural capital by producing their own original programming in order to compete and distinguish themselves in an increasingly crowded cable marketplace. In the late 1990s, in particular, both channels presented biographical and historical documentaries or, in some cases, developed original productions to accompany the exhibition of classic films. Like the festival programming, these documentaries have tended to focus on stars (such as TCM's *Louise Brooks: Looking for Lulu* or AMC's

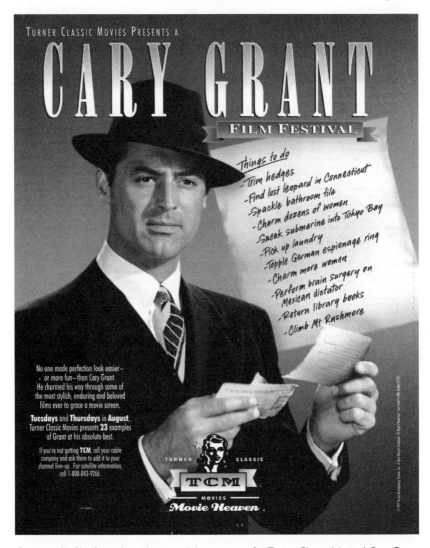

Bringing the film festival to television. Advertisement for Turner Classic Movies' *Cary Grant Film Festival*, featuring twenty-three of Grant's films, 1997. Author's collection.

Marlon Brando: The Wild One), directors (such as TCM's *Going through the Roof* on the career of Busby Berkeley or AMC's *The DeMille Dynasty*), genres, studio histories, and more general trends in film and television history. TCM also revived *Hollywood*, a critically acclaimed but rarely seen thirteen-part documentary on American silent film completed in 1979 by respected English scholars and

Tackling historical taboos and Hollywood censorship. Advertisement for Turner Classic Movies' *Risqué Business* festival, 1997. Author's collection.

producer-historians Kevin Brownlow and David Gill. TCM, and until recently AMC, basked in the praise critics bestowed on their televisual attention to film history.[30] For these cable channels, association with legitimate film historians, documentarians and critics imparted a gloss of prestige, lending credence to their existence and programming activities.

In some cases, the programmers and executives at these cable channels have viewed themselves as pioneering the cause of film history through television. As Karsch commented with regard to *A Separate Cinema* in 1998, "We feel this is a very important part of our film history. . . . The message hasn't gotten out nearly as loudly as it should." Karsch further admitted, "We might not get watched by mass audiences, but we felt so strongly it was important to be seen."[31] With this statement to the press, Karsch marketed this TCM program as part of a significant public service mission. Along with TCM's weekly Sunday night screening of silent-era films, a 2004 joint venture with the Film Foundation and IBM to promote film study in middle schools across the United States, and a monetary and programming commitment to promote FilmAid International in its efforts to educate refugees in East Africa, Karsch's public service perspective proved legitimate.[32]

Similar to the rhetoric historically employed by universities and museums such as MoMA, Karsch emphasized the importance of bringing film culture and film history to an uninitiated public. Here, TCM seemed to trade in on commercial interests in order to capitalize on a different and potentially more lucrative image as a pedagogical and philanthropic outlet for film culture. The commercial value of such cultural distinction cannot be ignored, however. TCM's image as popular educator and public service provider has distinguished the channel in both the cultural marketplace as well as the cable television marketplace. Such a relationship between culture and commerce was not lost on either TCM or AMC. As AMC learned when it started to show ads during its films, programming or branding that smacks too much of commercialism meant losing cultural cachet and the channel's primary audience.

To further their public service images and reinforce their cultural status, TCM and AMC constructed strategic affiliations with well-established and high-profile film institutions such as the Academy of Motion Picture Arts and Sciences, the American Film Institute (AFI), and the Congressional National Film Registry. Each year, both cable channels have paid tribute to the Academy Awards and the Academy of Motion Picture Arts and Sciences through programs such as TCM's aforementioned *31 Days of Oscar* and AMC's *Beyond Awards Week* that feature former best pictures, best actors, and best actresses. Since 1988, when Congress established the National Film Registry to recognize and preserve American films and shorts, and later with AFI's Top 100 film list, TCM and AMC learned to use their institutional connections to fuel new programming and marketing opportunities.

Preservation heroes saving film heroes. Advertisement for Turner Classic Movies' original documentary feature *The Race to Save 100 Years*, 1998. Author's collection.

In 1993, AMC took a more direct, active, and high-profile stand on its relationship to film history through an annual *Film Preservation Festival* during which restored classics were shown, as well as short programs highlighting the American film archives behind the preservation. The festival also included a three-day live television fundraising drive, donations from which totaled nearly $1.5 million over several years and went to the Film Foundation, an organization of filmmakers founded by Martin Scorsese in 1990 that distributes monies to film archives across the United States. Like its other affiliations with the academy, AFI, and Congress, AMC's preservation drive reflected an attempt to confer legitimacy and historical import on the cable channel as both an exhibition venue and a preservationist. AMC's cable reach to nearly eighty-four million homes potentially offered a built-in audience for the cause of film preservation.[33] AMC marketed the festival accordingly, focusing each annual drive on a popular genre such as the musical, film noir, war films, documentaries, newsreels, and in its last year, rock and roll films, in order to target the widest possible audience. Whether their drive was effective in stimulating interest in film preservation is difficult to say, however, especially given the negative press surrounding AMC's use of commercial advertising during films and their discreet elimination of the festival as an annual programming venture in 2003.

Such programming, whether tied to accolades or institutionally derived lists of "best" or "top" films, represented an uncritical, unselfconscious celebration of Hollywood. In paying tribute to those institutions that promote the film industry and its history, AMC and TCM benefited from an implicit association and shared the conferred legitimacy these institutions enjoy. The cultural-commercial crossover manifest in these alliances further revealed an insidious institutional power dynamic that continues to shape a range of public arenas devoted to film and Hollywood history.[34]

Commercial Concessions and Changing Directions

The mutual benefits of cultural-commercial affiliations for TCM and AMC reflect the ever-present blurred lines between public service, institutional pedagogy, and commercialism. As noted in previous chapters, academic and nonprofit arenas, particularly in the case of museums and universities, have historically understood the importance of industry ties and corporate sponsorship. Therefore, it is not surprising that they continue to welcome the affiliation with certain commercial entities. As David Francis, formerly chief of motion picture broadcast and sound division of the Library of Congress, commented, "The industry is actually talking about restoration and using restoration [as a tool] for selling classic films like 'Lawrence of Arabia.' Once I feel the industry takes the work of the film archivist into the commercial arena, it shows that everyone is getting aware of the importance of film preservation."[35]

The relative importance of film preservation for the industry depends on the potential profit margin stemming from each conglomerate's individual archival holdings. Thus, all archival materials are not created equal, and like film history, film preservation becomes subject to commodification. Without a clear market value tied to preservation and restoration, such projects potentially languish. Whether storing artifacts and papers or funding restoration endeavors, media conglomerates have discovered that their histories often prove expensive, if not burdensome.

Since 1999, in an attempt to compete with TCM and target a new demographic, AMC radically changed its formatting, adding commercials and expanding its programming beyond the purely "classic" to focus on so-called popular and quality motion pictures from the 1930s through the 1980s. With these changes, AMC showed less interest in a rigorous historical canon and more interest in promoting a broad-reaching fandom based on a looser and more lucrative picture of classic film.[36] In an effort to alter its branding and demographic, the channel further invoked the label "TV for movie people," while claiming its dedication to "the American movie fan."[37] The channel's advertising campaign furthered this populist image by featuring ordinary, everyday "movie" people (identified by first name), commenting on their love of movies ("a good movie should make you . . . wonder how they did that, make you feel, make you dream, make you laugh, scare the pants off you"), their favorite stars, their favorite movie lines, and their favorite villains. Like the American Film Institute's spate of television specials beginning in the 1990s that celebrated the popular appeal of film at the medium's centennial (including *AFI's 100 Years . . . 100 Movies*, *AFI's 100 Years . . . 100 Stars*, *AFI's 100 Years . . . 100 Laughs*, *AFI's 100 Years . . . 100 Thrills*, *AFI's 100 Years . . . 100 Passions*, and *AFI's 100 Years . . . 100 Heroes and Villains*), AMC targeted the everyday consumer as Hollywood fan or film lover over cinephile or collector. In doing so, the station showed little interest, especially in comparison to TCM, in retaining ties to the traditional arenas of film culture and a classical Hollywood canon. AMC, in its latter incarnation, renegotiated the meaning of classic film as it renegotiated the canon of classic film fare and history. By AMC's standards, history implied recent past, while classic got conflated with popular hits and blockbusters.

AMC ventured away from film history and a traditional canon of classic films and moved toward a focus on Hollywood production and behind-the-scenes industry gossip, a move that had historical precedent but also foreshadowed the popularity of Internet sites devoted to these topics beginning in the mid-2000s. Through an affiliation with the New York Film Academy, AMC offered production courses for adults and high school students in locations including Los Angeles, New York, Boston, Florida, and London. Following their corporate motto, "producing filmmakers, not film students," the AMC Movie Academy prided itself on a "learn by doing" approach. This approach solidified AMC's populist stance and reversed a hierarchical approach to learning. Empowering potential students by positing that "anyone with drive and ambition can make films," the AMC Movie Academy implicitly equated filmmaking with film fandom, reframing the value of film history and film culture in the context of a film-it-yourself ethos.

In keeping with its revamped image and industry-oriented interests, AMC added *Sunday Morning Shootout* in 2003, programming that blatantly celebrated the film business. The program featured *Daily Variety* editor Peter Bart along with producer, former studio head, or as he is known in the show's promotional advertising, "entertainment industry guru," Peter Guber, discussing insider gossip about the industry with star guests such as Ed Norton, Dustin Hoffman, Sylvester Stallone, Laura Linney, Anthony Hopkins, and former Sony studio head John Calley. The program had its roots in a seminar series Guber taught at UCLA as well as the anecdote-heavy industry guidebook authored by Bart and Guber, *Shoot Out: Surviving Fame and (Mis)Fortune in Hollywood*. In promotions for the program, Bart claimed that he and Guber take the movie scene seriously and promote serious and respectful dialogues about movies, "not in an E! Channel way."[38] Bart and Guber's "serious" discussions took place in a coffee house setting implicitly suggesting (high) cultural engagement. In a *Los Angeles Times* piece around the program's launch, Bart further attested to *Shootout*'s serious image by associating it with NBC's Sunday hard news program *Meet the Press*. The same article quotes Robert Rosen, dean of UCLA's School of Theater, Film and Television, who legitimated Bart and Guber's endeavor as a "significant new type of commentary about the industry."[39] Therefore, even industry gossip got framed as valuable, if not cultural, on AMC, despite similarities to the channel's other programming that was decidedly and explicitly more on par with E! Channel, namely, *Hollywood Hunt Club: Shooting Stars*. This reality program, which examined the world of Hollywood paparazzi (and followed *Shootout* in the AMC schedule on Sunday mornings), clearly emulated not only E! Channel but also other mainstream network entertainment programs, such as *Entertainment Tonight*, *Extra!*, *The Insider*, and *Access Hollywood*. The focus on gossip and promise of insider secrets necessarily diminished the channel's earlier efforts to distinguish itself from more mainstream movie fare on television while decidedly fitting in with the channel's populist goals.

Such programming attested to the needs of both AMC and TCM to attend to their commercial sides. At its height, TCM regularly promoted Hollywood history and nostalgia through glossy advertising of its themed programming in entertainment magazines such as *Premiere* or on its sister station, TBS. Following in the footsteps (or adhering to the directives) of its powerful global conglomerate parent, Turner Entertainment and, subsequently, Time Warner, TCM has regularly exploited a variety of commercial tie-ins. In order to broaden its range and market appeal, TCM occasionally shared programming and promotion

An insider's perspective on contemporary Hollywood. Advertisement for American Movie Classics' *Sunday Morning Shootout*, 2005. Author's collection.

with its more mass-oriented sister station, TNT. During "Bogie Week," for example, TNT presented the 1996 biography *Bogart: The Untold Story*, while TCM programmed classic Bogart films such as *Casablanca, Treasure of the Sierra Madre,* and *The Maltese Falcon*. In November 2003, TCM more blatantly showed its allegiance to parent company Time Warner when the station fairly explicitly promoted a Warner Bros. feature film that was slated to open the following week. Tom Cruise and director Ed Zwick hosted an evening dedicated to the films of Akira Kurosawa dubbed "Introduction to Samurai Classics," a clear marketing tie-in to the release of *The Last Samurai* designed to pass as educational outreach and foster a connection between contemporary Hollywood and art cinema.

TCM also established alliances with Reel.com, Hollywood Video, Rhino, and Barnes & Noble, revealing the channel's desire to brand itself through commercial cross-over strategies with established corporations. Both AMC's and TCM's websites include sections devoted to online shopping where such alliances manifest themselves. In 1996, TCM struck a more overt outside alliance with El Portal Luggage for the company's sixtieth anniversary. With the help of a commissioned designer, the luggage company created limited edition handbags inspired by classic films. Bags including "Maltese Falcon," "Singin' in the Rain," "Haunted Honeymoon," "High Society," "Doctor Zhivago," and "Anchors Aweigh" were marketed with the slogan "Classic Films You Can Carry." This slogan and the El Portal affiliation evoked a sense of travel, fulfilling the myth that Hollywood could be appropriated, packaged, and transported into other arenas and other times. The handbag promotion further recalled clear links between merchandising, retail empires, and Hollywood that date from the 1920s and continue in the present day with theme parks and other themed environments discussed in the previous chapter.[40]

In 2002, TCM continued this commercial cross-over trend with Pottery Barn, Starbucks, Chronicle Books, and Graphique de France under the banner of the "TCM Archives Program." Framed as a marketing initiative and designed by a brand consulting firm, this endeavor marked a conscious effort to use the aura of Hollywood's past and the promise of film acculturation in commodified terms. Brooks Branch, president of the brand consulting firm behind the project, asserted that classic films serve as repositories of glamour and style. Therefore, the goal in these commercial alliances moved beyond commemoration, and archiving for that matter, to "capture an essence and attitude of a movie or genre in a hip way."[41] It is not surprising that hipness in this context was equated with a younger demographic and a playful sense of irony. TCM's Karsch even admitted that these alliances were attempts to garner an audience younger than the channel's median 55.3 age.[42] Given its highly branded and mass-market corporate partners, TCM carefully chose the most easily digestible and familiar genres and themes, often putting a deliberate ironic spin on classic movie reception. The irony mixed with nostalgia has, in turn, become part of the branding and the selling of film history.

Chronicle's line particularly played up this irony with flashcards featuring classic movie lines designed to "improve your gangster speak" or find a new (albeit appropriated) pickup line. They also produced coasters with a film still on one side and, on the other side, recipes for classic cocktails such as the Earthquake or the Cure All, which according to TCM, evoked "a time when spirits ran high, in and out of the movies."[43] Echoing the cocktail motif, Pottery Barn produced a TCM-inspired set of stoneware Hollywood Plates. The plates featured four original Turner Classic Movies posters from Hollywood classics *King Kong*, *An American in Paris*, *Singin' in the Rain*, and *Casablanca*. According to the retailer's catalog, the purchase would allow its customers to "bring Hollywood favorites

El Portal and Turner Classic Movies Present

Classic Films You Can Carry

Limited Edition handbags inspired by classic films.

Anchors Aweigh™
$215

High Society™
$210

Doctor Zhivago™
$210

In 1910, the first film was shot in Hollywood – and the era of great screen storytelling was born. They've lifted your heart with laughter and touched it with emotion. They've awakened it with adventure and softened it with tears. They're the classic Hollywood films - an American Tradition.

On our 60th Anniversary, El Portal celebrates this tradition with the *Classic Films You Can Carry Collection*. One-of-a-kind, limited edition pieces inspired by classic Hollywood films and created in conjunction with Turner Classic Movies. We've brought these films to life... and put them in the palms of your hands.

Singin' in the Rain™
$135

Treasure Island™
$195

EL PORTAL®
LUGGAGE
Since 1936
60TH ANNIVERSARY

Las Vegas • Los Angeles • Palm Springs
Sacramento • San Diego • San Francisco
1.800.723.7568 http://www.el-portal.com

See the greatest movies of all time on Turner Classic Movies. TCM has the most comprehensive movie collection in the world with thousands of classics from the '20s through the '80s, all uncolorized and commercial-free. For over 350 movie choices every month, call your cable company and tell them to add Turner Classic Movies to your channel line-up.

TCM
TURNER CLASSIC MOVIES

Doctor Zhivago™ ™1965 Turner Entertainment Co. All Rights Reserved. Treasure Island™ ™1934 Turner Entertainment Co. All Rights Reserved. High Society™ ™1956 Turner Entertainment Co. All Rights Reserved. Anchors Aweigh™ ™1945 Turner Entertainment Co. All Rights Reserved. Singin' in the Rain™ ™1952 Turner Entertainment Co. All Rights Reserved

Classic films you can carry, from "High Society" to "Singin' in the Rain." Advertisement for El Portal limited edition handbag collection, 1996. Author's collection.

to the dessert table or cocktail hour."[44] Like other branding ventures discussed in relation to multinational media corporations in the previous chapter, and in line with TCM's relationship to Time Warner, these retailing endeavors were designed to insert the TCM brand into a variety of arenas that included home decor, publishing, stationery, paper goods, home furnishings, fashion and accessories, collectibles, bath and beauty, food and confections, and interactive games and music. Securing a place in everyday life, such promotional programs strategically aligned Hollywood history with personal lifestyle.

In 2004, TCM embarked on a more concrete and visible marketing venture at The Grove shopping mall in Los Angeles. This three-month retail experiment, dubbed "In the Picture," combined a memorabilia exhibition and retail storefront aimed to extend the TCM brand beyond basic advertising or a well-placed logo on the back of a book, plate, or box of note cards. Karsch went so far as to claim that this storefront could "bring the classic films we show on the network to life."[45] According to press releases, "In the Picture," which also served as a launch pad for a Chronicle book of the same name, exhibited the largest collection of memorabilia from the classic and popular favorite *Casablanca*, as well as artifacts from other crowd pleasers including *The Wizard of Oz*. In their self-proclaimed attempt to create an "interactive" "experience" of classic films—one that moved beyond but nevertheless promoted their cable network exhibition and Hollywood's classic star icons—TCM emulated both moving image museums and movie theme parks discussed in previous chapters. Indeed, the designer of the exhibition-retail space formerly headed Walt Disney's Imangineering group. Despite geographic proximity to the real Hollywood, this themed retail space at the center of The Grove's themed design functioned, like the cable channel and other examples discussed in this book, as an imaginary Hollywood site.

Through a wide variety of promotional programs, TCM and AMC, like other home entertainment media, offered opportunities for audiences to consume Hollywood in a different way. The channels allowed audiences to not only bring Hollywood history into their living rooms but also bring it with them wherever they go. Thus, the cocktail hour afforded an opportunity to insert film history (or trivia) into one's everyday conversation. As the channel promised in earlier self-promotions, "Turner Classic Movies is truly your passport to movie heaven."[46] The passport metaphor is significant. TCM conveyed the idea that Hollywood—its stars, films, and history—could be reduced to portable and consumable nostalgic merchandise. Taking advantage of its brand-name recognition and the authority of its association with Turner Entertainment and Time Warner, TCM, along with AMC and many of their contemporaries, whether corporate or cultural institutions, simultaneously and strategically coded Hollywood as *both* merchandise and culture.

DVD, Home Schooling, and the Promises of Home Theater

The drive to appeal to a wide audience as well as serve the interests of multiple exhibition formats and products shaped the supplemental content on both cable movie channels as well as the burgeoning DVD market. Illustrating the synergy in the home entertainment market, many of the documentaries and other supplemental programming originating on cable stations could also be found on DVD titles, while in other cases, TCM and AMC directly imitated DVD content.[47] TCM's website, discussed in more detail in the following chapter, has a "multimedia" section, where one can watch trailers and excerpts of classic films, view behind-the-scenes featurettes and short subjects, and look at production stills in the "Photo Gallery." These supplemental materials, like those on many DVD titles, have offered viewers a guide to the film and the viewing experience. Adhering to the same model that structures its programming and host introductions, the website instructed viewers on how to watch and interpret TCM's film content and canon.

AMC went farther, making the parallel to DVDs more concrete, with its DVD_TV, which ran from 2002 to 2008 on Sunday nights. In these program specials, one could watch a "Hollywood top hit" (generally indicating monetary success and critical acclaim), including such films as *Alien Resurrection*, *Platoon*, *Deer Hunter*, *Moonstruck*, *Groundhog Day*, and *Rain Man*, with running on-air commentary and trivia that appeared in a text banner running at the bottom of the screen. With DVD_TV, AMC contended that "television blasts into the information age." The AMC website further claimed that the DVD-like features enhanced the viewer's enjoyment of the film, pointing out, "You don't just watch your favorite movies—you get to experience them as never before. . . . DVD_TV offers endless ways for you to re-discover the movies you love—and thought you knew."[48] In framing this programming stunt as a rediscovery, AMC used the same rhetorical strategy employed by industry executives, trade papers, and popular media to celebrate the experiential and interactive potential of the DVD format. The channel therefore underscored a change in television and film, as not only media but also sites of exhibition.

AMC's DVD_TV signaled one response to the threat posed by the increasing availability of classic films on DVD. Another answer to such threats arose in synergistic cross-promotion strategies. In 2004, TCM and its Time Warner cohort, Warner Home Video, partnered with over four hundred Barnes & Noble booksellers to promote TCM's annual televised *31 Days of Oscar* festival. Consumers who purchased a Warner Home Video "classic" DVD at Barnes & Noble received what was touted as a Barnes & Noble "exclusive"—a free sampler of five new-to-DVD Academy Award–winning short films (not available for sale or rental). This seemingly simple promotion involving a cable network, a studio home video division, a national bookseller, and implicitly, the Academy of Motion Picture Arts and Sciences was synergistically designed to reap profits by attracting new subscribers to TCM, highlighting Warner Bros. DVD catalog and driving point-of-sale purchases at Barnes & Noble stores. At the same time, the tie-in was banking on the consumer's desire to own a classic, bring home a piece of Hollywood history, and support the academy's long-standing mythical powers to canonize Hollywood through its annual awards show. The promotion, then, legitimated an established group of Hollywood films, the corporations promoting them, and the consumers who purchased them for their home collections. It also singled out the DVD as a key player in the promotion and a historical artifact one could collect.

Like early television programming such as *Warner Bros. Presents* and the themed environments discussed in the previous chapter, DVDs offered studios a chance to brand themselves and attach a different kind of value to their products. More explicitly, the marketing and popular rhetoric around DVDs celebrated the studios' ability to reinvent the original film and shape their cultural impact. According to these marketing ploys, DVDs offered a level of interactivity, consumer empowerment, and even pedagogy unmatched by previous home entertainment products.

In addition to the DVDs themselves, a similar discourse of reinvention surfaced in relation to television as an exhibition site. With the popularity of HDTV and flat screen televisions in the 1990s and 2000s, contemporary consumers, like those of the postwar era, received advice about transforming their homes into home theaters.[49] In her book *Make Room for TV: Television and the Family Ideal in Postwar America*, Lynn Spigel points out that postwar consumers were taught how to replicate the "entire theatrical experience" in order "to create a total exhibition environment."[50] The idea of a total exhibition environment resonates in the present, paralleling the inclusive or totalizing attributes assigned to contemporary home entertainment products and programming, not to mention the themed environments discussed in the previous chapter. In the case of DVDs, which often get marketed based largely on their extratextual features, the concept of total exhibition or a totalizing experience is especially important.[51]

Through the late 1990s and into the 2000s, studios, along with industry trade papers and popular journalists, positioned DVDs as unique and "even more exciting than the movie."[52] Home entertainment divisions frequently claimed through advertising and other public relations channels that the theatrical product was unfinished, that DVDs offered a "new" reinvented and rewritten version of the original film not only through never-before-seen director's cuts but also through outtakes, audio commentary, deleted scenes, and alternate endings.[53] The idea that a DVD was more than or better than the original version of the film worked against the idea that the original theatrical film experience was authentic.

Since the DVD was introduced as a format to American consumers in 1997, industry trades and popular press, including the *Los Angeles Times, New York Times, Newsweek, The Wall Street Journal,* and *USA Today,* largely perpetuated Hollywood studio rhetoric that celebrated the DVD's value, versatility, and distinction. In August 2003, the *New York Times* devoted its "Arts & Leisure" section completely to the DVD, with the celebratory headline "The DVD Comes of Age." The entire section, organized around a technological determinist model, argued that each of the paper's regularly featured arts or "cultural offerings" (including film, television, music, fine art, theater, and even dance) had been affected in some significant way by this new media-storage platform. The various articles discussed, and in some cases praised, a range of technological features (and pleasures) that the DVD afforded its users, highlighting the platform's interactivity and accessibility as well as its storage capacity and suggestion of permanence. One article even contended that the DVD revolution was more significant than the coming of sound in terms of the way it had impacted not only home-viewing and industry revenue but also the film medium itself. Each of these articles, despite the focus on technology and technological promise, framed the DVD in the context of its impact on traditional realms of art and culture.

Critics and film buffs initially celebrated the DVD for the technological enhancements to picture and sound quality, particularly over VHS video. Thus, the rhetoric of authenticity was tied early on to a distinction between formats and technologies. The so-called early adopters of DVD in the late 1990s were cinephiles and technophiles who appreciated these attributes over pan-and-scan versions of film commonly seen on television.[54] The target audience for DVDs widened as big box chain stores and supermarkets increasingly sold the discs. DVDs entered the mainstream consumer marketplace on a scale that VHS, and certainly laser disc, never did. The breadth of this market reach reconceived the mass consumer as collector, intent on amassing a personal library of film titles.

Walmart, Target, and Best Buy accounted for more than half of all DVDs sold in the mid-2000s, with more than 60 percent of a new title's revenue coming in the first six days of its retail release.[55] In large part, the surge in DVD sales revolved around the average consumer's willingness and desire to purchase as opposed to rent films. In order to conquer this mainstream market and court the consumer, studios worked to reframe the technology as easy to use and accessible to all ages, educational backgrounds, and income brackets. Moving beyond technophiles and cinephiles, studios asserted that the DVD, unlike its digital forerunner the laser disc, was designed for families and mainstream audiences.

According to industry estimates, the extra features, or so-called value-added material (VAM), largely drove DVD consumer purchases. A 2003 survey claimed that 63 percent of DVD owners named value-added materials as a determinant in their DVD purchases.[56] DVD distributors capitalized on such findings by widening the scope of supplemental materials and using this content as a primary marketing tool. The extra features found on DVDs included an array of audio commentaries from directors, actors, and crew members; behind-the-scenes featurettes and interviews; marketing materials (posters, trailers, etc.); correspondence; memorabilia; newsreels and other period shorts; outtakes; galleries of stills and conceptual drawings; production notes; storyboards; alternate endings; games; and film-it-yourself activities.

The question remains: did this admittedly extensive selection of "value-added material" offer the consumer any real value? As discussed in the previous chapter, the terminology "value added" suggests that a DVD's otherwise incidental or supplemental material can add perceived value to the original product or film in the eyes of the consumer, whose purchase brings economic value to the corporate producer. Early on, such value-added material was found primarily on two types of DVD products. A nonstudio independent DVD production company, which had its roots in laser disc and educational CD ROM production in the mid-1980s, the Criterion Collection has produced widely and critically celebrated supplemental material on over three hundred DVD titles aimed at traditional cinephiles since 1997. On the studio side, action and science-fiction titles targeted at technophiles and young male consumers tended to represent the forerunners in mainstream DVD supplemental materials.

In both scenarios, value-added material was initially geared toward niche audiences. As collectors, these niche audiences typically wanted to own the film on DVD and, with it, the supplemental materials. Over time and certainly by the mid-2000s, DVD sales reflected an alternative economic and cultural model, one in which the everyday consumer became not only fan but also collector, and the commodity comprised an often extensive library.[57] Whether or not DVD purchases reflected the taste of a connoisseur-cinephile, much industry rhetoric and popular media discourse frequently applied cultural value to

Anyone can be a collector. Advertisement for Warner Home Video DVDs, 2003. Author's collection.

DVDs by framing supplemental materials as educational. DVDs were frequently called "film school in a can" or "film school in a box." In 2003, Dreamworks publicized its Spielberg releases AI and *Minority Report* as "an educational film school." In several stories on the DVD revolution, the *New York Times* highlighted the fact that extra features "illuminate and explain," "bring the medium close to a scholarly edition of a book," and that, "even as amusements, the supplements impart a good deal of information."[58] When director Michael Bay released his two mega-blockbusters, *Armageddon* and *The Rock,* on DVD through Criterion, he commented, "It's a cool way for film students and filmphiles to see [a movie] in more depth."[59] Bay's use of the term "depth" may seem generous—especially in relation to his own films, but juxtaposing these mainstream Hollywood films alongside Criterion's canon of art cinema classics necessarily offered Bay and the blockbuster a certain clout.

Celebrating the accessibility of the technology and the significance of two contemporary American film directors, *New York Times* film critic Elvis Mitchell called Martin Scorsese's audio commentary on *Taxi Driver* "a master class" and Sydney Pollack's on *Tootsie* "just the kind of education one would hope to get at film school, without having to echo the professor's thoughts in a paper."[60] Mitchell praised the DVD for the valuable input it provided on directors, the craft of filmmaking, and historical insight on certain titles. A *Los Angeles Times* story confirmed Mitchell's sentiments about the pedagogical value of DVDs, citing courses at UCLA Film School that employed DVD extras as part of the classroom curriculum.

In highlighting the DVD's potential to bring film education to the masses, several of these stories further echoed the rhetoric employed by early film libraries and museums such as MoMA. Complementing the programs in these public venues as well as those on cable movie channels such as TCM and AMC, DVD box sets and supplemental features were often built around famed directors, thereby reaffirming the auteur-based nature of film culture and study. Critiquing such a focus, Phil Alden Robinson, director of *Field of Dreams* and *The Sum of All Fears*, claimed that such a focus limited the DVD's full potential. He sought to involve more craftspeople in the commentaries and other features claiming, "It would be *cubist* in a way to show the film through different eyes" (emphasis mine).[61] In addition to such explicit highbrow associations, popular press often reverted to a high-low film divide in pitting Criterion's "gold standard" of traditional art house, European films in comparison to Hollywood studios and smaller DVD production companies, which featured cult classics and exploitation films.[62]

Peter Becker, president of the Criterion Collection, upheld such a divide in his view of the added value or supplemental material sold on many studio products. Distinguishing Criterion's DVDs from the average studio product, Becker commented,

> The attitude that you see represented very often in the sales material for studio DVDs refers to this stuff as "added value" or "bonus," which gives you a sense that this is really being driven by the marketplace. That's not inherently bad, but it's different from what we're doing. We generally don't like to use those "the making of" programs because they tend to be designed only to lure viewers into theaters or to convince exhibitors that they're going to make a lot of money.[63]

Becker framed Criterion along the lines of a nonprofit film institution. Their mission, he claimed, was to provide "a film archive for the home viewer." Criterion certainly cornered the DVD market on high film culture and, even with titles like *Armageddon*, tried to frame the Hollywood blockbuster as part of a "huge cultural cross-pollination" that influenced tastes, shooting styles, and visual references in a wide range of media.[64]

Following Criterion, many mainstream studio products with supplemental material, particularly those featuring audio commentary, adhered to conventional formal analysis and highlighted film directors. Many DVD titles included a release version of the film as well as the director's cut. The director's cut as well as the almost de rigueur commentary on contemporary DVD titles fetishized the director, again reinforcing traditional auteur studies. Both the focus on formal analysis (through audio commentary as well as how-to production exercises) and the auteur suggested an approach to film education dating back to the earliest days of film studies as an academic discipline. They further suggested a populist approach to learning that, in many cases, underscored admiration for Hollywood, the spectacle of the production process, and the value of a three-act story.

Another tactic, borrowed largely from the success of the Criterion Collection and employed by major film studios, promoted Hollywood history through the incorporation of a rich body of archival materials. Certain studios with extremely well-stocked and critically lauded vaults, particularly Warner Bros., Twentieth Century Fox, and Disney, created distinct lines for many of their classic titles while amassing a wide range of supplemental elements in order to frame these titles in a broader historical context.[65] Typical archival features included original source material; screen tests; storyboards; theatrical trailers; publicity stills; poster art; period newsreels, interviews, and radio theater broadcasts based around the film; and Academy Awards footage.

Under the banner label "Fox Studio Classics," Twentieth Century Fox has released over forty titles since 2003 that consisted of restored versions of classic films as well as archival supplemental materials including their own Movietone newsreels. Disney rereleased special edition DVDs of animated classics, paired with a wealth of archival material and interactive games. With a far more extensive vault and higher production value on DVD packaging and menu design, Warner Bros., too, released a number of classic titles with similar archival supplements. The fiftieth anniversary of John Ford's canonized *The Searchers*, for example, inspired an *Ultimate Collector's Edition*, featuring a leatherette-embossed slipcase that included color reproductions of the original film press book; a Dell comic book inspired by the original release; ten film stills; and correspondence,

Behind-the-scenes "exclusive" access to director Peter Jackson's production diaries in a "limited edition work of art." Advertisement for *King Kong* collectible two-disc DVD set, Universal Home Entertainment, 2006. Author's collection.

including Warner Bros. interoffice communication, regarding the production. Like the other audio and video supplemental features, these print materials both unearthed and made tangible the spectacle of Hollywood's historical film production. Here, Warner Home Video not only made film culture and film history available outside the archive but also integrated these materials and their celebration of Hollywood history directly into the home-viewing experience.

Some DVDs, like *Treasure of the Sierra Madre*, framed supplements in the context of classical-era theatrical exhibition. Grouped together as a single supplement entitled "Warner Bros. Night at the Movies, 1948," the DVD featured a trailer for *Key Largo* as well as a period newsreel, comedy short, and cartoon, simulating the movie experience in the late 1940s. Not only the archival materials, but in this case their presentation as well, offered educational value.[66] The presentation and packaging of the supplemental materials further paralleled the sleek packaging on many of Warner's classic titles, especially those designed as box sets, highlighting Hollywood genres and stars, including collections de-voted to gangster, noir, and controversial films, as well as Bette Davis, Joan Crawford, Errol Flynn, James Dean, and Elvis.

Hollywood studios that released films from their vaults also typically in-cluded audio commentaries by scholar-historians as well as contemporary documentaries, most of which previously aired on classic movie channels like AMC and TCM, or biographical and other historical programming from cable stations such as A&E and the History Channel. Based on their common corpo-rate parent, such synergy in promoting Hollywood history and the studio brand was particularly apparent in the use of TCM programming and specially labeled "TCM Archives" material (such as silent Greta Garbo films) in Warner Home Video releases. Securing links to Hollywood's past and present, many classic titles offered supplemental material that celebrated the film's legacy from a contemporary perspective with testimonials from current iconic Holly-wood filmmakers, such as Steven Spielberg, Ridley Scott, George Lucas, and Martin Scorsese, lauding a film's significant influence and place in film history. These contemporary inclusions, whether scholarly or peer homage, offered the titles a weight and legitimacy, distinguishing them from the mainstream con-temporary DVD market as well as more basic classical-era releases from other studios that offered little in the way of supplemental material.

The advertising for classic DVDs also played on the films' legacies and the viewer-consumer's implicit need to collect. Like the classic movie channels, stu-dio home entertainment divisions commonly marketed DVDs as collectibles in relation to the label "classic" as well as the awards a film has received. Fox Studio Classics specifically used the legitimacy attached to the Academy Awards as a tie-in to its marketing of classic Hollywood DVDs. On their promotional web-site, a red curtain parted to reveal the Oscar statuette flanking the Studio Clas-sics DVD packages, all with simple white backgrounds and a gold banner iden-tifying their connection to the awards show (as nominee or winner).[67] One Warner Home Video advertisement, which featured an Oscar statuette and eleven DVD boxes arranged chronologically from 1939's *Gone with the Wind* to 1992's *Unforgiven*, more directly addressed the consumer's implicit respect for the awards show, asking, "How Many Oscars Are on Your Shelf?" The ad strate-gically framed the iconic Academy Award–winning titles as part of the Warner Bros. studio library ("Warner Home Video Presents Eleven Oscar-Winning Best Pictures on DVD"), thereby conferring legitimacy on the studio and its brand. According to the logic of the ad, the studio could transfer this legitimacy to the

DVD consumer-collector ("no collection is complete without these 2 best picture gift sets"). The DVD collection implicitly legitimated the consumer's home (or at least the shelf that housed the DVDs).

For classic films or rereleases, restoration was also sold as part of the novelty. Film restoration projects and digital remastering of soundtracks motivated the marketing behind studio rereleases of films housed within their archives. Studios and marketing departments framed these revisions and restorations as laborious efforts that accurately upheld Hollywood history. Again emulating Criterion, some studios, including Twentieth Century Fox, included restoration comparisons as a routine part of their DVD supplemental materials, showing the value and technical feat behind such endeavors. In some cases, however, the "restoration," when equivalent to a simple cleanup of the print negative, took advantage of the consumer's desire for value and potential ignorance of restoration standards. Such marketing strategies, however spurious, added to the legitimacy and historical significance of the merchandise. Beyond studio-sponsored projects, Martin Scorsese and the Film Foundation sponsored the restoration and rerelease of classic films on home video as well as in commercial theaters under the series banner *Martin Scorsese Presents*.[68] Like the Criterion brand, Scorsese's name along with the studio labels "classic," "elite," "premiere," and "deluxe," bestowed authority and a gloss of prestige to home video merchandise. Whether playing on the distinction of such labels, the inclusion of archival materials, or scholarly analysis, the marketing of these home entertainment products largely emulated a film appreciation model. These products both recycled a vision of film culture cultivated in and by art cinema venues and renowned institutions such as MoMA and nostalgically celebrated Hollywood's classical era.

Access Hollywood • Empowering the Home Viewer

In addition to "selling" restoration, distinction, and legitimacy, studios also sold DVDs as a reinvented medium that could "bring audiences backstage" and "behind closed doors." The DVDs promised a different kind of education, based on access to Hollywood trade secrets and trivia. In some cases, such claims of accessibility were commensurate with film instruction; the viewer-consumers learned by listening and potentially doing on their own.[69] Like the supplemental materials on classic films that seemingly offered a direct conduit to history, film canons, and collecting, such behind-the-scenes supplements similarly positioned the DVD as a legitimate source of valuable information. When packaged on DVDs, the focus on the creative process and direct access to experts involved in a production paralleled the professional training and production-oriented courses introduced at major universities in the 1910s and 1920s. The archival materials and access to industry professionals with trade secrets served a similar function. Both were valued for their authenticity and ties to "real" Hollywood. At the same time, both types of supplemental features clearly served as marketing ploys in the construction of perceived value. Indeed, many of the behind-the-scenes features screened first as publicity filler on movie channels such as HBO or in a feature film's electronic press kit.

Paralleling the utopian discourse surrounding DVDs in the popular press, studios focused much of their advertising and public relations on the platform's uniqueness and distinction from theatrical exhibition. Studio marketing typically framed such behind-the-scenes access in terms of technological potency. Flaunting the DVD as a revolutionary technology, Warner Home Video took out a full-page ad in a 2000 issue of *Variety* that featured a larger-than-life DVD imprinted with the company's insignia, claiming, "The world is watching." For their own commercial gain and branding potential, the studios (especially Warner Bros., which has a patent stake in the format) hyperbolically lauded the |DVD as a distinctive format, whose value resided not only in the marketplace but also in the shaping of a film's legacy. Some titles, extolling interactivity and an "ultimate entertainment experience," allowed viewers to access such features while watching the film. The rhetoric of reinvention, uniqueness, and interactivity placed value on the supplemental materials, framing them as crucial elements in defining, and even potentially changing, the meaning of the original film. In celebrating what these supplemental features potentially added to a film, the rhetoric strategically worked to the advantage of the film's (and studio's) commercial value as well as its cultural value.

Many advertisements for DVDs, in focusing on the product's superiority in relation to the theatrical release, implicitly suggested that the tallied hours of value-added material (supposedly more than thirty-five hours for the ten-disc *Matrix* collection released in 2004) justified the DVD purchase. The ads framed the purchase rhetorically and in imperative terms, suggesting the need to own, amass, and collect the DVD product. In many cases, the studio insidiously coerced the consumer to make the DVD purchase, suggesting that "no collection is complete without . . ." the advertised title. In this way, the purchase took on significance and cultural value in granting the consumer access to the studio vaults, as well as the secrets of Hollywood filmmaking and the aura tied to its stars.

Selling Hollywood grandeur, even excess, studios also elaborately packaged and branded DVDs. Since the video era, studios marketed the exclusivity of home entertainment products through special labeling, packaging, critical reviews, and promotions. However, while video promotion previously worked along similar lines, the exponential growth of DVD in the 2000s made these marketing ploys more significant for the home video market.[70] Special releases warranted exhaustive (even ornate) box sets that hyped stars, genres, and directors and touted historical import (in the case of canonized, award-winning, and studio-labeled "classics"). Depending on the studio and its lexicon, DVDs were sold as part of a Platinum Series or a "gift set," as well as any number of distinctly labeled editions, including Deluxe, Limited, Collector's, Extended, Ultimate, Anniversary, and Special.

The packaging of such commemorative, classic, and reissued titles definitively betrayed a studio's use of history and Hollywood mystique to sell corporate merchandise.[71] Studios used similar tactics on high-market contemporary titles. First entering the mainstream marketplace around 2000, such packaging distinguished products in an increasingly crowded DVD marketplace. *Fight Club* and *Se7en*, two David Fincher–directed titles released that year, offered fold-out "keep cases" using heavy graphics and supplemental print materials (booklets and posters) that interweaved the films' themes into the package design.[72] *Terminator 2*, also a 2000 rerelease in Artisan Home Entertainment's "ultimate edition," came in a metallic casing, promising in the enclosed booklet, "If you think you've seen it all, look again." Under the Vista Series banner, which celebrated "the filmmaker's vision with imagination and content," Touchstone Home Video released the director's cut of *Pearl Harbor* in 2002.[73] This four-disc model of over-the-top packaging intertwined an intricate overview of the film with a historical perspective on the Pearl Harbor attack. The packaging, in what appeared to be a weathered leather photo album or scrapbook, set up a running motif of realism and authenticity that fed into all of the supplemental material. The album unfolded into four distinct compartments. The first compartment held a distressed and aged facsimile of the telegram President Roosevelt sent to Congress regarding the attack. Another compartment featured four vintage-looking postcards held in place by a khaki strap. The postcards, designed in the style of wartime propaganda posters with slogans such as "Keep Him Flying . . . Buy War Bonds," cleverly and tactically sutured in the star faces of Ben Affleck,

Cuba Gooding Jr., Josh Hartnet, and Kate Beckinsale, thereby reframing history as marketing gimmick. The rest of the album was filled with film stills masquerading as worn archival photos, smudged, and affixed with yellowing tape, as well as a stained, tattered booklet that outlined the content of the DVDs. The booklet, too, unself-consciously intermixed archival photos with behind-the-scenes shots from the film's production, pointedly blurring the line between filmed reality and historical reality in order to confer legitimacy on the film and instill nostalgia in DVD consumers.

The DVD's packaging and design further intertwined the historical offerings and behind-the-scenes production features by framing both as educational. The booklet offered an extremely brief historical overview of the attack, ending with a statement ostensibly designed to conflate and explain both the historical events and the film's narrative drive: "It was war." The booklet overviewed certain scenes from the film that directly correlated with actual events, such as an attack on Hickham airfield. Moving beyond the history of Pearl Harbor, the booklet also featured information about technology used during the filming (such as a gimbal), difficult stunts, and underwater shooting. Unrelated to the film, the DVD offered an additional supplement designed as a teaching tool entitled "Why Letterbox?" While concealed in one of the menus as an "Easter egg" (a hidden feature produced for the pleasure of fans and technophiles), the inclusion of this material, according to the packaging, reflected "an effort to educate the video consumer." The pairing of a World War II education with one revolving around Hollywood special effects, while random, catered to and ideally perpetuated the DVD and the film's value as they related to (often dubious) claims of authenticity.

The rhetoric of authenticity not only guided packaging and thematic DVD design but also served as the foundation and justification for a studio's rerelease of specific titles. In fact, it was common studio practice to strategize marketing and packaging around a consumer's need to purchase a film more than once, based on additional supplemental features or different versions of a film. These tactics distinguished the product from earlier home video releases, often basing these distinctions on claims of authenticity and superiority. A 2005 ad for the *Gladiator* DVD that read "A Hero Rises Again" referenced not only the film's plot but also the DVD itself, which was rereleased in a three-disc extended edition following the original release of a two-disk "signature collection" in 2000.[74] Meanwhile, between 2001 and 2005, Dreamworks released *Shrek* in four different versions, each at different price points, from $14.95 for a basic full-frame release to $42.99 for a box set including *Shrek*, *Shrek 2*, *Shrek 3-D*, and an entire disc devoted to supplemental features. Not all features could sustain such attention and rereleasing, especially when studios did not always generate completely new content, but the strategy proved successful as another branding avenue, especially for blockbuster titles with an abundance of supplemental features and a wide range of potential audiences.[75]

In order to sell DVDs as valuable collectibles, home entertainment divisions often included the director's cut, a tactic that also had precedent in video. In the past, such inclusions (whether on an original or rerelease) offered the director an opportunity to exhibit a version of the film that the studio, usually for economic reasons, did not release. With the popularity and monetary value of supplemental materials, however, studios increasingly fabricated such directors' cuts during the production process. No longer reflecting a David-Goliath tale of the angst-ridden auteur fighting the corporate giant's studio bosses then, the director's cut more frequently reflected a studio marketing ploy. In the case of some titles, the promise of a director's cut potentially offered a film new life and ideally new revenue. An advertisement for Oliver Stone's 2004 box office flop *Alexander* attempted such a resurrection. The ad positioned the film as superior to the theatrical version based on the inclusion of never-before-seen footage and a "newly inspired" perspective that supposedly enhanced "the acclaimed director's breathtaking final cut of his sweeping film."[76] Framing the DVD around Stone in a transparent attempt to regain cultural and monetary currency, the ad highlighted the director's audio commentary, his filmmaking "vision," and the creation of "awesome" battle scenes.[77]

Like the director's cut, which gave access and insight into Hollywood productions not available in public venues, many DVDs employed a range of audio commentaries and other featurettes that offered consumers virtual proximity to Hollywood craftspeople and actors. Some titles, such as *The Lord of the Rings* trilogy, used a multitude of discs and supplemental features to walk the viewer through the filmmaking process from preproduction to postproduction. Constructing an intimate connection between viewer and filmmaker, other titles offered video diaries or first-person accounts of the filmmaking process. For example, the *Godfather* DVD included a featurette in which Francis Ford Coppola sits on a sofa in an informal office setting, casually talking to viewers while thumbing through his original production notebook for the film. In this cozy exchange, Coppola excitedly shares how he made the notebook by pasting pages of Mario Puzo's novel onto loose-leaf notebook paper so he could jot

INTRODUCING THE ACCLAIMED
DIRECTOR'S BREATHTAKING
FINAL CUT OF HIS SWEEPING FILM.

NOW WITH ACTION-PACKED
NEVER-BEFORE-SEEN FOOTAGE.

OWN IT ON DVD AUGUST 2

Better than the real thing. Advertisement for director's cut, two-disc, widescreen special edition DVD of *Alexander* (2004), Warner Bros. Home Entertainment, 2005. Author's collection.

down his impressions and ideas beside Puzo's text. The how-to featurette reveals close-ups of Coppola's extensive notes, while also offering his nostalgic reminiscences of regularly toting his typewriter to a café in San Francisco's North Beach to work on the script. The use of such video diaries that mingle practical instruction alongside production trivia and nostalgia is typical of behind-the-scenes supplemental material. The line between education and entertainment, while blurred in such material, nonetheless offered access for budding filmmakers and historians to Coppola's copious documentation on this canonical film.

Highly structured in design and presentation, such content did not offer a radically "new" or particularly interactive experience. Focusing on the spectacle of a process rather than explaining how to achieve it or the labor and costs involved, these features remained rudimentary and often superficial (if not incomplete) in their educational aims. This was especially true of special effects and sound design featurettes that had to do with computer animation. Some DVDs used "animatics" (or animated moving storyboards) as a pedagogical device to help explain a technical process visually. The lack of information about exorbitant production costs and labor practices complicated any real-life application of this instruction. Given the target audience of mainstream consumers as opposed to future practitioners, however, such omissions were not surprising.

While erasing costs and labor involved in film production, some DVD titles claimed authenticity in their approach to historical realism. In *Pearl Harbor's* "Journey to the Screen" segment, the director, producer, and various cast members individually commented on the film's realism and uniqueness as a "movie that really hasn't been done." The DVD then set up and addressed the viewer-consumer as someone who wanted to know why and how it hadn't been done. Director Michael Bay discussed his reluctance to do the film "unless we can do it right . . . and we can create the world as real as possible." This purported desire for realism rhetorically helped to situate the film and the DVD as legitimate endeavors. Supporting this aim for realism, actor Cuba Gooding Jr. claimed, "You really felt like you were in a war," while Ben Affleck upheld the historical import of the project stating with great sincerity: "This story means an awful, awful lot." Stars such as Affleck and Gooding Jr. thereby served as points of identification for the viewer-consumers, telling them how to feel in relation to the event as well as the film, its production, and the other supplemental material.

The supplemental materials interwove Hollywood trade secrets, earnest proclamations from cast and crew, and archival features about the actual attack in order to foreground Hollywood spectacle paired with realism. Other titles similarly linked a fictionalized feature with historical events by using commentaries or archival audio tracks from real people depicted in films (such as the hotel manager Paul Rusesabagina in *Hotel Rwanda* or John F. Kennedy in *Thirteen Days*), historical documentaries, historian commentators, or Internet links to topical and historical sites (*JFK, Nixon, Into the Arms of Strangers*). The problematic mixture of fiction and fact in these features necessarily compromised the use of archival material.[78] Titles such as *Pirates of the Caribbean* further complicated the DVD representation of history with an ironic and playful tone. This DVD framed commentary by a British (read highbrow) maritime historian detailing the history of pirates within a gamelike interface of a three-dimensional pirate ship. Navigating through different parts of the ship allowed the user to access different historical information. While such a playful design scheme accurately evoked the film's tone, it necessarily devalued, if not mocked, traditional history.

In a similar spirit of authenticity mixed with play, many titles featured interactive explorations of different facets of filmmaking. Using a familiar discourse also tied to (and critiqued in relation to) the Internet, DVDs were celebrated as interactive. The "user" could interact with not only storytelling but also the filmmaking process. A rhetoric of empowerment securely situated the DVD as a form of interactive new media, one that created both an alternative viewing experience to theatrical exhibition and stereotypically passive television viewing. Even DVD menus were deemed noteworthy if they could put the viewer in the film world, capturing the "emotional experience of a film."[79] One of the most sought after DVD producers and menu designers contended that "interactivity empowers both the filmmaker and the consumer."[80] While this might have been nominally true for consumers who used the "record your own commentary" DVD-ROM feature available on a few titles (*Spiderman: 3-Disc Deluxe Edition*, *Pulp Fiction: Collector's Edition*, and *Jay and Silent Bob Strike Back*), such a statement seemed more applicable to the filmmaker and DVD producer than the average consumer.[81] The idea that DVD extra features empowered a viewer, and changed the nature and meaning of the original film, remained debatable. Not only was the level of interactivity still highly limited by virtue of technology and cost, but also the film's director, studio, and to varying degrees, DVD producer strictly controlled these extra features.

Many studios nevertheless framed such do-it-yourself activities as more directly accessible and potentially superior behind-the-scenes features. For example, the *Die Hard* DVD set up each instructive exercise with a user-friendly explanation tailored to its audience that placed the viewer in a privileged position. For the editing exercise, the preceding text explained, "We've given you access to three short sequences from *Die Hard* which you can edit together in several different ways so that you can see how even subtle differences in cutting can radically change the tone of a scene." Other titles offered similar promises of access through editing (*Men in Black*, *Star Wars, Episode I*, and *Scream 3*), multiple-angle viewing (*Fight Club*, *Moulin Rouge*, *Se7en*, *Speed*, *Pearl Harbor*, and *Die Hard*), and audio track mixing (*Se7en* and *Die Hard*). *Final Destination 3* promoted interactivity at the level of narrative, including a "Choose Their Fate" feature that allowed viewers to use additional footage (over one million dollars' worth) to rewrite the original film text. The DreamWorks family title *Spirit: Stallion of the Cimarron* went even further, encouraging the (mostly young) viewers to create their own animated film using the film's backgrounds and characters, recording their own voice over narration, and even importing their own photographs to personalize the film. While seemingly interactive and implicitly touting a film-it-yourself ethos on the surface many of these features served as play more than education.

In an effort to enhance the user-friendliness of its supplemental features and the DVD interface, New Line Home Entertainment (a Time Warner subsidiary) launched and trademarked a niche DVD brand in 2001 dubbed "infinifilm." Designed to expand the interactive potential on select titles, this so-called portal to extra features allowed the viewer-consumer access to supplemental material through automatic navigable pop-up menus. The pop-up feature presented a more direct and instantaneous incorporation of the behind-the-scenes features into the film itself, according to New Line's promotional rhetoric, transforming the overall viewing experience.[82] According to a PC *World* review of the design, infinifilm worked along the same lines as footnotes in a text, allowing access in a way formerly afforded only by DVD-ROM features.[83] New Line touted the technology as a "viewer-directed experience," highlighting the means to "explore, escape, and interact" in a way not possible on standard DVD titles. The studio thus framed the technology as empowering as well as unique in its ability to highlight Hollywood's mystique by taking viewers "beyond the movies" and the "movie watching experience to a whole new level."[84] While New Line's technology and others like it used by studio competitors certainly changed the viewing experience by interrupting the feature film with various featurettes and then returning to it, the value of this kind of integration remains difficult to assess.[85] Certainly film purists would not seek out these kinds of interruptions, and based on the limited number of titles featuring infinifilm (less than twenty), the average consumer did not seek them out either.

Many of the interactive trends in DVD extra features that used embedded content (such as New Line's infinifilm or the Easter eggs that can be found on hundreds of titles) mimicked computer games, another highly profitable arena in contemporary home entertainment. Some DVDs, particularly family, science-fiction, action, and comedy titles, clearly imitated the viable computer game market and, in many cases, advertised actual tie-ins for other ancillary game products. They transformed film characters or stories into games, allowing users to revoice (or sing, Karaoke style) characters in the film (*Shrek, Austin Powers: Goldmember*, and *Elf*); read along on *Stuart Little 2* or *Elf*; learn about Egyptology on *The Mummy Returns*; take a quiz to see which Disney princess they most resemble; or study the art of hula dancing on *Lilo and Stitch*. Like the infinifilm features, the level of interactive play on these games remained limited, especially in comparison to contemporaneous game platforms such as Xbox and Playstation. Meanwhile, as the DVD market declined in the late 2000s, Easter eggs and other interactive features plateaued, reserved for Blu-Ray science-fiction titles.

Given their vested financial interest, studios often skewed and potentially compromised the purported interactivity and educational value of extra features. As Barbara Klinger points out, "Viewers do not get the unvarnished truth about the production; instead, they are presented with the 'promotable' facts, behind-the-scenes information that supports and enhances a sense of the 'movie magic' associated with the Hollywood production machine."[86] The *Die Hard* DVD admitted as much, claiming before one of its exercises, "The actual process of mixing the soundtracks of a motion picture is, of course, much more complex and involved than this DVD-based workshop can allow, and requires talent and years of experience to master. It is hoped that this feature affords you a simple but entertaining experience of the craft." This unusually honest, if not self-conscious, declaration remained rare.[87] Much of the supplemental materials as well as the studio marketing and rhetoric surrounding it must be viewed as purely promotional. Less interested in training new professionals, giving real access, or teaching viewers how to understand or "read" a film by listening to a director's commentary, studios used a combination of Hollywood mystique paired with the authenticity and realism of a backstage pass to sell their products. Whether these titles truly educated or merely "edutained" therefore depended on not only how the consumer used them but also how they were produced. Beyond the nonprofit repertory image proffered by the Criterion Collection, DVD production, for the most part, revolved around economic return, branding, and sustaining Hollywood fervor and nostalgia over the more altruistic goal of education or archival posterity.[88]

The supplemental material on DVDs nevertheless served a variety of purposes during its heyday in the late 1990s through the 2000s. Each reflected slightly different visions of film acculturation and Hollywood memorializing tied to film's artistry, history, trivia, and production. The value of the DVD production itself was also celebrated as an artistic endeavor. Articles in both popular press and trade papers frequently featured the DVD producer, who worked independently and under contract with the major film studios, hailing him as DVD "auteur."[89] At the "The DVD Exclusive Awards," the industry's own awards show, these auteurs received further attention for their menu design and creation of unique supplemental material. Additionally, the DVD empowered the filmmaker because, as one DVD producer commented, the format "has gone from being just another ancillary avenue to becoming part of the filmmaking process itself."[90] The contention that the DVD market affected filmmaking had validity on an economic level, considering the fact that home entertainment division heads frequently sat in on development meetings and helped to decide whether or not to "green light" a film. Studios also hired DVD producers along with the rest of the crew at the outset of preproduction. Certain A-list directors like Steven Spielberg and Ridley Scott worked with the same DVD producer on all of their feature films.

The combination of industry self-promotion and popular press adulation, along with the packaging, marketing, and advertising of DVDs during the 2000s, transformed them into what Universal Home Entertainment president Craig Kornblau called "must-have entertainment properties."[91] Such must-have properties not surprisingly paralleled the top grossing films at the box office and typically fell within certain genre and demographic categories. The best-selling DVD titles included family films, action, and science fiction, and studios spent the most time and money producing value-added material for these titles. With such a limited scope of Hollywood genres and the slow collapse of the DVD market in the late 2000s, we must ask again about the value of these "value-added materials" and whether such value can be sustained in ever-evolving media platforms. Did DVD supplemental materials hold real pedagogical promise? Could they be classified as artifacts of culture? Or were they mere novelties and a new kind of attraction, offering posterity for a director and revenue for a studio? Are they, as director Frank Darabont suggested, simply "cultural white noise"?

The utopian discourse surrounding contemporary home entertainment and the lack of concrete statistics on how these media actually were used render questions pertaining to value difficult to address. Clearly, there was great consumer demand for supplemental materials both on DVD and through cable channels during the height of the DVD market in the mid-2000s. But it remains unclear what drove this viewer-consumer. Peter Staddon, a marketing executive at Twentieth Century Fox, admitted that most consumers only spent ten or fifteen minutes exploring the many hours (ten or more on some titles) of value-added materials, yet the list of features on the box (the more the better) somehow justified their purchase.

On the one hand, then, supplemental materials served as a marketing ploy, and the extra content sold had little value other than economic. At the same time, these extrafilmic materials, whether on DVD or cable, offered insight into

the way Hollywood as a cultural symbol and economic reality has been reimagined. In addition to the public exhibition site, the film itself may no longer play
the starring role in Hollywood. Within the home entertainment arena specifically, films represented simply one part of a larger ensemble of satellite texts.
These satellite texts imparted scholarly insight, historical information, practical
filmmaking tips, trivia, and nostalgia while perpetuating a still viable Hollywood mystique. Similar to the themed environments and themed retails spaces
discussed in the previous chapter, these outlets redefine the spatial and conceptual limits of Hollywood. Paralleling the early days of television when the living
room was reimagined as a home theater, the popularity of home entertainment
reinforced the significance of the home as a primary site of film exhibition and
Hollywood memorialization. As the final part of this book suggests, even as
platforms continue to change with the rise of on-demand viewing as well as the
prominence of the Internet and mobile devices in everyday life, many of the
economic and cultural values driving this content remain the same.

Handheld Hollywood

If you type "Hollywood Walk of Fame" into the search field of Apple's iTunes store, six different iPhone applications dedicated to the site pop up. In 2010, two of the application creators, the Hollywood Chamber of Commerce and an independent organization called the Hollywood Walk of Fame (HWOF), announced their respective versions of competing applications (apps) that allow users to locate and access information about the nearly 2,400 stars on the iconic Walk of Fame. Both free apps (in addition to four others for sale) primarily serve as virtual tour guides with GPS navigation directing consumers to specific star locations on the Walk of Fame. The unofficial but self-purported "best" guide created by HWOF also promises an account of the star's history and, where applicable, connects the user to current headlines from more than thirty-five news sources, photos (of the Walk of Fame and the star), a "StarRank" that claims to reflect the star's current Internet popularity, and links to more information via IMDb and Wikipedia. Paul Nerfer of HWOF explained the value of the app to Webwire, claiming that "millions of tourists come to Hollywood each year and when they look down at the sidewalk, they see names they know, names they barely remember, and names that they have never heard of and now they can learn about the person behind the name."[1] The app, in turn, Nerfer suggests, helps give *meaning* and history to these names.

But whose meaning is this? And whose history? More to the point, who is driving the story and symbolic image of Hollywood and its past? While these apps may be gimmicks with little seeming relevance outside of Hollywood tourism, their growing number nonetheless serves as a prime example of Hollywood's interminable migration into the digital arena since the Internet boom of the mid-1990s. As real geographic sites, such as the Walk of Fame, the star footprints at Grauman's Chinese Theatre, and the Hollywood Forever cemetery transform into Hollywood monuments of a new "virtual" order, we must question whether or not the meaning of Hollywood transforms with them. Do these virtual representations of Hollywood offer a well-worn and familiar, yet exponentially expanded, story? Or in opening up the meaning making to fans and users as well as an information-rich Internet landscape, do we see the development of a modified or alternative Hollywood imagination? Further, how do the motives, whether for commerce or pleasure, for telling Hollywood's story differ and intermingle?

Beyond the spate of third-party mobile applications on the rise since 2008, a plethora of Hollywood Internet sites confirms Hollywood's cultural relevance and staying power in the digital arena. Such sites reflect a popular interest in Hollywood's industry politics and business practices as well as an increased fixation with and access to celebrity culture. Broadly paralleling the geographic, institutional, and televisual sites and products discussed throughout this book, many of these sites center on Hollywood and its history, sometimes emulating and other times rearticulating the functions of their "real" world counterparts. In large part, Hollywood-themed Internet sites perpetuate many of the same stories and images that have laid the groundwork for the other sites and products discussed throughout this book.

Out of necessity, the nonprofits and corporate entities I've discussed in various chapters all maintain Internet correlates or profiles. While many of these sites simply house information, others have used the unique properties of the Internet (storage capacity, connectivity, global reach, immediacy, and a do-it-yourself ethos) to explore and write Hollywood's story from a myriad of perspectives and depths. Many of these sites, particularly in their extensive scope and access, embody and exude a kind of Hollywood excess. They historically imagine, give meaning, and even bolster Hollywood (financially and symbolically) within a digital landscape that uniquely and immediately offers accessibility to all things Hollywood. More than affording access, however, many Hollywood sites (particularly those that originated on the Internet) reflect a note worthy hybridization—one that aggregates divergent content and, in turn, manifests not only a culture-commerce crossover but additionally a more complicated picture of the multiple meanings and uses Hollywood simultaneously generates.

Just as the range and assemblage of sites and examples throughout this book underscore Hollywood's contested meanings, the excess embodied by the Internet potentially maps a similarly complicated terrain with a range of players including media conglomerates, nonprofit institutions, entrepreneurs, fans, cities, and chambers of commerce. The proliferation of Hollywood Internet sites corresponds to the polysemic meanings tied to Hollywood throughout its history and across the globe. However, the implications of this contested arena for the user remain unfixed. On the one hand, the user is privy to multiple meanings and is empowered to choose a given Hollywood story. At the same time, though, many of these Hollywood stories capture a fairly similar, historically sanctioned narrative and image, leaving the user with a range of sites, yet minimal variation in core content.

Rather than provide an encyclopedic overview of these sites and their specific content, I want to consider how the *type* of site and its author (whether corporate, nonprofit, or user) leverage Hollywood's symbolic image and history to different ends. Moving beyond the home entertainment examples discussed in the last chapter, the digital content discussed here further broadens Hollywood's scope by redefining its geographic and symbolic boundaries. This content shows that the "idea" of Hollywood continues to carry symbolic weight and monetary value, even as it gets further removed both temporally and spatially from its origins, riding on the Internet's greater capacity over traditional media to traverse time and space.

Yet, a discussion of the Internet and mobile applications should not be read as the next step in a teleological trajectory. While this book loosely adheres to a linear history exploring the negotiation of Hollywood's meaning in a range of sites, from MoMA's Film Library in the 1930s to the DVD revolution of the 2000s, I find it limiting to frame the Internet as some kind of final frontier for reimagining Hollywood. Not only do many of the sites and products discussed throughout this book still exist, but as I suggested in the previous chapter, a shift in platform from cable to DVD to Video on Demand (VOD) to the Internet does not necessarily indicate a corollary shift in the core cultural and economic values tied to Hollywood. Even as the Internet offers the potential for fans and users to generate their own content and develop their own Hollywood meanings and images, much of this content still largely adheres to or at least works in dialogue with a predictable, if not sanctioned, narrative. Therefore, this conclusion underscores the persistent significance Hollywood and its history play as they interface with both conventional institutions and corporations discussed throughout this book as well as new media content and technology platforms.

What's Old Is New Again • Finding a
Site on the Internet

Public exhibition sites and other ancillary branding platforms that memorialize Hollywood clearly have not evaporated with the rise of digital media. Nonetheless, this digital landscape yields an ever-increasing array of sites and activities devoted to Hollywood that underscore two key ways it continues to be memorialized. One approach taps into the mythological and timeless side of Hollywood associated with stars, glamour, and excess. The other approach, decidedly more concrete, logs industry facts and figures primarily through searchable databases. These approaches reflect two interrelated but different understandings of Hollywood that often share common ground in an extensive span of corporate-sponsored Internet sites. They also manifest an alternative way to promote, celebrate, nostalgize, institutionalize, and profit from Hollywood and its history. On the nonprofit side, while many organizations use the Internet simply to stake out a digital presence, others have used their primary sites to more deliberately extend their public service missions and engage in public pedagogy. Given limited resources, many nonprofits also experience financial pressure to digitize their holdings for the general public. Like many of the museums and archives discussed in earlier chapters, including the Museum of Modern Art's (MoMA) Film Library, the Cinémathèque Française, and the failed Hollywood Museum, these nonprofit institutions value, prioritize, and need to foster their public outreach. At the same time, with difficulties in funding and the need to compete with for-profit leisure outlets, many of these same nonprofits increasingly use the Internet, not only for public pedagogy, but also, like their corporate counterparts, to self-brand and self-promote. The public pedagogy itself can be an avenue to self-brand as the brand and the branded products become strategically fundamental to the instruction. Therefore, the lines between public service and self-service are often difficult to distinguish for nonprofits adopting what appears to be a corporate sensibility.

Taking advantage of the virtual storage capacity afforded by the Internet, many nonprofit organizations offer searchable databases for the public, and in some cases online exhibits of their collections of Hollywood history and artifacts. For example, the Academy of Motion Picture Arts and Sciences (AMPAS) offers several searchable databases of their library and archives. While some searches yield results only accessible in person at the Margaret Herrick Library in Los Angeles, AMPAS has made a good amount of material accessible online, including motion picture credits and some of its poster collection. Given the popularity and media spectacle, not to mention financial boon, that emanates from the annual Academy Awards, much of the institution's online material centers on the telecast with acceptance speeches and other highlights from awards shows. Beginning in 2010, the academy offered live feeds via its Facebook site and Twitter feeds from backstage insiders.[2] AMPAS also posts a range of videos on its website featuring members discussing individual facets of crafts including editing, screenwriting, and acting in the digital age. In conjunction with some of its public programs, such as a tribute to film noir, the website also displays videos of members discussing the historical and contemporary impact of the classical genre. The combination of this type of public pedagogy and awards show boosterism reflects the academy's complicated negotiation between serving the public while promoting, preserving, and even protecting itself, especially given the institution's and industry's acknowledged piracy woes.

More than the nonprofits, studios have strategically benefited from online branding. They use their websites as platforms to advertise and sell products as well as to promote a total package and image that interweaves current products, ancillary divisions, and studio history. Such a totalizing scope harkens back to the theme parks and other themed environments discussed in chapter 3 that proliferated in the 1980s and 1990s, and suggests a penchant for exploiting the Internet in similar ways to reach the widest possible demographic. Each studio site includes a catalog of media properties (including film, television, DVDs, and in some cases games), with both contemporary and archival content increasingly available to directly stream or download. In addition to the core media properties, these sites also feature a range of other activities such as trivia, polls, and online quizzes; downloads; e-cards; widgets; mobile content; and do-it-yourself exercises designed to add value by enhancing or expanding visitors' experiences and, in turn, encouraging retention and repeat visits. There is perhaps a dual function tied to these sites; they market and advertise traditional properties while existing as self-sustaining web-only content, both ultimately serving the brand.

Representing key ancillary elements in their corporate properties, Disney and Universal Studios' theme park websites serve as an additional platform for studio branding. These websites inform potential visitors about the parks, filmmaking and television production, Hollywood history, and most often, the studios' big budget intellectual properties. Such Internet sites clearly function as promotional vehicles, while sharing many similarities with the extra features found on contemporary home entertainment products. Universal Studios Hollywood uses its website as a virtual supplement for its latest themed attractions. In conjunction with Revenge of the Mummy: The Ride, for example, a specially designed website functions like a movie trailer, beckoning visitors to a ride that offers "no way out." With a "making of" section including photographs of the production; the musical score; an interview with the film's director and producer of the ride; and relatively cursory information about the audio system, the actor who voices the part of Imhotep, and the supposedly authentic Egyptian relics that inspired the ride's design, the website clearly emulates special features on many DVD releases.[3]

King Kong 360 3-D similarly offers a video gallery with behind-the-scenes footage on the conceptualization and making of the attraction, featuring the film's director Peter Jackson and the 3-D effects supervisor. The site also includes entries from a video contest and video records of guest reactions, animatedly attesting to the immersive quality of the ride. Such purported interactivity necessarily reflects a kind of pseudo-personalization in which the creator or corporate entity largely directs and regulates guest responses so they align with the brand.[4] Meanwhile, the success of Disney's *Pirates of the Caribbean* movies spawned a website that synergistically ties the film franchise to the history of the original Disneyland ride, its 2006 makeover by current Disney Imagineers, a game based on the films, a dictionary of "pirate speak," and links to facilitate planning a Disney vacation.

Specialty spinoff sites such as King Kong and Pirates intertwine historical and current properties, helping to reinforce a studio's ties to Hollywood history. Of all the studios, Sony Pictures most explicitly uses its website to establish a connection to the studio's early Hollywood roots, ironic perhaps given its corporate ownership since 1989 by a Japanese multinational electronics company. Providing a link to a separate site, the interactive Sony Pictures Entertainment Museum, which embraces the tenets of a powerful and prevalent Hollywood nostalgia industry, greets visitors with the familiar musical score and image from its historical Columbia Pictures company logo. According to the website, the image of the "Columbia Lady" is "bigger than a single individual—she's the trademark of filmmaking quality."[5] Like Hollywood itself, this iconic image transcends time and locale and, in turn, grants the studio cachet and historical import. The site further leverages its history with sections devoted to studio founder Harry Cohn, director Frank Capra, producer Irving Thalberg, screen siren Rita Hayworth, and its still operating Culver City lot.

While the *Hollywood Reporter* heralded the online museum, which launched in 2003, as an "innovative move to further [Sony's] brand online," this branding uniquely unfolds in an archival format.[6] The site provides a catalog of the studio's theatrical films, similar to many other studio websites, and also includes information about the preservation process with video clips demonstrating a behind-the-scenes look at Sony's preservation efforts and the before-and-after impact they have had on certain titles. Here, the corporate site parallels the nonprofit model, emulating websites of other preservation organizations, such as Martin Scorsese's Film Foundation. Sony highlights its seemingly selfless dedication to the safeguarding of Hollywood history, while financial motives for its preservation efforts strategically remain hidden in the background. And Sony's site adheres to a museum model by explaining the steps involved in a film's production process. With still images, text, and some video, visitors can learn about the basics of filmmaking as well as the visual and special effects used in recent Sony blockbusters such as *Spiderman 3*, *Hancock*, and the animated *Cloudy with a Chance of Meatballs*. Couching such instruction firmly in Sony's history and films, the museum fits the *Hollywood Reporter*'s assessment of the site as a branding platform. Like the classical DVD titles put out by studios such as Sony, Fox, and Warner Bros. discussed in the previous chapter, this site largely capitalizes on the profit potential of Hollywood nostalgia. At the same time, it emulates more contemporary DVD titles by leveraging the value and spectacle of behind-the-scenes access to contemporary film production.

Websites for television networks such as Turner Classic Movies (TCM) and American Movie Classics (AMC) serve similar functions as many of the studio sites. At a fundamental level, they offer an online presence with television schedules and online stores for DVD purchases. Under the Time Warner corporate umbrella, TCM's site also offers an extensive array of material, rivaling many nonprofit archives and libraries. TCM's "MediaRoom" contains hundreds of film excerpts, trailers, and interviews, while the "Archive" section of the site's database features online galleries of lobby cards, posters, costume sketches, internal studio memos, publicity photos, press books, screenplays, and on-set photos. TCM also provides video podcasts (with monthly schedule overviews made in-house with commentary by TCM employee-curators) as well as audio podcasts of archival interviews with stars. In addition to the archival material, the site adheres to Internet convention in soliciting visitor interaction through games, trivia, contests, polls, e-cards, and screensavers. Similar to the studio sites that promise interactivity, such interfacing with users largely facilitates consumption more than genuine empowerment.

TCM goes further, however, by encouraging visitors to "become a part of history." Visitors can essentially construct their own canons by making playlists from TCM's database. They can also upload their own images and historical documents (as long as the title is already in the database, and thus vetted and copyright protected), thereby playing the role of researcher, historian, and archivist. While TCM's scope is limited by the archival holdings of its corporate parent, Time Warner, the site shows another outlet for studios to use the digital landscape to preserve and celebrate their history, and for fans and collectors to take part in it. TCM's parent clearly understands the financial benefits reaped from the network's association with Hollywood history.

Once Removed • Fans, Entrepreneurs, Startups, and Digital Hollywood

TCM's classic cable compatriot, AMC, does not possess a studio parent rich in archival holdings; however, when its parent corporation, Rainbow Media (a division of Cablevision) took filmsite.org under its umbrella in 2008, the company's online presence greatly expanded. Filmsite.org (also known as Greatest Films) started in 1996 when Tim Dirks developed the site content peripherally as text that could serve as the material foundation of a class he taught on HTML coding. According to *Variety*, Dirks's website and interest in film had humble and nonprofit origins, as a hobby more than a business model.[7] Dirks started with a few of what he deemed "great" moments in film history and soon thereafter began writing reviews of his self-conceived "100 Greatest Films" list. Within its first few years, the site received both substantial visitor traffic and acclaim from the computer world as well as the film world (notably Roger Ebert). As someone familiar with programming and hyperlinking, Dirks seems to revel in the expansiveness and encyclopedic potential of the site as well as the multiple ways of categorizing, organizing, and cross-referencing film titles. Hyperlinking almost exclusively within his own site offers a limited, controlled, and ultimately insular overview of Hollywood. The site features several lists, including greatest films; greatest directors and stars; "best of" lists ("Best of James Bond Girls," "Best of Chick Flicks," and "Best of Film Editing Sequences");

great film quotes; great scenes (chases, crowds, deaths, and disasters); a section on the Oscars and genres; and poster images from several hundred films.[8] Wearing multiple hats as reviewer, curator, and historian, Dirks continues to solely author all of the content, again limiting the range of Hollywood stories and meanings. He has penned reviews for numerous films ranging from D. W. Griffith's 1916 *Intolerance* to the latest in the *Mission Impossible* series and, in the "History" section, provides a decade-by-decade breakdown of Hollywood cinema. Dirks further schools his visitors in the critical viewing of a film (with "fundamental" as well as "in more depth" viewing tips). The video section, clearly added by AMC, remains limited to behind-the-scenes featurettes, trailers, and AMC *News* reports. According to Dirks, AMC's most recent network slogan "story matters" compliments the content on filmsite.org; however, for AMC, the traffic generated by his site (now branded on each page with AMC's logo) was certainly key to its buyout, with over eight million unique visitors (i.e., unduplicated) and over thirty-one million page views between January and September of the year of acquisition.[9]

Like filmsite.org, Rotten Tomatoes, IMDb (Internet Movie Database), Film.com, and MRQE (Movie Review Query Engine) launched on a small scale in the 1990s, only to be subsequently bought out by larger media corporations that saw potential profits in each site's substantial visitor traffic. MRQE and Rotten Tomatoes started in 1993 and 1998 respectively as hobbies of their movie enthusiast creators who each had day jobs in the tech world (as computer science instructor and web designer). Both sites grew substantially over the decade with praise from critic Roger Ebert among others in the new business of rating Internet sites. Within Rotten Tomatoes' first year, Yahoo! and Netscape highlighted the site as a key Internet destination. With its promising Internet traffic, Rotten Tomatoes was subsequently absorbed into the corporate arena, first by Fox News Corporation's IGN Entertainment in 2004 and, later, in 2010, by movie social networking site Flixster.[10] Other sites followed suit. MRQE developed a strategic partnership with New York business development and investment firm The Loft Group, while RealNetworks launched its own version of Film.com, founded in 1994 by a Seattle film critic.

As aggregate sites, Rotten Tomatoes and MRQE continue to offer reviews from select and therefore vetted critics. Rotten Tomatoes claims that its reviewers are mostly affiliated with accredited media outlets and online film societies, setting up a distinction between "top" critics and all others. Using the same critics to evaluate each movie allows for a certain consistency in the ratings system (the Tomatometer) as well as "fresh" and "rotten" designations applied to individual titles. With its metric system and accredited list of critics, Rotten Tomatoes produces an authorized collection of information. At the same time, given the sheer multiplicity of reviews, encompassing a varied range of media outlets (from the traditional and respected *New York Times* to the less-known and more irreverent Internet sites such as Cinematic Happenings Under Development or CHUD), Rotten Tomatoes presents visitors with an opportunity to cull their own information about a given title.

In addition to the reviews from selected critics, Rotten Tomatoes, along with fellow entertainment aggregate sites such as MRQE, IMDb, and Yahoo! Movies, offers user reviews from its Rotten Tomatoes "community" as well as an audience score that measures the percentage of users who enjoyed or would like to see a given movie. In some cases, the user reviews for a particular title outnumber the critics, rendering a potentially more democratic landscape of criticism. IMDb qualifies the value of its user reviews by quantifying them. In its "Top 25 User-Rated Movies of 2010," for instance, the site claims that the list is based on actual ratings by unique monthly users and that each film received at least five thousand user votes.

Given the ubiquitous presence of user reviews on many Hollywood news and information sites, sanctioned knowledge clearly works in tension with such user-authored content and ratings. The impact of this tension ultimately depends on the respective Internet site as well as specific film titles. Regardless of the site, the consistency otherwise guaranteed within the critic reviews is typically not applicable to the user reviews. Certain titles may garner few, if any, user ratings, making the pool of user ratings difficult to consistently assess and compare. Therefore, it remains difficult to determine how much of a given site's user-generated content is central to the average site visit. Although many of these sites include areas for user-generated content, such interactive arenas remain, for the most part, a small portion of the overall site content.

In its corporate transitions, Rotten Tomatoes shifted from an aggregate site of movie reviews to a more broad-based Hollywood entertainment news site, with film reviews and critic profiles as well as box office statistics, showtimes, "best of" lists (based on reviews, awards ceremonies, and the Library of Congress's National Film Registry), a celebrity rating system (the "star power meter"), celebrity profiles, and entertainment news (produced in-house and culled from a variety of sources ranging from the *Los Angeles Times* and the *Hollywood Reporter* to Moviefone and Deadline Hollywood). The site, which also features numerous trailers, film excerpts, and stills, reported more than ten million visitors at the end of 2009. MRQE and Film.com similarly expanded beyond reviews and ratings to feature a comparable range of additional material. In 2009, MRQE further produced a spinoff, Flicktweets, which aggregates real-time movie reviews posted by Twitterers, and manifests yet another trend in digital entertainment.[11]

IMDb has a similar origin story to these movie review sites. Also with a background in software authoring, its creator turned hobby into business in 1996. Col Needham started working on the site and researching movies in 1990 in England—decidedly outside of the mainstream Hollywood industry. With its growing success after incorporating in 1996 and gaining advertising revenue, IMDb was subsequently "discovered" and subsumed within a corporate industrial structure. Needham met with Amazon executives in 1998 and soon thereafter sold the business to the burgeoning online retail group, while keeping IMDb a separate entity. Amazon's interest in IMDb centered on the database's ability to synergistically support Amazon's online movie sales through direct solicitation to buy the product via an amazon link. The site's traffic is notable. In 2006, in one month alone, IMDb had over eighteen million unique visitors and, by 2010, was used by over one hundred million unique users per month worldwide, while remaining ranked one of the top twenty-five trafficked sites in the United States.[12] Like Rotten Tomatoes, the site's content has expanded beyond the database of film credits (organized by title, year, name, genre, awards, companies, user ratings, country, language, and keyword) to cover more general entertainment news (amassed from over 150 sources); box office statistics; DVD rental charts; film, television, and DVD releases; reviews; quotations from film and television; film festival listings; best and worst of lists; photo galleries (with celebrity photos, publicity shots, and behind-the-scenes images); trailers; and trivia and games. In 2004, the company launched a subscription-only supplementary site, IMDb Pro, in order to target industry insiders and wannabes with more specific information on budgets, contact information, resumes, agency representation and management, and more specific data about production and crew. In 2008, IMDb again expanded its offerings by allowing free streaming access to a limited number (six thousand at the outset) of full-length film and television episodes, provided largely by online video service Hulu.[13] That same year, IMDb also acquired Box Office Mojo, another popular site that tracks box office statistics, which was originally created by a movie fan-analyst in 1999.

Given their common origin stories, it seems the creators of filmsite.org, Rotten Tomatoes, IMDb, MRQE, and Box Office Mojo did not necessarily envision, let alone predict, that their hobbies would turn a profit or, at the very least, garner value from the corporate arena. If we take these stories at face value, the creators were passionate fans and film geeks who happened upon the Internet at the right time. In the mid-1990s, when these sites launched, the Internet was still a fairly open playing field. Hollywood fans, with some tech expertise, had new outlets to express their interests, amass their extensive knowledge, and share it with the like-minded visitors who happened to log on. The sites not only attracted fellow fans and geeks but also bred them.

Visitors to these sites encountered a Hollywood with multiple identities and uses. They could read reviews from professional critics as well as fans; they could get Internet-curated film lists (to see or to avoid); they could get news and insider gossip on current releases; they could get complete film credits on current and past films; they could read about a film's production history; and they could get access to data on industrial successes and failures. Everyday fans and users could also generate their own images and ideas of Hollywood and its history, expressing personal connections, nostalgia, and pleasure. Such user-generated content exhibited the agency of the authors; however, such agency must be read alongside the historical power of Hollywood narratives. The promises of access and authorship fail to address industrial and institutional realities of the Internet and the political economy that defines it. In large part, user-generated content tied to Hollywood necessarily derives from and negotiates with a set of long-standing ideas and images of Hollywood proffered over time by the studios, publicity, and news outlets as well as established libraries, archives, and museums. While the ideas and images are not necessarily unique to the Internet, these sites nonetheless provided a more widespread access to Hollywood's past and present, and illustrated a demand for a different kind of knowledge. They also attracted a new kind of Hollywood consumer and Internet user, one who typically works outside of Hollywood's proverbial gates and may not be classified as an avid fan or a cinephile. These sites, like those conceived in large numbers by the corporate arena in the mid-2000s, target a broad demographic of mainstream consumers, likely corresponding to the target audience for the mainstream media those same conglomerates produce.

Hollywood 2.0

When Yahoo! Movies launched in 1998, the same year as Rotten Tomatoes, the sites embodied two extremes of Hollywood's place on the Internet. Given

Yahoo!'s corporate role as an already established global Internet media company, "Yahoo! Movies" was at a distinct advantage in the late 1990s. When the site debuted, Yahoo! touted its comprehensive content and services, including showtimes, upcoming releases, box office information, news and reviews, and an actor index. Yahoo! Movies survives with a comparable, though extended, format, while many other sites dating from the same period have become victims of corporate shuffling, either folding or being folded into larger conglomerates, as the examples above suggest.

By the mid-2000s, there was a decisive shift in the Hollywood Internet landscape, one that in many ways paralleled broader changes on the Internet at large, generally associated with the term "Web 2.0." Media conglomerates and investment groups enveloped many preexisting and high-performing user-generated sites, while many corporations also launched their own income-generating Internet brands that featured social networking. While fan- and user-generated sites still exist in great numbers, especially with the proliferation of blogs in the 2000s, they must now compete with a slew of other sites that often feature the same content and have venture capital or major corporations behind them. Niche and fan sites certainly still exist (associated with stars, films, genres, and even formats like widescreen), but they do not attract the same kind of traffic, and therefore advertising, as their corporate counterparts.

Many general entertainment sites that debuted since the mid-2000s and possess secure financial backing bank on a conventional set of content categories, designed to appeal to the widest demographic. The sites present an overarching picture of Hollywood, with a generic, if not nebulous, focus on contemporary entertainment products and culture. Visitors can access a wide range of information that is similar, if not identical, to content on Yahoo! Movies as well as the expanded and now corporate-owned versions of Rotten Tomatoes and IMDb. Sites such as Hollywood.com (which relaunched in 2008 under new ownership) epitomize this approach with a range of content, including showtimes and DVD releases, reviews, news, editorials, trailers, photos, best of lists, box office statistics, social networking, and a celebrity section with photos, videos, news, and style. Despite the similarity in content, each site seeks to stand out as a primary online destination. Given the numerous sites devoted to Hollywood, standing out seems difficult. Indeed, the excess and breadth of Hollywood content across the Internet captures not only Hollywood's staying power but also the ambiguous and ineffable identity it possesses, particularly in the contemporary digital landscape.

General interest entertainment sites, while broad in scope, do manifest a notable focus on two facets of Hollywood culture — celebrity and industry. Internet attention to the Hollywood industry first surfaced on specialty sites and blogs like Box Office Mojo and The Numbers in the late 1990s, both of which exclusively track movie business information. Paralleling changes in traditional print and television news, the Internet has witnessed marked growth in consumer interest in Hollywood's business dealings. Since the early 1980s, when data companies began recording and studios began disseminating box office figures, mainstream entertainment news outlets and programs such as USA Today, the Los Angeles Times, and Entertainment Tonight began reporting the numbers to the general public.[14] Such information promised another kind of behind-the-scenes access to Hollywood. The public could potentially uncover Hollywood's cultural currency by mathematically dissecting the popularity of its films. While it is difficult to determine whether such reports responded to or drove audience interest in the 1980s and 1990s, it is common, if not requisite, for Internet sites that report Hollywood news to regularly and prominently feature such data. Thus, the Hollywood that exists on the Internet goes beyond fan or student interest in stars, films, filmmaking, and their histories. The concentration on industry brings another side of Hollywood's story into focus. Beyond the glamour and spectacle of its stars and productions, Hollywood's import, even appeal, lies in the scale of its budgets and profits, signaling the relationship between its economic and symbolic value.

In addition to the industry tallies found on many general interest sites, two types of gossip increasingly and prominently figure on sites that expose and celebrate Hollywood spectacle and excess. Celebrity gossip has become de rigeur on most general entertainment and movie sites as well as the many sites that focus on insider industry gossip.[15] The gossip that has historically driven celebrity culture in fan magazines and tabloids has crossed over into the realm of Hollywood deal making, casting, and daily production. While the history of Hollywood gossip considerably predates the Internet, the plethora of celebrity sites in the digital age suggests a marked and expanded reach and interest in celebrity culture, not to mention the increased speed that gossip can travel.

The popularity of celebrity Internet sites not only manifests a migration of content from traditional media (print and television) to new media (Internet and other mobile applications); these sites also underscore a significant intersection of the popular interest in Hollywood with the digital promise of instantaneous communication and global access to information. In addition to general interest Hollywood sites that feature celebrity news and gossip, other wholly celebrity sites gained Internet prominence within both the corporate arena and the blogosphere in the mid-2000s, with the likes of TMZ, PerezHilton.com, and Defamer (now under the Gawker umbrella). Using tabloid tactics, these sites uncover and immediately report on all things celebrity. The content, which runs the gamut from salacious celebrity scandals to everyday errands, draws substantial traffic and garners cachet among a growing pool of daily (even hourly) celebrity watchers. Sites like TMZ cater to and feed a desire for immediacy, with regular updates on its main site in addition to text alerts and mobile phone applications. The site also engages visitor interaction by soliciting tips and photos.[16]

Comparable to print and television celebrity news, tabloid Internet sites compete and coexist with more polished (and publicist-vetted) sites that center on star power, style, and glamour.[17] Yahoo! launched celebrity news site OMG! in 2007 with content amassed from *Access Hollywood* and other mainstream sources. In 2009, digital media firm mail.com Media Corporation received thirty-five million dollars in financing to underwrite a handful of celebrity and entertainment websites including Hollywood Life, Deadline Hollywood, and Movieline. Hollywood Life focuses primarily on Hollywood style and fashion. Editor and president Bonnie Fuller intimately addresses her readers as "BFFS" and seeks out their input on celebrity dos and don'ts. Fuller shifted to the celebrity Internet arena from traditional print periodicals, having overseen successful makeovers of the *Star* and *US Weekly*. Fuller's track record for tapping into mass-market interest in Hollywood celebrity easily transfers to the Internet.

The scope of such celebrity sites continues to expand as blogs and fan pages devoted to Hollywood stars regularly launch. While some of these sites adhere to a catchall approach highlighting any and all celebrity news, others focus on individual stars (created by a star's publicity team or by fans). The prevalence of stars and fans on Twitter further solidifies the illusory though powerful connection between Hollywood and Hollywood followers. In many respects, as I've suggested, the digital incarnation of celebrity news and gossip mimics the content and images of Hollywood found in the context of traditional media; the digital arena nonetheless offers and promotes simplified and accelerated access to Hollywood at any time and from any location.

The abundance of celebrity-watching sites further parallels, if not directly influences, an interest in industry gossip dating from the mid-1990s. Leading the industry gossip train in 1996, Ain't It Cool News (AICN) not only produced veritable competition for established Hollywood trade papers such as *Variety* and the *Hollywood Reporter* but also forced Hollywood insiders to reckon with the Internet and its impact on the general public. Founder Harry Knowles (along with his minions and followers) dig up and report information on behind-the-scenes Hollywood, offering visitors access and perspective unavailable in conventional entertainment news or trade papers.

While Hollywood studio marketers and publicists initially maligned and feared Knowles's posts, many insiders subsequently embraced the self-professed film geek who surveyed them virtually from Texas and attempted to win him over with private screenings, food and drinks, and a show of respect. Knowles has nonetheless maintained financial independence from the corporate arena, while his more recent Internet competitors, Deadline Hollywood and The Wrap, which launched more than a decade after AICN, receive backing from deep corporate coffers. Deadline Hollywood's Nikki Finke and The Wrap's Sharon Waxman began as journalists at traditional print publications (*LA Weekly* and the *New York Times* respectively) and subsequently struck respective deals with mail.com Media Corporation and venture capital group Maveron to support their blogs.[18] The popularity of these blogs along with AICN shows how the industrial side of Hollywood and information previously protected behind closed doors or privy only to those who subscribed to the trades is now widely available. With access to "insider" information, visitors are treated as privileged and enticed by the promise (or illusion) of social capital.

While sites such as Deadline Hollywood and The Wrap capture the boardroom side of the Hollywood industry, other behind-the-scenes sites focus on the craft and artistry behind Hollywood filmmaking. "Makingof.com" and "Movieclips.com," which both launched in 2009, retain the feel of 1990s user-generated sites in their avoidance of the all-encompassing model of Hollywood sites. Rather, these sites maintain a niche focus on individual aspects of films and film production yet have more capital and name recognition than their 1990s user-generated predecessors. Actress Natalie Portman and Silicon Valley entrepreneur Christine Aylward developed Making Of to serve as a central resource for behind-the-scenes interviews and featurettes. While emulating DVD extra features, the site acts as a hub of information that extends beyond the craftspeople attached to a single film title. Highlighting its breadth and crossover, the site categorizes content not only by film or artist name but also by craft area and, in turn, ostensibly functions as a forum for public pedagogy. Portman's insider role in Hollywood has no doubt helped Making Of score many high-profile interviews. A *Vanity Fair* profile on the site's launch characterized it as "insiders speaking to insiders," underscoring the privileged Hollywood access the site grants its visitors. The site also includes a separate blog as well as a social networking component and forum that allows visitors to discuss common interests in a genre, questions about equipment, or potential job leads.

The crossover between Hollywood sites and social networking that took hold in the mid- to late 2000s reveals what has become a prevailing intersection of industrial and social media. Hollywood, one of many creative industries currently exploiting social media, has a track record of inviting outsiders inside, offering audiences behind-the-scenes access through print, television, and home video. The addition of audience or user participation afforded by social media in many respects therefore serves as an extension of historical efforts to engage and immerse audiences in the "idea" of Hollywood.

A startup such as Movieclips reveals another way Hollywood studios have taken advantage of the Internet and social networking formats to exercise influence and gain revenue through the backdoor. Six major Hollywood studios (Warner Bros., Paramount, Universal, Sony, Fox, and MGM) licensed content to the site, founded by Zach James, a former investment banker, and Richard Raddon, former director of the Los Angeles Film Festival.[19] The studios and Movieclips share ad revenue, while the site encourages visitors to share clips with friends. Featuring clips from more than twelve thousand films chosen by self-described "movie freaks," the site organizes and makes clips searchable by actor, title, genre, occasion, action, mood, character, theme, setting, prop, and dialogue.[20] The site, in framing user visits as a process of discovery, encourages users to purchase the full-length films on DVD or via download. On the "about us" page, the creators celebrate their site's connections and legal arrangements with Hollywood studios. These connections not only facilitate access to multiple studio libraries but also offer the site a measure of authenticity. Movieclips both legitimates its own motives and redeems potential users; fans do not have to "resort to piracy" or "wade through mismarked user-generated crap to find the 'real' scene."[21] In offering up the "real" scene, Movieclips implicitly offers access to the "real" Hollywood and, in turn, privileges industry-controlled over user-generated content.

Where Is Hollywood?

One of the implicit questions raised throughout this book is whether or not there is a "real" Hollywood and, more importantly perhaps, who names it, constructs its image, and tells its story. If the digital age increasingly manifests a battleground between user-generated and industry-controlled representations of Hollywood, then in many ways, it retreads earlier struggles over Hollywood's meaning and relative import. As I have suggested throughout this book, many of these struggles have been site specific, played out in different historical moments, different institutional contexts, and with different sets of players in different geographic locales: New York, London, Paris, Berlin, Los Angeles, the living room, the retail store, the restaurant, the theme park, and most recently, the computer and mobile device—all have played host to Hollywood, leveraging to varying degrees its symbolic and economic power. Uniting these examples is a common spotlight on Hollywood as a central player in a larger story, institutional mission, and in many instances, bottom line.

Many of these struggles over Hollywood embody underlying tensions between art and commerce that date back to the filmmaking capital's inception. Alongside this art-commerce divide, institutions and products that memorialize Hollywood have faced other competing priorities. On the one hand, they must preserve Hollywood's mystique and aura, while on the other, they must grant a degree of access to its backstage secrets. Historically, in negotiating these divides, Hollywood studios have demonstrated a vested interest in upholding their cultural and financial value as well as the value of their products. Nonprofits, as I discuss in the first chapter, must also contend with these same competing values. The expansive scope of the digital landscape paired with the potential for fan and user-generated content ostensibly promises a more open and diverse field for Hollywood representation. Bloggers and fans can easily appropriate content and images and present their own stories, evidenced by the plethora of sites devoted to niche genres, film styles, title sequences, film frames, movie quotes, memorabilia, and other fan and cinephile proclivities.[22] At the same time, however, corporations continue to poach high-volume sites and employ social media tools to perform market research on unwitting users. With competing content producers, the digital arena represents a truly contested space where the multitude of sites, producers, and consumers wrestle to control Hollywood's past, present, and future.

As an inherently contested terrain, the digital landscape presents an ideal end point to *this* narrative, particularly given the fact that Hollywood's history, mythology, and profit potential will undoubtedly continue to generate valued content. However, the Internet and other incarnations of the digital should not, as I've suggested, be treated as a simple end point to Hollywood's larger tale.

From the movie theater to television and back again. Advertisement for Turner Classic Movies' *Classic Film Festival*, 2010. Author's collection.

Indeed, it is crucial to remain wary of the significance we attach to any single medium or site. While the Internet clearly represents a key site of our digital age, Hollywood also continually migrates back to older media sites and, in some cases, to its original geographic locale. TMZ and Rotten Tomatoes, two of the most successful and well-trafficked Hollywood Internet sites, spawned television offshoots in 2007 and 2009 respectively, while in 2010, classic television movie network TCM debuted an annual film festival held at iconic Hollywood sites, including the Hollywood Roosevelt Hotel, Grauman's Chinese Theatre, and the Egyptian Theater. The Academy of Motion Picture Arts and Sciences will open a museum at the corner of Wilshire and Fairfax. These examples, though seemingly minor, point to a cross-pollination of media and sites that not only exemplifies the synergistic motives of conglomerates but also indicates Hollywood's ability to travel temporally and spatially. The examples discussed throughout this book further manifest a range of historical and contemporary sites, both physical and mediated, that shed light on and work to uphold Hollywood's cultural and commercial power. The perpetual changes in mediascapes, urbanscapes, and corporate ladders necessarily impact the way Hollywood is socially and culturally perceived, defined, represented, historicized, and preserved. The sheer multiplicity of sites, both physical and virtual, testifies to the symbolic and monumental status Hollywood continues to hold. The sites may change as technologies fluctuate and develop, but clearly, Hollywood will remain a constant site of fascination, memories, and dreams.

Acknowledgments

Given the long gestation of this project, I am overwhelmed and humbled by the number of people I want to thank. The project began as a dissertation in the Critical Studies department at University of Southern California's School of Cinema-Television, where I was mentored by an awe-inspiring faculty committee. My advisor, Lynn Spigel, significantly shaped my thinking and approach to history and historiography in many thought-provoking graduate seminars and at each stage in the book's development. I am indebted to Marita Sturken, who not only gave me entrée to the Annenberg School for Communication as a new PhD but also served as mentor in the true sense of the word, always generous with her time and attention to detail. David James pushed me to think outside the Hollywood bubble in a way that I still greatly appreciate and admire.

Others have given their time to read and offer indispensible input. Dana Polan proved consistently accessible and always encouraging with his feedback and praise for the scope of my study. Chris Horak, who has personally navigated much of the institutional terrain I explore throughout the book, provided sage and trusted advice at key points in my writing and revision. Sarah Banet-Weiser, Barbara Hall, Mark Latonero, Jennifer Peterson, and Scott Curtis also read drafts and offered insightful critiques at various stages. Barbara Hall and Val Almendarez steered me toward some amazing collections at the Margaret Herrick Library and were always open to talking about Hollywood history over a coffee, a drink, or a homemade meal. Over the years, I regularly crossed paths with colleagues Peter Decherney, Christel Schmidt, Dan Streible, and Haidee Wasson, whose work in similar arenas fostered my curiosity and intellectual growth.

I am grateful to Herb Farmer, David Francis, JoAnn Hanley, Bud Lesser, and David Schwartz for granting me interviews during the research stages of the book. Linda Barth at the Los Angeles Department of Recreation and Parks, historian Richard Koszarski, and Donata Pesenti Campagnoni at the Museo Nazionale del Cinema helped me piece together undocumented histories. I also extend thanks to Ron Magliozzi and Charles Silver at the Museum of Modern Art's Film Library and to the Museum of the Moving Image's Carl Goodman, who unknowingly inspired my initial investigation of film museums. More recently, Mark Williams, as editor of the visual culture series of which this book is part, saw the potential in this project despite much time lying dormant. I would also like to extend thanks to UPNE editor Richard Pult for encouraging me to listen to and trust my inner voice and to the helpful production editor Amanda Dupuis and copy editor Naomi Burns.

When the contents of this book were merely fledgling ideas, my graduate student peers, including Steve Anderson, Vicky Johnson, Mary Celeste Kearney, Christie Milliken, Jim Moran, Sarah Nilsen, Luisa Rivi, Bhaskar Sarkar, Valentin Stoilov, Sophie Siddique Harvey, Michelle Torre, Christina Venegas, Karen Voss, and Bill Whittington, shared with me the sometimes rocky road of dissertating with good spirit and welcome diversions. Having been at USC for many years, the line between mentor and colleague has become fuzzy. Over these years, Rick Jewell, Marsha Kinder, Michael Renov, and Ellen Seiter have offered much appreciated encouragement. Many of my colleagues at USC, including Todd Boyd, Taj Frazier, Priya Jaikumar, Abby Kaun, Josh Kun, Tara McPherson, Christopher Holmes Smith, and Stacy Smith, have proven to be uncommonly astute listeners and good friends. While I've been at Annenberg, a number of students have also assisted me, reading drafts, doing research, and making site visits. Many have also become colleagues and friends, including Beth Boser, Joyee Chatterjee, Eric Hoyt, Jade Miller, Alex Minton, D. Travers Scott, Shayne Thomas, Cara Wallis, Lauren and David Weinzimmer, and Cynthia Wills. Additionally, Larry Gross and the Annenberg School for Communication and Journalism deserve special mention for their steadfast support through the years.

While the project began in graduate school, the critical thinking that drove my research and writing came much earlier. I would like to particularly recognize King Schofield, who directed me toward authors that opened my academic mind at an impressionable age. Rachel Adams, Eden Allswang, Jenny Eisenberg, Dana Garcetti, Lenna Lebovich, Karyn Morse, Kristin Nesburn, Lisa Parker, Lori Quon, and Carolyn Wessling, a truly extraordinary group of women, shared my academic drive yet also understood the need to decompress, go to the movies, eat tacos, and just talk. Marie Szurszewski and I wrote side by side and page by page, keeping each other in check. Whitney Wilson provided an always-available and much-appreciated sounding board. These friends have journeyed with me through the years and, in many instances, have lived through this project. Since becoming a parent, I've had the pleasure to know, rely on, and commiserate with a new kind of support group who helped keep me sane and focused through the tumultuous years of new parenthood.

As the cliché goes, parenthood has made me appreciate my own parents, Linda and Sorrell, whose unswerving and continued support, enthusiastic encouragement, and impact remain unparalleled. My father, in particular, stimulated my interest in history — both academic and popular. His encyclopedic knowledge of classical Hollywood films paired with personal memories of old Los Angeles haunts brought history to life for me. Beyond a love of popular history, he taught me to think critically and, to his detriment perhaps, question authority. Daily conversations and catch-up with my mother helped ground me in everyday rituals and routines, offering me needed perspective on the running list that life sometimes becomes. My sisters and brother, Laura, Donna, and Michael, have always been there for me when I have called on them, and my grandmother, Lila, who will be ninety-five when this book is published, continues to warm my heart with baked goods and an optimism I will always admire. I also owe thanks to my in-laws, Harriet and Al, for their willingness and availability to babysit on a regular basis.

This is a book about Hollywood and Los Angeles, a place where I grew up and briefly fled from during college and shortly thereafter. At the time, I wanted to escape much of the superficiality I had come to associate with my hometown and to uncover what I thought was a more authentic kind of life. It was in moving back to Los Angeles to attend graduate school that I found that authentic life—with Tom Kemper—my intellectual partner, friend, and soul mate. It is beyond my ability to innumerate the ways in which he has patiently, humorously, and lovingly shared in this often arduous process—reading the text more times than I can remember. He has also been instrumental in raising our two wonderfully energetic boys, Jack and Dashiell, whose high spirits, passion, and sense of fun continually bring perspective and sheer joy to my life. I look forward to sharing whatever the future holds with them all.

Notes

Introduction

1. Hortense Powdermaker, *Hollywood, the Dream Factory: An Anthropologist Looks at the Movie-Makers* (Boston: Little, Brown, 1950), 16.

2. "Hollywood" circa 1950s. Brochure prepared by the Hollywood Chamber of Commerce with the cooperation of the Association of Motion Picture Producers. "Hollywood Tours and Tourism," General Subject Files, AMPAS. This brochure poses and answers ten frequently asked questions about Hollywood, suggesting another attempt to offer behind-the-scenes access to film production and Hollywood glamour.

3. Bob Sehlinger and Arthur Frommer, *The Unofficial Guide to Walt Disney World 1998* (New York: Macmillan, 1998), 163.

4. Sarah Banet-Weiser, *Authentic™: Political Possibilities in Brand Cultures* (New York: New York University Press, forthcoming).

5. Robert Sklar, *Movie-Made America: A Cultural History of American Movies* (New York: Vintage, 1975), 69.

6. In both the late 1970s and 2010, Hugh Hefner unleashed a media frenzy in support of preserving the sign. In 2010, he funded the remaining nine hundred thousand dollars needed to purchase the land around the sign and restore it. For more on the Hollywood Sign, see Leo Braudy, *The Hollywood Sign: Fantasy and Reality of an American Icon* (New Haven: Yale University Press, 2011).

7. Douglas Gomery, *Shared Pleasures: A History of Movie Presentation in the United States* (Madison: University of Wisconsin Press, 1992); Gregory Waller, *Moviegoing in America: A Sourcebook in the History of Film Exhibition* (Malden, MA: Blackwell, 2002); Gregory Waller and Charles Musser, eds., *Main Street Amusements: Movies and Commercial Entertainment in a Southern City* (Washington, DC: Smithsonian, 1995); Kathryn Fuller, *At the Picture Show: Small-Town Audiences and the Creation of Movie Fan Culture* (Washington, DC: Smithsonian, 1996); Janna Jones, *The Southern Movie Palace: Rise, Fall, and Resurrection* (Gainesville: University Press of Florida, 2003); Barbara Wilinsky, *Sure Seaters: The Emergence of Art House Cinema* (Minneapolis: University of Minnesota Press, 2001); David E. James, *The Most Typical Avant-Garde: History and Geography of Minor Cinemas in Los Angeles* (Berkeley: University of California Press, 2005); Haidee Wasson, *Museum Movies: The Museum of Modern Art and the Birth of Art Cinema* (Berkeley: University of California Press, 2005); Peter Decherney, *Hollywood and the Culture Elite: How the Movies Became American* (New York: Columbia University Press, 2005); Barbara Klinger, *Beyond the Multiplex: Cinema, New Technologies and the Home* (Berkeley: University of California Press, 2006); William Boddy, *New Media and Popular Imagination: Launching Radio, Television and Digital Media in the United States* (New

York: Oxford University Press, 2004). Ina Rae Hark's anthology *Exhibition: The Film Reader* (New York: Routledge, 2002) also includes essays from the 1980s, such as Russell Merritt's on nickelodeon theaters and Charlotte Herzog's on architectural styles in early movie palaces. Other work on the subject of contemporary exhibition includes Janet Wasko, *Hollywood in the Information Age: Beyond the Silver Screen* (Austin: University of Texas Press, 1995); Charles R. Acland, *Screen Traffic: Movies, Multiplexes, and Global Culture* (Durham, NC: Duke University Press, 2003); and Anne Friedberg, *The Virtual Window: From Alberti to Microsoft* (Cambridge, MA: MIT Press, 2006). Other work that tangentially considers exhibition in the home includes Frederick Wasser, *Veni, Vidi, Video: The Hollywood Empire and the VCR* (Austin: University of Texas Press, 2001); and Chuck Tryon, *Reinventing Cinema: Movies in the Age of Media Convergence* (New Brunswick, NJ: Rutgers University Press, 2009).

8. Tony Bennett, "Museums and 'the People,'" in *The Museum Time Machine: Putting Cultures on Display*, ed. Robert Lumley (London: Routledge, 1988), 63; Carol Duncan, "Art Museums and the Ritual of Citizenship," in *Exhibiting Cultures: The Poetics and Politics of Museum Display*, ed. Ivan Karp and Steven D. Lavine (Washington, DC: Smithsonian, 1991). For a discussion of personal collections, see James Clifford, "On Collecting Art and Culture," in *The Predicament of Culture: Twentieth-Century Ethnography, Literature and Art* (Cambridge, MA: Harvard University Press, 1988), 218.

9. Brian Wallis, "Selling Nations: International Exhibitions and Cultural Diplomacy," in *Museum Culture: Histories, Discourses, Spectacles*, ed. Daniel J. Sherman, Irit Rogoff (Minneapolis: University of Minnesota Press, 1994), 265–81.

10. Spencer Crew and James Sims, "Locating Authenticity: Fragments of a Dialogue," in *Exhibiting Cultures: The Poetics and Politics of Museum Display*, ed. Ivan Karp and Steven D. Lavine (Washington, DC: Smithsonian, 1991), 168–69.

11. Tony Bennett, *The Birth of the Museum: History, Theory, Politics* (New York: Routledge, 1995), 10, 177–86. Bennett comments that the museum was frequently conceived as (if not directly named) a "machine of progress" during the late nineteenth and early twentieth centuries, and was often custom built to construct linear routes.

12. Andreas Huyssen, *Twilight Memories: Marking Time in a Culture of Amnesia* (New York: Routledge, 1995), 14.

13. Anna McCarthy makes a similar argument about television's place outside of the home in *Ambient Television: Visual Culture and Public Space* (Durham, NC: Duke University Press, 2001).

Chapter 1 • Essential Hollywood

1. Terry Ramsaye, "Of Time and the Films," *Motion Picture Herald*, July 8, 1939, 12–13.

2. "March of Time Correspondence, 1935–1941," March 21, 1939, file 02.02, box 2, Film Study Center, Special Collections, MoMA. In 1939, the library planned to produce an educational film directed by Paul Rotha to explain various film techniques. Once again, the interest in film production activities marked an affinity with Hollywood's in-

dustrial practices, in which the museum showed it could value the film process as much as the product. The library further considered producing a feature film in 1938 in conjunction with the major Hollywood studios. The library's director, John Abbott, traveled to Hollywood in order to enlist the cooperation of the studios to help produce this piece on the history of the motion picture industry. The *March of Time* episode was the result.

3. "The Movies March On," *The March of Time Presents American Lifestyles 1939–1950* (1939; Los Angeles: New Line Home Video, 1995), VHS.

4. David Bordwell, *On the History of Film Style* (Cambridge, MA.: Harvard University Press, 1997), 24–27. Bordwell uses MoMA to set up his own argument about the origins and development of film style.

5. Miriam Hansen, *Babel and Babylon: Spectatorship in American Silent Film* (Cambridge, MA: Harvard University Press, 1991), 61–65.

6. Hansen, *Babel and Babylon*, 64.

7. Haidee Wasson and Peter Decherney discuss the establishment of MoMA's Film Library at length. Wasson focuses on MoMA's founding, while Decherney offers a more extensive overview of the institutional attempts to define cinema as an art form that includes MoMA as well as the work of other cultural and industry leaders. Haidee Wasson, *Museum Movies: The Museum of Modern Art and the Birth of Art Cinema* (Berkeley: University of California Press, 2005); Peter Decherney, *Hollywood and the Culture Elite: How the Movies Became American* (New York: Columbia University Press, 2005).

8. Wasson, *Museum Movies*, 111, 113.

9. Amy Newman and Irving Sandler, eds., *Defining Modern Art: Selected Writings of Alfred H. Barr, Jr.* (New York: Abrams, 1986), 126, 142. Barr's diary, which compares Vsevolod Pudovkin's *Mother* to the poor quality of most American films, expresses such sentiments.

10. In 1943, Barr was fired by the museum's board. Sybil Gordon Kantor, *Alfred H. Barr, Jr. and the Intellectual Origins of the Museum of Modern Art* (Cambridge, MA: MIT Press, 2002), 352–61.

11. For more on the development of film studies as a discipline, see Dana Polan, *Scenes of Instruction: The Beginnings of the U.S. Study of Film* (Berkeley: University of California Press, 2007).

12. Barr's list was based on Paul Rotha's 1930 publication of *The Film Till Now: A Survey of the Cinema* (London: Cape, 1930), though Mary Lee Bandy admitted Barr's original list could not be located. Mary Lee Bandy, "Nothing Sacred: 'Jock Whitney Snares Antiques for the Museum,'" in *The Museum of Modern Art at Mid-Century: Continuity and Change*, Studies in Modern Art 5 (New York: Museum of Modern Art, 1995), 101n35. For more information on Barr's thinking at this time, see Kantor, *Alfred H. Barr, Jr.*, 423n143. See also Alice Goldfarb Marquis, *Alfred H. Barr: Missionary for the Modern* (Chicago: Contemporary Books, 1989).

13. Iris Barry, "The Motion Picture, 1914–1934: Ninth Program, the Sociological Film," file 01.03A, box 1, Iris Barry Collection, Film Study Center, MoMA. This quote is taken from program notes for a screening at the Wadsworth Atheneum in Hartford, Connecticut, in 1934.

14. Edward M. M. Warburg, "Unstuffing the Self-Important," in *Remembering Iris Barry*, ed. Margareta Akermark (New York: Museum of Modern Art, 1980), 4.

15. Iris Barry, review of *Stella Dallas*, quoted in Marsha McCreadie, "Iris Barry: Historian and All Around Critic," in *Women on Film: The Critical Eye* (New York: Praeger, 1983), 98, 101.

16. Warburg, "Unstuffing the Self-Important," 4.

17. Arthur Knight, "It Has All Been Very Interesting," in *Remembering Iris Barry*, ed. Margareta Akermark (New York: Museum of Modern Art, 1980), 9.

18. Iris Barry, "Art in America," 1934, scrapbook 1: April 1935–November 1935, Film Library Scrapbooks, MoMA.

19. John Abbott and Iris Barry, "An Outline of a Project for Founding the Film Library of the Museum of Modern Art," April 17, 1935, file 01.05, box 1, Film Study Center, Special Collections, MoMA. Also reprinted in its entirety in *Film History* 7, no. 3 (Autumn 1995): 325–35. A modern art collector, Whitney also had an interest in the film industry, leading him to invest in Technicolor and the founding of Pioneer Pictures. Later, Whitney went on to form Selznick International with David O. Selznick and had an important financial role in the productions of *Gone With the Wind* and *Rebecca*. Mary Lea Bandy, "The Movies at MoMA," *Film Quarterly* 22, no. 4 (Summer 1969): 27. For more information on Whitney, see E. J. Kahn Jr., *Jock: The Life and Times of John Hay Whitney* (Garden City, NY: Doubleday, 1981).

20. John E. Abbott, "Organization and Work of the Film Library of the Museum of Modern Art," *Journal of the Society of Motion Picture Engineers* 28, no. 3 (1937): 297. The focus on American cinema should be contextualized vis-à-vis other trends in the museum at large as well as trends in other American museums and universities. While American art was not always considered a worthy subject for academic attention, World War II necessitated a change in exhibition practices. Marquis, *Alfred H. Barr*, 35, 79, 141–42, 190, 229, 231.

21. This list included nearly all films produced outside the United States, namely, in France, Germany, Sweden, and England (except those from the USSR that were easily obtainable by film societies and student groups); all films by Chaplin made after 1918; all of Griffith's work from 1904 to 1914 and *Intolerance* (1916); early American Westerns from 1909 to 1917; and the majority of American films "of importance" produced prior to 1932.

22. Abbott and Barry, "An Outline of a Project." With few exceptions, the report does not list actual film titles.

23. Abbott and Barry, "An Outline of a Project," 15.

24. "Inter-Office Memo: Addendum to Memo June 12th on Museum of Modern Art," June 18, 1935, MPAA General Correspondence Files, 1930–1935, Special Collections, Margaret Herrick Library, AMPAS. These files also include direct correspondence between Will Hays, John Abbott, and John Hay Whitney. The correspondence includes a list of films for the "text-book of film art in film." This list reveals which films the library sought

from Hollywood in 1935. With a few exceptions, most of the films later appear in the Film Library's programs. Subsequent MPPDA memos indicated an attempt to trace the ownership of these films. In regard to some of the early Griffith and Ince films, the MPPDA indicated that Harry Aitken was "tracing" them. Other titles were speculatively attributed to Mary Pickford, W. R. Hearst, the George Kleine collection, Adolf Zukor, Charlie Chaplin, Harold Lloyd, Cecil B. DeMille, Douglas Fairbanks, Marion Davies, and Joseph von Sternberg, as well as the major studios.

25. "An Equal Responsibility," *Washington Post*, July 15, 1935, 8, scrapbook 1: April 1935–November 1935, Film Library Scrapbooks, MoMA.

26. Iris Barry, "The Film Library and How It Grew," *Film Quarterly* 22, no. 4 (Summer 1969): 22.

27. Wasson, *Museum Movies*, 136.

28. Iris Barry used the phrase "talk turkey" in relation to Abbott, also citing his ability to "conjure with figures." These were assets she admittedly did not possess. Barry, "The Film Library and How It Grew," 21.

29. Tip Poff, "Good Old Days," *Los Angeles Times*, September 1, 1935, scrapbook 1: April 1935–November 1935, Film Library Scrapbooks, MoMA.

30. Wasson, *Museum Movies*, 134.

31. Iris Barry, untitled and undated manuscript, file 02.03, box 2, Iris Barry Collection, MoMA.

32. Barry, manuscript. It is unclear whether or not this was the actual speech given or merely a discarded draft.

33. These arguments and national sentiments would be used again by Hollywood leaders themselves in the 1960s.

34. Barry, "The Film Library and How It Grew," 23.

35. "Old Films for Archives," *Daily Variety*, September 11, 1935, scrapbook 1: April 1935–November 1935, Film Library Scrapbooks, MoMA. For more on early donations, see Tom McGreevey and Joanne L. Yeck, *Our Movie Heritage* (New Brunswick, NJ: Rutgers University Press, 1997), 77–78. Discussions of copyright holdings and negotiations with rights holders can be found in Mary Lee Bandy and Eileen Bowser, "Film," in *The Museum of Modern Art*, ed. Sam Hunter (New York: Abrams, 1984), 527; see also A. Conger Goodyear, *The Museum of Modern Art* (New York: Museum of Modern Art, 1943), 119.

36. Barry, "The Film Library and How It Grew," 23.

37. Bandy, "The Movies at MoMA," 29.

38. Discussion of Hollywood film acquisitions can be found in "A Report on the Film Library, 1941–1956," *Bulletin* 24, no. 1 (Fall 1956): 4. See also Bandy, "Nothing Sacred," 56, 101n555; and Iris Barry, "Why Wait for Posterity?" *Hollywood Quarterly* 1, no. 2 (January 1946): 131–37.

39. Barry, "Why Wait for Posterity?" 131, 133.

40. *Bulletin of the Museum of Modern Art: Exhibition of American Art in Paris* 5, nos. 4–5 (April–May 1938), box 18, Film Library, Special Collections, MoMA.

41. For a discussion of the rising archive movement in the 1930s, see Penelope Houston, *Keepers of the Frame: The Film Archives* (London: British Film Institute, 1994); Richard Roud, *A Passion for Films: Henri Langlois and the Cinémathèque Française* (New York: Viking, 1983); Anthony Slide, *Nitrate Won't Wait: Film Preservation in the United States* (Jefferson, NC: McFarland, 1992); Paolo Cherchi Usai, *Burning Passions: An Introduction to the Study of Silent Film* (London: British Film Institute, 1994).

42. Henri Langlois, "La Cinémathèque de la Foundation Rockefeller de New York," *La Cinématographie française*, June 27, 1936, quoted in Glenn Myrent and Georges P. Langlois, *Henri Langlois: First Citizen of the Cinema* (New York: Twayne, 1995), 35.

43. Kristin Thompson, *Exporting Entertainment: America in the World Film Market, 1907–1934* (London: British Film Institute, 1986).

44. Biographers Roud and Myrent both attest to Langlois's acceptance of all film. Roud, *A Passion for Films*, 24, Myrent and Langlois, *Henri Langlois*, 130–31.

45. Henri Langlois, "Trois cents ans de cinéma," *Ecrits, Cahiers du Cinéma: Cinémathèque Française* (Paris: Fondation Européenne des Métiers de l'image et du Son, 1986), 49, quoted in Donata Pesenti Campagnoni, "Tra Patrimonio Filmico e Patrimonio Cinematografico: Alcune tracce storiche sui musei del Cinema e dintorni," *Notizario Dell'Associazione Museo Nazionale Del Cinema* 49–50 (1997): 27.

46. Roud, *A Passion for Films*, 26.

47. Roud, *A Passion for Films*, 47–49; Myrent and Langlois, *Henri Langlois*, 99–102. Given the murkiness of the details of this wartime history and the lack of an actual contract between Langlois and the Hollywood studios, it is difficult to definitively establish the veracity of this deal. However, it is clear that Langlois was an expert at negotiating with, even indulging, those whom he admired or possessed objects that he coveted.

48. For more on *Cahiers*, see Jim Hiller, ed., *Cahiers du Cinéma: The 1950s: Neorealism, Hollywood, New Wave* (Cambridge, MA: Harvard University Press, 1985).

49. Myrent and Langlois, *Henri Langlois*, 215–16.

50. Myrent and Langlois, *Henri Langlois*, 13.

51. The first temporary exhibit of the work of Georges Méliès took place in 1938. For a more detailed history of exhibitions, see Laurent Mannoni, "Henri Langlois and the Musée du Cinéma," *Film History* 18 (2006): 274–87.

52. Such rumors likely stem from the loose exchanges and deals Langlois proffered tied to his wartime preservation of American film titles.

53. Mannoni, "Henri Langlois," 278.

54. Mannoni, "Henri Langlois," 278.

55. Myrent and Langlois, *Henri Langlois*, 293.

56. Roud, *A Passion for Films*, 178–79.

57. Myrent and Langlois, *Henri Langlois*, 183–87.

58. Myrent and Langlois, *Henri Langlois*, 286–88.

59. For extensive overview and images from the exhibitions, see Huguette Marquand Ferreux, *Musée du Cinéma Henri Langlois* (Paris: Maeght éditeur, 1991).

60. See Thomas Elsaesser, *European Cinema Face to Face with Hollywood* (Amsterdam: Amsterdam University Press, 2005).

61. For a discussion of federal government's impact on German film exhibition, see Thomas Elsaesser, *New German Cinema: A History* (New Brunswick, NJ: Rutgers University Press, 1989), 20.

62. This is further supported by the attention paid to Hollywood by New German Cinema filmmakers such as Wim Wenders and Rainer Fassbinder.

63. It is unclear exactly why MOMI closed. The BFI press release posted on its website in 1999 offered little in the way of explanation, claiming initially that the closure was temporary and the museum would reopen in 2003. Later press releases claimed the closure was permanent. Some have speculated that attendance flagged since first opening and that the BFI had overly optimistic attendance projections. At its close, visitor numbers estimated at over 350,000 per year. Others claim that those in positions of power at the BFI were not interested in the museum and viewed it as a financial drain on an already taxed institution. Deac Rossell, "Museum Closes," *Domitor Bulletin* 13, no. 2 (August 1999): 10–11. David Francis indicated that audiences were declining because the BFI had not invested in the museum in order to keep it updated. David Francis, e-mail message to author, November 2, 2000.

64. MOMI, press release, November 1987, General Subject Files, Margaret Herrick Library, AMPAS.

65. MOMI, press release.

66. Robert Osborne, "Rambling Reporter," *Hollywood Reporter*, November 2, 1988, 5, MOMI, General Subject Files, Margaret Herrick Library, AMPAS. The British cinema, censorship, animation, documentary, and various television exhibits spanned several decades (generally from the 1920s or 1930s to the present) within a single installation area.

67. Rinella Cere, "'Exhibiting Cinema': The Cultural Activities of the Museo Nazionale del Cinema, 1958–1971," *Film History* 18 (2006): 303.

68. For more information on his projects, see François Confino, "Museum and Exhibition Design," accessed March 16, 2011, http://www.confino.com/.

69. This percentage is based on listing of films by theme provided by the MNC press materials.

70. Museum of the Moving Image, "About," accessed March 16, 2011, http://www.movingimage.us/about.

71. Without an equivalent museum in Hollywood, New York's Museum of the Moving Image has been able to tap the Hollywood industry for money. Its English counterpart, on the other hand, had no national film industry on a Hollywood scale to tap for financial assistance and instead relied on patrons like Getty. The academy's plans for a museum may change the New York museum's fundraising strategies; however, the New York site managed to complete its renovation despite the academy's fundraising efforts and the late 2000s recession.

72. In 2010, board members included such Hollywood power brokers as Dreamworks' Jeffrey Katzenberg, former president and CEO of NBC-Universal Jeff Zucker, director Ang Lee, and Sony Picture Classic's copresident Michael Barker.

73. Tony Bennett discusses the museum as social reformer. See Tony Bennett, *The Birth of the Museum: History, Theory, Politics* (London: Routledge, 1995), 28–33.

74. Edward Rothstein, "When Pictures Leap to Other Screens," *New York Times*, January 14, 2011, C23.

75. "An Interview with Rochelle Slovin, Founder and Director, American Museum of the Moving Image," AMMI Press Kit, 1996.

Chapter 2 • The Great Whatzit?

1. "Star Studded Crowd of 6000 at Museum Groundbreaking," *Hollywood Reporter*, October 21, 1963, 1, 3.

2. T. K. Peters, "A Museum of Motion Picture History," *Transactions of the Society of Motion Picture Engineers* 22 (September 1925): 54, 61–62.

3. SMPE committee notes reveal debates over the location of a suitable repository for its collection, including the Museum of Peaceful Arts in New York, the Smithsonian Institute, the Julius Rosenwald Museum of Science and Industry, and the Museum of the University of Southern California in Los Angeles. "Report of the Historical Committee," *Journal of the Society of Motion Picture Engineers* (January 1931): 102–5. A later report suggested that the West Coast locale was preferred over the east as many of the desired collections were available only for a West Coast museum. "Report of the Museum Committee," *Journal of the Society of Motion Picture Engineers* (August 1932): 203–6.

4. For more on Theissen's activities as head of the Museum Section of the SMPE's Historical Committee, see Earl Theissen, "The Historical Motion Picture Exhibit at the Los Angeles Museum," *Journal of the Society of Motion Picture Engineers* (March 1936): 259–64.

5. Other attempts to build a museum in Hollywood and about Hollywood during the mid-1930s, which may have complemented this Los Angeles museum exhibit, are poorly documented.

6. In 1936, Harry Crocker, member of the famed California banking and oil family and sometimes actor in Charlie Chaplin's films, proposed a museum on Sunset Boulevard furnished with props and other equipment from notable historical movies. Like many others, this venture failed due to lack of studio cooperation as well as, according to Crocker, a lack of cooperation from transportation and sightseeing lines. Philip K. Scheur, "Films of the Past Will Live Again: Eastern Art Patrons Movie to Perpetuate Hollywood's Bygone Days," *San Antonio Texas Express*, July 12, 1936, D11, scrapbook 3: February–September 1936, Film Library Scrapbooks, MoMA. Frank Whitbeck (Hollywood golden age studio publicist, hired at MGM by Thalberg from 1934 to 1937) also discussed museum plans, according to the Los Angeles Parks and Recreation Department conversation with Linda Barth.

7. For more, see Dana Polan, *Scenes of Instruction: The Beginnings of the U.S. Study of Film* (Berkeley: University of California Press, 2007).

8. "Excerpt from Minutes of the Academy Board of Governors Meeting," August 2, 1940, AMPTP Files on the Hollywood Museum, Special Collections, AMPAS. Gledhill does not mention the Los Angeles museum exhibit in this statement.

9. "Excerpt from Minutes of the Academy Board of Governors Meeting."

10. "Excerpt from Minutes of the Academy Board of Governors Meeting."

11. "What the Motion Picture Exposition Will Be," c. 1954–1955, "Motion Picture Exposition and Hall of Fame" promotional brochure, Motion Picture Exposition and Hall of Fame, General Subject Files, AMPAS. Like the Motion Picture Exposition and Hall of Fame project, the records of this endeavor were targeted to benefit the Motion Picture Relief Fund.

12. Joel Kotkin, "The Powers that Will Be," *Los Angeles Times*, December 14, 1997, M1.

13. "Financing Expo Thru Bond Sale," *Daily Variety*, March 15, 1955, Motion Picture Exposition and Hall of Fame, General Subject Files, AMPAS.

14. "Movie Exhibit Plan Dropped," *Los Angeles Herald Examiner*, August 13, 1955, Motion Picture Exposition and Hall of Fame, General Subject Files, AMPAS. Similar headlines were found in *Daily Variety*, the *Hollywood Reporter*, and the *Los Angeles Times*.

15. "Hollywood Summary: Industry Prestige Project Misfires," *New York Times*, August 21, 1955, Motion Picture Exposition and Hall of Fame, General Subject Files, AMPAS.

16. Dick Williams, "Collapse of Museum Project Is Black Eye for Hollywood," *Mirror News*, August 20, 1955, Motion Picture Exposition and Hall of Fame, General Subject Files, AMPAS.

17. "Mary Pickford Attacks Lack of Movie Museum," *Mirror News*, March 20, 1956, fiche 6, Biography Files, Mary Pickford, Margaret Herrick Library, AMPAS.

18. File 39.31, Mary Pickford Collection, Special Collection, Margaret Herrick Library, AMPAS. This file is filled with letters from fans, tourists, and former industry employees clamoring for a museum, supporting Pickford's public outcry against the industry. Some letters from tourists directly express their disappointment over the lack of a museum on former visits to Hollywood. Pickford additionally received offers of collectibles from amateur historians and fans as well as an offer of land for a potential museum from a local Los Angeles realty company. Many other letters from the East Coast suggest Pickford give up on the Hollywood locale.

19. File 39.31, Mary Pickford Collection, Special Collection, AMPAS.

20. Sol Lesser produced many Tarzan films and founded the West Coast Fox theater chain. In the summer of 1955, Lesser approached Henri Langlois after seeing Langlois's exhibit "Sixty Years of Cinema" and offered to buy the entire collection. Langlois turned him down, supposedly telling Lesser to make his own museum where he came from. It remains uncertain whether Lesser would have added these materials to his own collection or was considering one of the fledgling, but still potentially viable, Hollywood mu-

seum projects. Glenn Myrent and Georges P. Langlois, *Henri Langlois: First Citizen of the Cinema* (New York: Twayne, 1995), 289.

21. Besides the Hollywood Bowl property, other options were considered, including Exposition Park adjacent to the main Los Angeles County Museum (the former resting place of the Society of Motion Picture Engineers collection) as well as Vine Street, at either Sunset or Hollywood boulevards.

22. Sol Lesser, "A Progress Report on the Hollywood Motion Picture and Television Museum Center," October 15, 1959, Hollywood Museum, 1959, General Subject Files, AMPAS.

23. Lesser, "A Progress Report."

24. Arthur Knight, "Curator's Choice," *Film Quarterly* (Spring 1962): 35–39. The museum's planners tended to conflate Hollywood with American film, making little distinction or place for non-Hollywood American film, notably independent and avant-garde.

25. Congressional Record, 87th Cong., 1st sess., June 1, 1961, vol. 107, pt. 91. For other relevant reports, see 85th Cong., 2nd sess., vol. 104, pt. 27 and pt. 141. Prior to these attempts, the Library of Congress had begun efforts to preserve films in conjunction with the academy in the late 1940s.

26. Congressional Record, 87th Cong., 1st sess., June 1, 1961, vol. 107, pt. 91.

27. Earlier, Kuchel introduced a bill to underwrite the academy's work preserving the Library of Congress paper print collection. For more on the Library of Congress, see Tom McGreevey and Joanne L. Yeck, *Our Movie Heritage* (New Brunswick, NJ: Rutgers University Press, 1997), 29–50.

28. Museum officials furthered this national cause and supplemented the cause of international diplomacy by sending a telegram to Robert McNamara, then defense secretary, claiming that the museum's representation of mass media would create better understanding among nations. Lynn Spigel outlines the Kennedy administration's discussion of television to solicit connections between art and diplomacy in "High Culture in Low Places: Television and Modern Art, 1950–1970," in *Disciplinarity and Dissent in Cultural Studies*, ed. Cary Nelson and Dilip Parameshwar Gaonkar (New York: Routledge, 1996), 314–46; and "The Making of a TV Literate Elite," in *The Television Studies Book*, ed. Christine Geraghty and David Lusted (London: Edward Arnold, 1998), 63–85.

29. "The Scope of the Hollywood Motion Picture and Television Museum, A Live Institution," 1961, Hollywood Museum, 1960, General Subject Files, AMPAS.

30. "The Scope of the Hollywood Motion Picture and Television Museum."

31. While this idea had entered theoretical and popular discourse earlier than the 1940s, Malraux's specific terminology had more cachet and application in everyday language. Specific reference was made to a "Museum without Walls" in a 1963 board of directors meeting. Hollywood Museum Board of Directors, Minutes of Meeting, April 24, 1963, file 39.33, Mary Pickford Collection, Special Collections, AMPAS.

32. Through televised broadcasts of the first American space flight in 1961, to presidential addresses on the space race, and to the space-age transformation of everyday

design and culture, the motif of space became firmly ensconced in the American imaginary. Spigel, "High Culture in Low Places," 338.

33. Theodore Fred Kuper, "Objectives of the Educational and Cultural Programs of the Hollywood Museum," December 17, 1964, Hollywood Museum, 1964, General Subject Files, AMPAS.

34. Theodore Kuper, "Topical Summary of the First Five Years in the Creation of the Hollywood Museum," December 1964, Hollywood Museum, 1964, General Subject Files, AMPAS.

35. Marshall McLuhan, *Understanding Media: The Extensions of Man*, ed. Lewis H. Lapham (Cambridge, MA: MIT Press, 1994), ix.

36. "Hollywood Museum: An International Center for the Audio-Visual Arts and Sciences," undated brochure (likely 1964), file 45.14, Mary Pickford Collection, Special Collections, AMPAS.

37. Sol Lesser, "Report on the Hollywood Museum," June 7, 1962, Hollywood Museum, 1961–1962, General Subject Files, AMPAS.

38. "The Scope of the Hollywood Motion Picture and Television Museum."

39. All subsequent references to the museum's architectural and interior design come from the film *Concept* (Burbank, CA: Walt Disney Productions, 1964), VHS, as well as drawings by Pereira and Associates from which the film was animated. Fletcher was chairman of the museum's animation committee.

40. Carolyn Marvin, *When Old Technologies Were New: Thinking About Electric Communication in the Late Nineteenth Century* (New York: Oxford University Press, 1988).

41. This design was similar to Pereira's Los Angeles County Museum of Art built at approximately the same time. Pereira, a well-known local architect, designed other important civic structures such as City Hall, UCLA's Dickson Art Center, and Pepperdine University.

42. Imagery of the multiple, sprouting television sets resembles 1960s television advertisements, in particular for Motorola, which depicted a crossover between interior and exterior, and technology and nature.

43. Several public relations efforts (through local radio and television stations, short films, souvenir booklets, postcards, and fundraising events) in the early 1960s were designed to garner museum support. The Hollywood Chamber of Commerce crusaded for the museum's cause, and Lesser toured several established institutions in New York, Washington, and Chicago to create an air of legitimacy for the museum project.

44. Despite the intent to represent all four industries, most stars featured in *Concept* are from film and television. As crossover stars, Ed Wynn and Bing Crosby were known for appearances in film and television as much as radio and recording.

45. Mike Davis, *City of Quartz: Excavating the Future in Los Angeles* (New York: Random House, 1992). See also Kotkin, "The Powers that Will Be," M1.

46. Dave Kaufman, "MCA Museum to Rival H'wood's?" *Daily Variety*, February 16, 1962.

47. When Universal became a subsidiary of MCA in 1962, the MCA tours at Revue likely served as precursor for the Universal tours begun in 1964.

48. "Creator of Movieland Wax Museum Realized Dream Via Sleeping Pill," *Box Office*, December 24, 1962, Movieland Wax Museum, General Subject Files, AMPAS. The museum closed in 2005.

49. The world-famous precinema Skot-Hansen collection was assembled by Danish producer-director, Mogens Skot-Hansen. Lytton acquired the collection in 1961, at which time it was listed among the acquisitions of the Hollywood Museum.

50. The sound stages were expected to be a major tourist attraction; however, the studios were reluctant to sign binding contracts for using them. By the end of 1964, the plans were considered controversial and too expensive, and were subsequently dropped.

51. Neal Graham, "Universal Studios Tours Have Mostly Class, with Few 'Bugs,'" *Hollywood Reporter*, July 20, 1964, Universal Studios Tour, 1964–1969, General Subject Files, AMPAS.

52. While most of the monetary and other donations were pledges only, by 1962, thirty committees had collected two million dollars' worth of artifacts and memorabilia, and had commenced restoration on several films. Donations came from reputable companies such as Kodak and Consolidated Film Industries, and from individuals such as Mary Pickford, Buster Keaton, Rudolf Valentino, and Walt Disney; the estates of Cecil B. DeMille, Carl Laemmle, and Jesse Lasky; collectors such as Sol Lesser and T. K. Peters; all of the major and minor studios, television networks, and corporations; and the U.S. government.

53. Like arrangements made with other county-supported arts projects, the county set up a lease-back arrangement with the museum. This arrangement guaranteed a loan (through bonds secured by the county) in the amount of four million dollars. At the end of thirty years, the property and the building ownership would revert to the county, while the museum would continue fundraising and daily operations. Early estimates suggested museum profits would be $1.5 million annually.

54. "LA County Okays Coin for Museum," *Daily Variety*, December 28, 1960, 1, 4.

55. "Risqué Movies Endanger County Film Museum Aid," *Los Angeles Mirror*, August 29, 1961, Hollywood Museum, 1961, General Subject Files, AMPAS.

56. The county previously condemned land for the County Court House complex and Dodger Stadium. Many homeowners protested the latter, upon learning the city planned to hand over the property without any lease agreements or legal obligations.

57. In March 1964, as the museum project lost credibility, the Television Academy decided to give its collection to UCLA rather than the Hollywood Museum. This rejection was echoed the following year when Roy and Walt Disney turned down a suggestion to build Cal Arts adjacent to the museum.

58. Anthony had changed his name from Vnuk when he had acquired a police record for misdemeanors ranging from drug possession and drunken disorderly conduct to vagrancy. "Home Defender," *Los Angeles Times*, April 9, 1964, 1, 2, Hollywood Museum, 1964, General Subject Files, AMPAS.

59. "Fort Anthony Razed Before Angry Crowd," *Herald Examiner*, April 14, 1964, 1, 4.

60. Zeman, "Film Museum Project Called Taj Mahal," *Los Angeles Times*, March 10, 1965, Hollywood Museum, 1965, General Subject Files, AMPAS.

61. One other means of salvaging the museum was compromising with Bart Lytton, whose initial rejection from the board had apparently been orchestrated by Walt Disney and Mary Pickford. "Hollywood Museum: Minutes of Meetings, Reports and Financial Statements," file 45.11, Mary Pickford Collection, Special Collections, AMPAS.

62. Dale Olson, "Museums Move to Preen Its Public Image Backfires," *Daily Variety*, April 17, 1964, 1, 4.

63. For more on projected museum costs and reactions, see "Hollywood Museum: Minutes of Meetings, Reports and Financial Statements"; Marshall Jay Kendall, "The Hollywood Museum Showdown," *Los Angeles Herald Examiner*, May 16, 1965, 1, 7, 11; "Museum Role to Be Fixed," *Los Angeles Herald Examiner*, November 22, 1964, B5.

64. Lytton's report to the County Board of Supervisors, March 9, 1965, in "Hollywood Museum: Bart Lytton's Criticism," file 45.20, Mary Pickford Collection, Special Collections, AMPAS.

65. Ray Zeman, "Reorganization and $5 Million Gift Sought for Hollywood Museum," *Los Angeles Times*, May 26, 1965, 1, 3.

66. John Anson Ford, letter to *Los Angeles Times*, undated (1965), Hollywood Museum, 1965, General Subject Files, AMPAS.

67. Kotkin, "The Powers that Will Be," M1.

68. Arthur Knight, "Does Hollywood Need a Museum?" *Hollywood Reporter*, September 3, 1976, 6, 14.

69. Real estate developers, among others, offered properties. Erwin Karz and Associates, letter to Hollywood Chamber of Commerce, March 25, 1965, "Museum: Hollywood Motion Picture and Television Misc. 1954–65," Mary Pickford Collection, Special Collections, AMPAS.

70. Minutes of board meeting, September 30, 1965, in "Hollywood Motion Picture and Television Misc. 1964–65," file 45.14, Mary Pickford Collection, Special Collections, AMPAS.

71. Jonathan Miller, "A Museum for Hollywood: At Long Last?" *Los Angeles Times*, September 23, 1984, calendar section, 18–22.

72. "Univ. Gets H'w'd Museum Artifacts," *Daily Variety*, August 28, 1972, Hollywood Museum, 1966–1975, General Subject Files, AMPAS.

73. The original donors signed no-strings releases to the museum and county, and had little recourse, even after the artifacts were sold to the city.

74. Debbie Reynolds had previously attempted to revive the museum project herself by forming her own nonprofit organization in 1972. In May 1970, Reynolds made several purchases at MGM's auction, outbidding the Cinémathèque Française's representative, Curtis Harrington. Reynolds had collected costumes since the 1950s, hoping to establish a costume museum. Myrent and Langlois, *Henri Langlois*, 286–87; Miller, "A Museum for Hollywood?" calendar section, 18–22.

75. Will Tusher, "Hollywood Museum Award Stirs Fight," *Hollywood Reporter*, February 12, 1974, Hollywood Museum, 1966–1975, General Subject Files, AMPAS.

76. The chamber was particularly criticized for its involvement in the Holiday Inn's plans to add a multimillion dollar entertainment complex of shops and restaurants onto its existing hotel at the corner of Hollywood and Highland boulevards. In response to the chamber–Holiday Inn alliance, a cross-section of industry guilds proposed a museum project underwritten by MCA/Universal. Gerry Levin, "Chamber Eyes Facility for Hollywood Museum," *Hollywood Reporter*, January 13, 1977, 1, 25; Knight, "Does Hollywood Need a Museum?"

77. In the late 1970s, Olender teamed with city council representative Peggy Stevenson, and together they sought a reputable institution equipped to store and care for the extensive collection. "H'Wood C of C to Get More Time to Decide on Film Museum Site," *Daily Variety*, September 8, 1976, 4, 26.

78. While Department of Recreation and Parks' Linda Barth sought to amend the loan agreement and permanently donate the collections to the four institutions, the city rejected the proposal because it violated the original agreement calling for the collection to remain within Hollywood. At the time, only AFI fulfilled this stipulation. Since the opening of its Hollywood and Vine site, the academy has also gained Hollywood property.

79. The so-called glamour items, including the costume collection, remained indefinitely at the Lincoln Heights Jail, until the Department of Recreation and Parks loaned them to the Fashion Institute of Design and Merchandising in the mid-1980s. Barth reorganized the materials at this time so each institution's collection was distinct. USC possesses most of the physical and technical artifacts as well as most of the Hollywood Museum's business records, other studio records, some interviews, and oral history transcripts. UCLA was given all of the film material as well as some of the recording material. They also hold some of the star ephemera and memorabilia, movie posters, and scrapbooks. The academy claims all of the photographic stills as well as the script collection, books, scrapbooks, film program notes, and some manuscripts. AFI has a limited collection of scripts and books that supplemented their already existing collections. Other ephemera, dating back to T. K. Peters's exhibitions, are in storage at the Los Angeles Natural History Museum's Seaver Center.

80. "At Last the Hollywood Museum," *Hollywood Studio Magazine* (November 1979).

81. In May 1982, after many unsuccessful attempts to locate a site, the trust turned over the Barn and money raised to Hollywood Heritage, Inc. Soon thereafter, Universal offered to house the Barn on its lot, but many in the Hollywood community rejected this proposal. Hollywood Studio Museum, General Subject Files, AMPAS.

82. Miller, "A Museum for Hollywood?"

83. Allen visited New York and participated in seminars for the American Museum of the Moving Image's planning.

84. For announcement of museum's opening, see *LA Weekly*, October 1–7, 1982, Hollywood Memories Museum, General Subject Files, AMPAS.

85. Avid collector John LeBold who had previously worked with Debbie Reynolds opened the Hollywood Museum in May 1984 along with Joan Whitenack and Robert Nudelman. For more on LeBold and Reynolds, see Rhys Thomas, "The Ruby Slippers: A Journey to the Land of Oz," *Los Angeles Times*, March 13, 1988, calendar section, 1–7.

86. The extra Hollywood in the name was added to differentiate it from the earlier Hollywood Hall of Fame. The complex, backed by entrepreneurs, a former actor, and a former Chippendale's manager, and curated by Dan Price (archivist, collector, and amateur historian), would house a restaurant, a Legend's Lounge, two nightclubs, a five-hundred-seat theater, and a basement speakeasy complete with flappers and a carpet club.

87. Following this announcement, several community activists and fans protested Proctor and Gamble's decision. In the end, Proctor and Gamble sold the building to Donelle Dadigan, a local Los Angeles developer. Dadigan continues to serve as president of the museum.

88. Much of the additional money came from the state.

89. Paramount was the only major studio contributor to the project during its twelve-year planning and development, offering legitimacy to the fledgling project.

90. Frank Barron, letter to the editor, *Daily Variety*, July 9, 1985, Hollywood Entertainment Museum, 1984–1987, General Subject Files, AMPAS.

91. A total of $785,000 in state funds (derived from the Department of Commerce) was approved as seed money in 1985. According to one report, the Department of Commerce surreptitiously prevented other nonprofit groups from bidding on CRA funds. The academy soon thereafter withdrew its plans for the Academy Cinema Center. Chip Jacobs, "History of Hollywood Museum Reads Like Horror Movie Script," *Daily News*, September 10, 1995, 1, 20.

92. Roberti hired many of his staff and allies to work in the museum. In addition to Caskey, Michael Woo—then on the city council but formerly Roberti's senior consultant—was designated secretary and treasurer. In 1991, the CRA offered to subsidize the museum in the amount of four million dollars and additionally proposed a special interest-free loan to those entertainment companies that would agree to stay in or relocate to Hollywood.

93. Jacobs, "History of Hollywood Museum."

94. The museum became the subject of a state audit by the State Attorney General's office, and the CRA was highly criticized for its indiscriminate and dubious handling of municipal loans.

95. For example, the museum sponsored outreach programs for at-risk youth largely supervised by the Los Angeles County Probation Department, justifying receipt of state funds totaling two million dollars in 1997. Between 2000 and 2002, the museum received an additional $2.5 million in state funds for a vocational training program.

96. The museum maintains a website that indicates plans to reopen the museum with an expanded mission, focusing on the story of Los Angeles. Details are scant on the

newly proposed focus, yet the description seems to mark a definite move away from Hollywood toward a broader focus on creative industries and the city's history.

97. Under the direction of Warner Bros. co-CEOs Robert Daly and Terry Semel, the museum and accompanying studio tour were designed to serve a corporate and studio-wide renovation. Without rides and other theme park attractions, however, the tour and museum can hardly compete economically with its rival, Universal Studios.

98. Chris Horak, "The Hollywood History Business," in *The End of Cinema as We Know It: American Cinema in the Nineties*, ed. Jon Lewis (New York: New York University Press, 2001), 33–42.

99. The Academy Awards revenue increased substantially following a new contract negotiation with ABC in 1998, a jump of 55 percent to forty-one million dollars in 1999. In 2004, the academy garnered more than fifty million dollars for broadcast rights. In addition to awards-related revenue, the academy also reaps substantial profits annually from an investment portfolio. Michael Cieply and James Bates, "Academy Flush with Funds, Plans Film Museum," *Los Angeles Times*, February 3, 2004, A1, 12.

100. As of this writing in 2010, the academy has not released a newsletter regarding the museum since 2008.

101. Nikki Finke, "Oscar: Academy's Bruce Davis to Retire," Deadline Hollywood, October 12, 2010, http://www.deadline.com/2010/10/oscar-academys-bruce-davis-to-resign. Nicole Sperling and John Horn, "Academy Has Long Sought to Build Prominent Film Museum in L.A." *Los Angeles Times*, October 6, 2011.

102. Part of these dreams for Hollywood Boulevard have since been tested with the opening of the American Cinematheque at the old Grauman's Egyptian Theater; the construction of a grandiose, state-of-the-art Kodak theater for the academy's annual award's ceremony at the Hollywood and Highland complex; and a number of hotels, restaurants, and nightclubs. However, it remains to be seen whether or not these ventures will change the face of the boulevard, reversing the area's long-standing economic depression but more importantly its cultural legitimacy.

Chapter 3 • Out of Bounds

1. Toby Miller, Nitin Govil, John McMurria, and Richard Maxwell, *Global Hollywood* (London: British Film Institute, 2001), 25. Miller et al. cite 1919 as a key historical moment when "overseas receipts were factored into Hollywood budgets."

2. Stephen Prince, *A New Pot of Gold: Hollywood under the Electronic Rainbow, 1980–1989* (New York: Scribner, 2000), 45–47, 92, 175; for more on global distribution and exhibition, see Toby Miller, Nitin Govil, John McMurria, Richard Maxwell, and Ting Wang, *Global Hollywood 2* (London: British Film Institute, 2005), 294–311.

3. Janet Wasko, *Hollywood in the Information Age: Beyond the Silver Screen* (Austin: University of Texas Press, 1995). See also Prince, *A New Pot of Gold*.

4. In the field of landscape architecture, most scholars point to the sixteenth-century

European gardens as theme park predecessors. Terence Young, "Grounding the Myth: Theme Park Landscapes in an Era of Commerce and Nationalism," in *Theme Park Landscapes: Antecedents and Variations*, ed. Terence Young and Robert Riley, 1–10 (Washington, DC: Dumbarton Oaks Research Library and Collection, 2002). Nineteenth-century public exhibition and display, including the department store, fair, and exposition, is discussed in William Leach's *Land of Desire: Merchants, Power, and the Rise of a New American Culture* (New York: Vintage, 1993); Curtis M. Hinsley's "The World as Marketplace: Commodification of the Exotic at the World's Colombian Exposition, Chicago 1893," in *Exhibiting Cultures: The Poetics and Politics of Museum Display*, ed. Ivan Karp and Steven D. Lavine, 344–65 (Washington, DC: Smithsonian, 1991); and Chantal Georgel's "The Museum as Metaphor in Nineteenth-Century France," *Museum Culture: Histories, Discourses, Spectacles*, ed. Daniel J. Sherman and Irit Rogoff (Minneapolis: University of Minnesota Press, 1994), 113–22.

5. Bluford Adams, *E Pluribus Barnum: The Great Showman and the Making of U.S. Popular Culture* (Minneapolis: University of Minnesota Press, 1997), 77, 80–82. Even after Barnum's museums waned, the patrician founders of New York's venerable museums continued to chastise him, determined to develop an antithetical approach that shunned commercialism and upheld decidedly nonprofit values.

6. "Skyscrapers as Art Museums" (1927), quoted in Neil Harris, "Museums, Merchandising and Popular Taste: The Struggle for Influence," in *Material Culture and the Study of American Life*, ed. Ian M. G. Quimby (New York: Norton, 1978), 164.

7. Anthony Vilder, "Architecture as Spectacle," *Los Angeles Times*, May 5, 1998, M1, M6.

8. Mark Gottdiener, *The Theming of America: Dreams, Visions, and Commercial Spaces* (Boulder, CO: Westview, 1997), 2. John Hannigan disputes Gottdiener's historical framing, citing earlier themed spaces including Coney Island. John Hannigan, *Fantasy City: Pleasure and Profit in the Postmodern Metropolis* (New York: Routledge, 1998), 84–86. See also Umberto Eco, *Travels in Hyperreality*, trans. William Weaver (New York: Harcourt, 1983).

9. David Lowenthal, "The Past as a Theme Park," in Young and Riley, *Theme Park Landscapes*, 11–23.

10. Nostalgia is a theme that historically links European aristocratic gardens of the eighteenth century with contemporary theme parks. Young, "Grounding the Myth," 2.

11. Colin Sorensen, "Theme Parks and Time Machines," in *The New Museology*, ed. Peter Vergo, 60–73 (London: Reaktion Books, 1989). Michael Bommes and Patrick Wright, "'Charms of Residence': The Public and the Past," in *Making Histories: Studies in History Writing and Politics*, ed. Richard Johnson, Gregor McLennan, Bill Schwarz, and David Sutton (London: Hutchinson, 1982).

12. Dustin B. Cherotoff, "Improving Presence Theory through Experiential Design," *Presence* 17, no. 4 (August 2008): 407–8.

13. Jack Rouse, quoted in Hannigan, *Fantasy City*, 89.

14. Prince, *A New Pot of Gold*, 135.

15. "Urban entertainment destination" is a term, now widely used, coined by the

urban land institute. These largely profitable public spaces can include entertainment-oriented retailers, high-tech entertainment centers, themed restaurants, cinema complexes and specialty film venues, theme parks, and festival marketplaces. Dennis R. Judd and Susan S. Fainstein, eds., *The Tourist City* (New Haven, CT: Yale University Press, 1999), 147.

16. Lowenthal, "The Past as a Theme Park," 15.

17. Gottdiener roots the development of themed environments in the 1960s. However, his contemporary examples of themed environments largely come from the 1980s and 1990s. Gottdiener, *The Theming of America*, 75.

18. Michael Sorkin, ed., *Variations on a Theme Park: The New American City and the End of Public Space* (New York: Hill & Wang, 1992), 206. Much has been written about the history of Disneyland and Disney's influence. See Sharon Zukin, *Landscapes of Power: From Detroit to Disneyland* (Berkeley: University of California Press, 1991); John M. Findlay, *Magic Lands: Western Cityscapes and American Culture after 1940* (Berkeley: University of California Press, 1992); Sorkin, *Variations on a Theme Park*, 206–32; and Hannigan, *Fantasy City*, 98. Other themed environments that more consciously blur the education-entertainment divide include heritage centers such as Colonial Williamsburg and Henry Ford's Greenfield Village. See, for example, Richard Handler and Eric Gable, *The New History in an Old Museum: Creating the Past at Colonial Williamsburg* (Durham, NC: Duke University Press, 1997). For a more historical discussion of museums and commerce, see Adams, *E Pluribus Barnum*; and Harris, "Museums, Merchandising and Popular Taste."

19. Sorkin, *Variations on a Theme Park*, 206–8; Hannigan, *Fantasy City*, 39, 87; Christopher Anderson, *Hollywood TV: The Studio System in the Fifties* (Austin: University of Texas Press, 1994), 133–55.

20. Bob Sehlinger and Arthur Frommer, *The Unofficial Guide to Walt Disney World 1998* (New York: Macmillan, 1998), 163.

21. Studio lore credits former studio manager Al Dorskind with the idea for the tour. Dorskind apparently approached Lew Wasserman, suggesting that the tour would offer promotion for the studio's films. Alan Leigh, "Universal Appeal: Poised for the New Millennium, the Theme Park Celebrates Its Milestone Anniversary," *Hollywood Reporter*, October 29, 1999, S2.

22. Army Archerd, "Just for Variety," *Daily Variety*, July 15, 2004, Universal Studios Tour (2000-), General Subject Files, Margaret Herrick Library, AMPAS.

23. Leigh, "Universal Appeal," S1–S2. The revamped tour opened in summer 2006. See also Greg Braxton, "Universal Studios, the Sequel," *Los Angeles Times*, July 6, 2006, calendar section, E22, 23.

24. Universal Studios Hollywood, "Park Overview," accessed July 22, 2004, http://www.universalstudioshollywood.com/park_overview.html.

25. Universal Studios Hollywood, "Park Overview."

26. The ride itself was comparable to a small film in its production. The twelve-minute piece included a forty-person cast, directed by three Oscar winners, and cost re-

portedly more than one million dollars per minute. David Bloom and John Woolard, "The Dimension beyond the Ultimate," *Long Beach Press Telegram*, March 7, 1999, J1.

27. The featured movies in the rides rotate to some extent based on current blockbusters. Some attractions such as E.T. Adventure that originate at Universal Studios Hollywood relocate to Orlando or Osaka, Japan. Certain popular attractions may exist simultaneously at all of Universal's parks. Universal's followers have mimicked the focus on blockbuster science fiction, fantasy, and adventure rides with attractions based on *Lara Croft: Tomb Raider, Top Gun, Crocodile Dundee,* and *Face Off* at Paramount Parks; *Lethal Weapon* and *Police Academy* at Warner Bros. Movie World; and *Indiana Jones* and *Armageddon* at Disney-MGM and Walt Disney Studios Park, respectively.

28. Time Warner has an entangled history with the theme park arena. The company bought shares of Six Flags in the early 1990s, owning a total of 50 percent of the company. In 1995, experiencing financial difficulties, Time Warner sold 51 percent of the shares. Premier Parks, Inc., bought Six Flags out in 1998 and, in 1999, also acquired Warner Bros. Movie World in Germany. That same year, Warner Bros. phased out its Warner Bros. International Recreation Enterprises, yet still maintained a presence in certain parks through licensing and other partnership agreements. To retain the brand loyalty associated with the Six Flags name, Premier officially became known as Six Flags in 2000. Warner Bros. continues to have licensing agreements with Six Flags. In 2004, Six Flags sold all of its European parks except Warner Bros. Movie World Madrid to a private investment firm, Palamon. The parks, including Warner Bros. Movie World in Germany, were subsequently renamed under the company's new moniker, Star Parks. Later that same year, Six Flags also sold off the Madrid location, which currently operates under a licensing arrangement with Warner Bros. Bob Weitkamp, Warner Bros. Licensing for International Theme Parks, telephone conversation with author, August 5, 2004; Antje Moeller, public relations manager, Warner Bros. Movie World, Bottrop-Kirchhellen, Germany, e-mail message to author, August 6, 2004. Paramount failed to open planned theme parks in Spain, Australia, and Japan, and in 2006, CBS Corp., Paramount's parent company, sold interest in five of its theme parks to Cedar Fair LP, a company devoted to theme and water parks.

29. In addition to Hollywood studio-backed theme parks, other movie theme parks opened in Europe in the late 1980s and 1990s. Babelsberg Studios, which opened in 1993 in Germany, is loosely modeled on U.S. theme parks offering visitors a studio tour of the original UFA studios, stunt shows, and other behind-the-scenes demonstrations. In 1987, Futurscope opened in Poitiers, France, with a broader take on media, including video games.

30. For more on the partnership between Warner Bros. and Village Roadshow as well as other partners with vested interests in the Australian theme park, see Warner Bros., Movie World, accessed March 31, 2011, http://www.movieworld.myfun.com.au.

31. Cedar Fairs subsequently removed the Paramount name, logo, and the parks' Hollywood elements.

32. "AFI Goes to Disneyworld," *Los Angeles Times*, December 8, 1997, F2.

33. Chuck Cisafulli, "A Hollywood Museum with Mustard, Mayo," *Los Angeles Times*, September 19, 1995, sec. F, 1, 9.

34. Cisafulli, "A Hollywood Museum," sec. F, 1, 9.

35. Planet Hollywood International Inc. also ran the Official All-Star Café, a sports-themed restaurant chain. Other themed restaurants popular in the 1990s included the Rainforest Café, Dive, Copperfield's Magic Underground, NASCAR Café, Harley Davidson Café, Motown Café, Fashion Café, Dick Clark's American Bandstand Grill, and Billboard Live. See Hannigan, *Fantasy City*, 96–97. See also Josh Stenger, "Consuming the Planet: Planet Hollywood, Stars, and the Global Consumer Culture," *Velvet Light Trap* 40 (Fall 1997): 42–55.

36. Planet Hollywood devised and publicly released several plans for expansion since these bankruptcy claims; however, most of them have never materialized.

37. Prices for Hollywood memorabilia swelled in the 1990s, largely due to Planet Hollywood's aggressive acquisition campaigns, and auctions held by houses like Julien's that specialize in celebrity memorabilia still see major profits.

38. While Hollywood has factored overseas receipts into its budgets since 1919 and, by the 1930s, foreign sales accounted for nearly half of Hollywood's revenue, in the early 1980s, there was a significant shift in the revenue from overseas audiences. This revenue had wavered and fluctuated since World War II. Of the top twenty-five box office titles of all time, only three since the late 1970s showed higher revenues for domestic as opposed to overseas box offices. See Miller et al., *Global Hollywood*, 3–15. See also box office statistics at Chuck Kahn, Worldwide Box Office, accessed March 31, 2011, http://www.worldwideboxoffice.com/.

39. Before declaring Chapter 11, Planet Hollywood positioned the memorabilia from its shareholder/stars' films (Bruce Willis, Arnold Schwarzenegger, Sylvester Stallone, Demi Moore) prominently in the restaurant.

40. As a for-profit corporation, Planet Hollywood is not required or expected to label artifacts as in a traditional museum space. However, it is clear that some artifacts have been recycled many times over. The handprints, in particular, seem largely inauthentic copies. The New York location even exhibits two handprints from Will Smith.

41. Mike Schneider, "Planet Hollywood Emerges from Bankruptcy . . . Again," *South Florida Sun Sentinel*, December 16, 2002.

42. These agreements likely hold similarities to Warner Bros.' relationships in the United States with big box retailers such as K-Mart and Walmart.

43. Tony Kent, "2D23D: Management and Design Perspectives on Retail Branding," *International Journal of Retail and Distribution Management* 31, no. 3 (2003): 131, 139.

44. Warner Bros., WB Shop, accessed March 31, 2011, www.wbstore.com/.

45. For a discussion of early attempts to legitimate animation as art, see Bill Mikulak, "Mickey Meets Mondrian: Cartoons Enter the Museum of Modern Art," *Cinema Journal* 36, no. 3 (Spring 1997): 56–72.

46. Warner Bros., WB Shop.

47. For a historical discussion of Hollywood tie-ins or "tie-ups," see Charles Eckart, "The Carole Lombard in Macy's Window," *Quarterly Review of Film Studies* 3, no. 1 (Winter 1978): 6–7.

48. The Pigeon Forge plans originally called for a theme park, which later was scaled down to twelve themed pavilions and a gift shop selling "original" pieces of memorabilia. In 2009, after major roadblocks in the development of the site, the museum filed for bankruptcy protection and announced plans to liquidate its assets.

49. Like other Paramount Park holdings, after 2006, Star Trek: The Experience came under the umbrella of Cedar Fair Entertainment Company. It is likely that this corporate shuffling led to the Las Vegas attraction closure two years later.

50. PR Newswire, "Planet Hollywood Resort and Casino Announces Agreement with Clear Channel Entertainment," press release, February 8, 2005. In 2006, the corporation also announced a casino in Philadelphia, Planet Hollywood Riverwalk Casino.

Chapter 4 ◦ Hollywood in a Box

1. Christopher Anderson, *Hollywood TV: The Studio System in the Fifties* (Austin: University of Texas Press, 1994), 159–63. All references to Sullivan's show come from Anderson.

2. Anderson, *Hollywood TV*, 165.

3. Anderson, *Hollywood TV*, 171, 191.

4. For an in-depth discussion of the rhetoric of early television, see Lynn Spigel, *Make Room for TV: Television and the Family Ideal in Postwar America* (Chicago: University of Chicago Press, 1992), 136–42; and Jane Feuer, "The Concept of Live Television: Ontology as Ideology," in *Regarding Television, Critical Approaches: An Anthology*, ed. E. Ann Kaplan (Los Angeles: American Film Institute, 1983).

5. Behind the Cameras Documentaries, *Rebel without a Cause*, "Special Features" (Burbank, CA: Warner Home Video, 1999).

6. Warner Bros. Presents Documentary Shorts, *The Searchers*, "Special Features" (Burbank, CA: Warner Home Video, 1997).

7. The ownership of cable movie channels, however fluctuating, reveals the widespread power of multimedia conglomerates. Time Warner owns HBO and TCM as well as AOL, TBS, TNT, Time Warner Cable, New Line Cinema, Warner Bros. Entertainment, and Time Inc.; Viacom owns Showtime, the Movie Channel, Sundance (along with Robert Redford and NBC-Universal), and FLIX; and Rainbow Media, a subsidiary of Cablevision, owns AMC, IFC, and WE: Women's Entertainment, among others. Rainbow also owns satellite television service VOOM; Rainbow Movies, owner of the Clearview Cinemas group; and video-on-demand service Mag Rack. Bravo, formerly owned by Rainbow Media, rarely shows films anymore and is currently owned by NBC-Universal.

8. Barbara Wilinsky, *Sure Seaters: The Emergence of Art House Cinema* (Minneapolis: University of Minnesota Press, 2001), 1–15. See also Barbara Klinger, "The New Media Aristo-

crats: Home Theater and the Domestic Film Experience," *Velvet Light Trap* 42 (Fall 1998): 11–15; and David E. James, *The Most Typical Avant-Garde: History and Geography of Minor Cinemas in Los Angeles* (Berkeley: University of California Press, 2005).

9. Klinger discusses the appeal of behind-the-scenes information, commenting on the way video collectors are addressed as film industry "insiders." While Klinger claims that these collectors are addressed as already knowledgeable, I contend that much of DVD supplemental material and cable programming is addressed not to the connoisseur but to the uninitiated, potential student of film. Barbara Klinger, "The Contemporary Cinephile: Film Collecting in the Post-Video Era," in *Hollywood Spectatorship: Changing Perceptions of Cinema Audiences*, ed. Melvyn Stokes and Richard Maltby (London: British Film Institute, 2001); Barbara Klinger, *Beyond the Multiplex: Cinema, New Technologies and the Home* (Berkeley: University of California Press, 2006).

10. *Project Greenlight* (on HBO initially and now Bravo), Sundance Channel's *Anatomy of a Scene*, NBC's *Next Action Star*, and even James Lipton's *Inside the Actor's Studio*, which has aired on Bravo since 1994, are a few examples. Meanwhile, the Independent Film Channel airs several programs that offer behind-the-scenes access to film production outside the studio system, for example, in film school and the festival circuit. They also offer shows such as *Film Fanatic* and *Dinner for Five* geared toward the serious cinephile.

11. Douglas Gomery, *Shared Pleasures: A History of Movie Presentation in the United States* (Madison: University of Wisconsin Press, 1992); Anderson, *Hollywood TV*. For more on early home archiving and exhibition, see Haidee Wasson, *Museum Movies: The Museum of Modern Art and the Birth of Art Cinema* (Berkeley: University of California Press, 2005).

12. This purchase was secured with a sell-back of UA to Kirk Kerkorian, the original owner. While the sale basically fell apart, forcing a debt-ridden Turner to sell off various parts of MGM, he kept over 3,500 films from the MGM/UA library. These films included not only MGM films from 1924 to 1986 but also the pre-1948 Warner Bros. library (previously acquired by MGM in its acquisition of UA in 1983). United Artists acquired the Warner Bros.' pre-1948 library from Associated Artists Productions in 1958. UA donated the Warner Bros. pre-1948 nitrates to the Library of Congress and post-1951 negatives to UCLA.

13. Stephen Prince, *A New Pot of Gold: Hollywood under the Electronic Rainbow, 1980–1989* (New York: Scribner, 2000), 72.

14. Turner was not the only one with such foresight. In the 1950s, Lew Wasserman's MCA purchased film properties as ancillary product for the company's television stations. However, no other executives managed to accrue the extensive collection Turner did in the 1980s.

15. Prince, *A New Pot of Gold*, 18–25, 136–38.

16. According to Stephen Prince's account based on industry trade papers, these rights had to be reacquired in order to finalize the Turner purchase. In turn, AMC used the buyout money to purchase other classic films, bolster its library, and expand its service. Prince, *A New Pot of Gold*, 73. AMC grew from three hundred thousand subscribers

in 1984 to seven million by 1987. Klinger offers statistics on AMC's growth in the 1980s and 1990s. Klinger, *Beyond the Multiplex*, 96.

17. Turner programmed TCM with films from both the MGM/UA library as well as New Line Cinema, which he acquired in 1994.

18. Fox Movie Channel typically shows films commercial free from the Twentieth Century Fox library. The channel also features behind-the-scenes featurettes of current Fox releases as program filler. Like AMC, the channel does not limit itself to classic fare and often exhibits films from the 1990s.

19. Klinger discusses the history of AMC in the 1980s and 1990s, focusing on the channel's symbolic use and representation of Hollywood's past, framing her discussion in terms of cultural memory and specific historical and cultural events of the period. Klinger, *Beyond the Multiplex*, 91–134.

20. It is difficult to make specific claims about TCM's or AMC's actual audience reach. AMC became a subscriber to Nielsen in 1999, and TCM still does not subscribe. Changes in cable networking and the increasing channel availability through basic cable, digital cable, and satellite necessarily impacts the availability of these channels. However, even with an increase in availability and a potential increase in audience share (AMC reaches 84 million homes and TCM reaches 63.4 million), AMC and TCM still only garner a small percentage of the cable-watching audience.

21. Turner Classic Movies, "Peter Bogdanovich: Host of the Essentials," accessed April 21, 2011, http://www.tcm.com/this-month/article/90224|0/Peter-Bogdanovich-Host-of -the-Essentials.html.

22. Mavis Scanlon, "Online Extra: Q&A with Turner's Tom Karsch," *Cable World*, March 21, 2005.

23. Scanlon, "Online Extra."

24. Turner Classic Movies, home page.

25. Spigel discusses a similar rhetoric employed in the early days of television, when the living room was promoted as a home theater. Spigel, *Make Room for TV*, 108–9.

26. During the 1980s and early 1990s, AMC also used old-guard celebrity guest hosts, akin to Dorian, including Debbie Reynolds, Shirley Jones, and Douglas Fairbanks Jr. Klinger, *Beyond the Multiplex*, 96. In 1999, AMC started airing commercials between feature films and, in 2002, regularly interrupted features with advertising. The channel introduced a younger host before doing away with hosts entirely. They also briefly had a *Wayne's World*–type show, *Movies at Our House*, in which two hosts, Rachel and Jimmy, screened a film in their living room and discussed it with friends and their own invited "experts." One Saturday night, Rachel invited "a hot single woman" from her gym, while Jimmy invited his "drumming circle leader" to discuss "What is a 21st-century man?" Other guests included a massage therapist, a dentist, and friends from high school. American Movie Classics, home page, accessed August 17, 2003, http://www.amctv.com/.

27. Turner Classic Movies, home page.

28. As Klinger argues, the focus on such classic stars facilitates the channel's produc-

tion of nostalgia as well as its commemoration of nation. Klinger, *Beyond the Multiplex*, 104–16. Not surprisingly, the quality and historical significance of AMC's productions has shifted since changing its format. While they still might produce a documentary on director Michael Cimino, they more frequently focus on gossip and sex with programming such as *Shirtless: Hollywood's Sexiest Men* and *Dish: Gossip in Hollywood*.

29. This film was previously packaged as a free giveaway in a 1997 Twentieth Century Fox Home Entertainment offer tied to the purchase of classic videos including *The Great White Hope, Island Sun,* or *No Way Out*. Klinger discusses the way AMC dealt with race and historical film in *Beyond the Multiplex*, 111–14.

30. Kenneth Turan, "There at the Creation," *Los Angeles Times*, June 1, 1997, calendar section, 7, 28. To be fair, AMC also received some of this praise before changing its formatting.

31. Susan King, "'Race' Movies: Separate and Unequaled," *Los Angeles Times*, June 28, 1998, calendar section, 21, 22.

32. For information on the middle school program, see the TCM press release "Turner Classic Movies Works to Support Film Projects That Enlighten and Inspire," accessed August 28, 2005, http://www.tcm.com/; Film Foundation, home page, accessed April 2, 2011, http://www.film-foundation.org/; and Film Foundation, *The Story of Movies*, accessed April 2, 2011, http://www.storyofmovies.org/. For more on FilmAid International, see http://www.filmaid.org/.

33. For a more detailed overview of AMC's preservation drive and other efforts, see Klinger, *Beyond the Multiplex*, 116–32.

34. Charles Eckert discusses a parallel insidious relationship between Hollywood and the commercial sphere, offering insight into power dynamics that increasingly shaped Hollywood and Hollywood's by-products as merchandise. Charles Eckert, "The Carole Lombard in Macy's Window," in *Fabrications: Costume and the Female Body*, ed. Jane Gaines and Charlotte Herzog (New York: Routledge, 1990), 4.

35. Susan King, "Save That Movie!" *Los Angeles Times*, October 23, 1997, weekend, 12.

36. Some question whether AMC was ever really devoted to the classics. Though it is in more homes than its rival station, TCM, AMC does not have licensing agreements with the studios that control most of the canonical classic film fare.

37. American Movie Classics, home page.

38. American Movie Classics, "Sunday Morning Shootout," accessed October 25, 2003, http://www.amctv.com/section/0,,111-EST,00.html.

39. Lynn Smith, "Shooting from the Hip: Peter Guber and Peter Bart Chat It Up on Their 'Insider' Show on AMC," *Los Angeles Times*, October 24, 2003, http://www.calendar live.com/.

40. Eckert, "The Carole Lombard in Macy's Window."

41. "Turner Classic Movies Creates Marketing Opportunities to Extend Brand beyond the Channel," Time Warner Newsroom, November 19, 2002, accessed April 21, 2011, http://www.timewarner.com/newsroom/press-releases/2002/11/Turner_Classic_ Movies_Creates_Marketing_Opportunities_11-19-2002.php.

42. Joe Flint, "Classic Movie Channel Thinks Young," *Wall Street Journal*, November 11, 2002, Turner Entertainment, General Subject Files, Margaret Herrick Library, AMPAS.

43. Turner Classic Movies, "Classic Cocktails: 15 Coasters," coasters, (San Francisco: Chronicle Books, 2004).

44. Pottery Barn, catalog (Winter 2003): 26.

45. Turner Classic Movies, "In the Picture: An Exhibition at the Grove, Los Angeles," accessed January 15, 2005, http://www.tcm.com/.

46. Turner Classic Movies, home page.

47. In addition to TCM and AMC, such documentaries as well as making-of featurettes and star bios also appear on other movie channels such as HBO, later appearing on DVD.

48. American Movie Classics, home page.

49. Klinger, "The New Media Aristocrats."

50. Spigel, *Make Room for TV*, 108.

51. Home theater technology, once the province of technophiles or consumers with extensive disposable income, is increasingly sold to the middle-class consumer. The *New York Times Sunday Magazine* devoted its cover story to home theater construction in 2004.

52. Thomas K. Arnold, "DVD Timeline," *USA Today*, October 17, 2002, E4.

53. Thomas K. Arnold, "Special Features Boost DVD Sales," *Los Angeles Times*, December 5, 2000.

54. In 2001, Columbia Tri-Star/Sony Home Entertainment started producing a specialty DVD line: the Superbit Collection, which offered higher resolution picture and sound by eliminating all special features and using all of the disc space for the film. This collection, which comprises some sixty titles, fulfilled the original goal of DVD for cinephiles and technophiles seeking a technological equivalent to theatrical exhibition. The titles, like early specialty DVD titles, tended to skew toward certain genres such as action, science fiction, horror, and a few classics.

55. John Horn, "How the Moguls Came to Love Retail," *Los Angeles Times*, April 17, 2005.

56. This statistic comes from a study done by the DVD (now Digital) Entertainment Group, an industry-supported trade coalition that was reprinted in the *Los Angeles Times*. Marc Saltzman, "The Behind-the-Scenes Art of Developing DVD Extras," *Los Angeles Times*, January 14, 2003, E12. The box office gross from these DVD titles (some sixteen billion dollars in 2005) also drives the increase in marketing (particularly print and television ads) for upcoming DVD releases.

57. DVD producers and home entertainment executives are frequently asked to speculate on differences between the VHS and DVD market. However, none can point definitively to a single factor that changed the economic model for home entertainment. In part, such a shift might be tied to any number of factors, including changes in home viewing and upgraded standards in home theater technology; increased desire for supplemental materials and interactive accessibility; DVD size (comparable to an already

successful CD) and packaging as compared to VHS; price point; and, probably less a factor for mainstream consumers, picture and sound quality.

58. Peter M. Nichols, "Producing DVD's with Lavish Extras," *New York Times*, August 27, 2000, 9; David Kehr, "Movies 'Deluxe': Definitely Bigger, Sometimes Better," *New York Times*, December 15, 2002, 45.

59. Susan King, "As DVD Popularity Grows, So Do Extras," *Los Angeles Times*, July 15, 1999, calendar section, 50.

60. Elvis Mitchell, "Everyone's a Film Geek Now," *New York Times*, August 17, 2003, sec. 2, 1, 15.

61. Richard Natale, "Press Play to Access the Future," *Los Angeles Times*, April 7, 2002, calendar section, 80.

62. Gina McIntyre, "Raiders of the Lost Art: DVD Entrepreneurs Discover an Unlikely Revenue Stream with Obscure Films from Years Past," *Hollywood Reporter*, December 11, 2001, 14–15. Such a high-low divide in exhibition parallels repertory and art house counterparts.

63. Gary Crowdus, "Providing a Film Archive for the Home Viewer: An Interview with Peter Becker of the Criterion Collection," *Cineaste* 25, no. 1 (December 1999): 49.

64. Michael Sragow, "The Disc Master: A Conversation with the Criterion Collection's Peter Becker, the Man Who Created the Ultimate DVD Versions of 'Grand Illusion,' 'This Is Spinal Tap,' and 'Armageddon,'" *Salon*, March 23, 2000, http://salon.com/ent/col/srag/2000/03/23/criterion.

65. Other studios have not exploited the classic collection angle to the same degree, in large part because they don't have the sizeable vaults that these studios have. MGM created a Vintage Classics line but does not offer extensive supplemental features. Universal released its horror cycle under a classic banner. Other studios like Paramount and Columbia Tri-Star tend to release classics collector's or limited editions.

66. AMC offered a similar program called "America's Movie Palace Memories." Klinger, *Beyond the Multiplex*, 102.

67. Best Picture winners also have a statuette as part of the cover art.

68. Martin Scorsese is well known and respected in preservation circles for his efforts. He is involved in the activities of the Film Foundation, has deposited films at the MoMA and the George Eastman House, and regularly speaks about preservation. He appeared before the U.S. House of Representatives in March 1992 as a Director's Guild of America (DGA) member to support the Film Disclosure Act, a bill that would require labeling of films materially altered for television broadcast, cable transmission, or video distribution. In 1992, he established a company, "Martin Scorsese Presents," to reissue and redistribute classic films such as Jean Renoir's *The Golden Coach*, Luchino Visconti's *Rocco and His Brothers*, Luis Buñuel's *Belle de Jour*, Nicholas Ray's *Johnny Guitar*, Anthony Mann's *El Cid*, and Abraham Polonsky's *Force of Evil*.

69. The Academy of Television Arts and Sciences created a DVD series beginning in 2005 devoted to such behind-the-scenes instruction entitled "Journey below the Line."

The DVD used popular television shows currently in production such as *ER* and *24* to examine individual below-the-line jobs including editing, props, and special effects.

70. The advertising budget on some titles in the early 2000s has been over twenty million dollars—not surprising given the revenues. The best-selling title for 2002, *Spider-Man*, made more than $190 million in its first weekend sales ($7 million sold on first day alone) as compared to its opening weekend box office take ($115 million). Studios were increasingly concerned with how a DVD would "open" and with securing a good "street date." For the most promising moneymakers, studios would throw DVD release parties. Universal threw a particularly lavish party for *Scorpion King* in 2002 including a movie reenactment with flaming explosions, belly dancers, snake handlers, jugglers, sword-slinging warriors, and a caravan of camels. Studios would also put on multiday advertising campaigns as well as promotions and giveaways at big retail chains like Target and Kmart for their most promising moneymaking titles. Gina Piccalo, "Studios Turn Up the Heat for DVD Sales," *Los Angeles Times*, October 2, 2002, F1, F4; James Bates, "DVD Sales Trend More than Hollywood Hype," *Los Angeles Times*, November 19, 2002, C1, C7.

71. Rerelease of classic titles was also popular during the video era. Warner Bros. also used the reissue of some of its films, notably *The Wizard of Oz* in 1998, to create themed merchandise available in its retail stores during the 1990s. And Turner Entertainment followed the studios' lead in creating a tie-in to TCM with a theatrical program Turner Classic Movies on the Big Screen in 1996.

72. *Se7en* (1995) was a rerelease put out by New Line's Platinum Series. Prior to DVD, the film was put out by Criterion on laser disc in 1996, and first released on DVD by New Line in 1997.

73. Other Vista Series titles include *Unbreakable* (the first in the series) as well as *Tombstone, Signs, The Sixth Sense, The Village,* and *Who Framed Roger Rabbit?*

74. The 2005 release included seventeen additional minutes, highlighted by a trivia track, "Are You Not Entertained?" The original *Gladiator* DVD, even in 2005, was still considered one of the top fifteen best-selling DVDs of all time. Susan King, "Context, Comment and, Yes, Cash," *Los Angeles Times*, August 23, 2005.

75. Some titles are released simultaneously in several versions, such as the three versions of *Spiderman* released in 2002, one in anamorphic widescreen, one in full frame, and a collectible box set with extra features. The film was also released later in a Superbit edition with higher resolution and no special features.

76. Oliver Stone's *Alexander* (2004), advertisement, *Time* magazine, July 26, 2005.

77. Glenn Abel, "*Alexander, Gladiator,*" DVD review, *Hollywood Reporter*, August 2, 2005, http://www.hollywoodreporter.com/.

78. For example, reviews of Pearl Harbor point to inaccuracies in the portrayal of Roosevelt.

79. Catherine Applefeld Olson, "DVD Puts the Squeeze on VHS," *Hollywood Reporter*, December 6, 2000, S1–S15.

80. Natale, "Press Play to Access the Future," calendar section, 80.

81. There are restrictions on titles that allow commentary recording. For *Jay and Silent Bob*, Miramax owns the rights to the commentary. On *Pulp Fiction*, one can only comment over select scenes. On *Spiderman*, one can only play back the commentary on the computer used to record it. Another trend that got its start in 2001 involves film fans recording their own commentary as MP3 files and making them available to others via the Internet. This unregulated mode fits more within a veritable do-it-yourself ethos; however, the site that previously stored these files, "DVD Tracks," is no longer operational.

82. Since 1996, VH1 has broadcast the popular *Pop-Up Video*, using pop-up text insertions on the screen to offer additional trivia about a recording artist, the video production, and so forth. Like the extratextual examples discussed in this chapter, this program exemplifies an attempt to re-create the music video. Gary Burns, "Pop Up Video: The New Historicism," *Journal of Popular Film and Television* 32, no. 2 (Summer 2004): 74–83.

83. Michael S. Lasky, "Infinifilm Brings DVD-ROM Features to DVD Players," *PCWorld*, July 10, 2001, http://www.pcworld.com/article/54834/infinifilm_brings_dvdrom_features_to_dvd_players.html.

84. New Line Home Entertainment, "Premium DVD Experience Invites Viewers to 'Go beyond the Movie,'" press release, April 16, 2001, accessed April 21, 2011, http://www.infinifilm.com/publicity.html.

85. Fox used a similar navigation technique with a pop-up green fairy in its DVD release of *Moulin Rouge* in 2001.

86. Klinger, "The Contemporary Cinephile," 140.

87. Other features on the *Die Hard* DVD reflect a similar degree of integrity and pedagogical value including a "Why Letterbox?" segment offering a detailed discussion of telecine transfer as well as a fairly extensive glossary of film terms.

88. The budget for supplemental materials generally correlates with the film's projected box office and home video revenues (action-adventure-type fare and animation having the highest budgets of studio DVDs).

89. David Bloom, "DVD's Extra Creative Lair," *Daily Variety*, October 18, 2002, A6.

90. Bloom, "DVD's Extra Creative Lair."

91. Thomas K. Arnold, "Movies To Go: DVD Revenues Are Beginning to Rival Theatrical Grosses," *Hollywood Reporter*, January 15–21, 2002, 18.

Chapter 5 • Handheld Hollywood

1. Paul Nerger, "Legendary Hollywood Walk of Fame Gets High Tech," Webwire, February 8, 2010, accessed April 21, 2011, http://www.webwire.com/ViewPressRel.asp?aId=112332.

2. Twitter correspondents in 2010 included Ben Lyons; Wolfgang Puck; Adam Shankman, the producer of the telecast; and Lorrin Millette from the marketing department of the telecast. Tammy Todd, "The Oscars Host a Twitter and Facebook Live Feed," March 7,

2010, http://www.examiner.com/twitter-entertainment-in-national/the-oscars-host-a
-twitter-feed-facebook-live-feed.

3. The older attractions such as Jurassic Park the Ride have pages devoted to them but do not offer the special links to such behind-the-scenes materials.

4. James Beniger, "Personalization of Mass Media and the Growth of the Pseudo-Community," *Communication Research* 14, no. 3 (1987): 352–71.

5. Sony Pictures Entertainment Museum, "Columbia Lady History," accessed April 6, 2011, http://www.sonypicturesmuseum.com/studio/history/columbia.

6. Josh Spector, "Web Museum Tells SPE History," *Hollywood Reporter,* October 10, 2003, Museums and Collections, 1996–1999, General Subject Files, AMPAS. The industry guilds, including SAG, DGA, and WGA, as well as AMPAS and ATAS, have recorded oral histories that serve as alternate or supplemental historical artifacts to traditional exhibition. Michael Goldman, "Preserving Hollywood's History," *Los Angeles Times,* November 29, 1997; Barbara Isenberg, "Capturing the Glory: Stories of the Small Screen's Earliest Days from Those Who Lived It," *Los Angeles Times,* November 29, 1997, F1, F10, F12.

7. Travis F. Smith, "Filmsite Has Unique Spin on Top Pix," *Variety,* July 8, 2003.

8. The poster images come from an affiliate relationship with Allposters and Moviegoods.

9. Tim Dirks e-mail message to author, August 25, 2010. These statistics come from Dirks's Google Analytic Reports, e-mail message to author, September 10, 2010. By 2010, two years after the acquisition, traffic has almost doubled.

10. Fox will retain a minority equity share in Flixster with some speculation that the media giant may buy back the combined company in the future. Ben Fritz, "News Corp. Sells Movie-Review Website," *Los Angeles Times,* January 5, 2010, B.3.

11. Twitter-based review sites also include fflick, flixup, mombo, and miso. Jason Kinkaid, "fflick's Sentiment Engine Turns Twitter into a Crowdsourced Movie Critic," *TechCrunch,* August 3, 2010, http://techcrunch.com/2010/08/03/fflick-movie-search-twitter.

12. Richard Siklos, "From a Small Stream: A Gusher of Movie Facts," *New York Times,* May 28, 2006; Col Needham, "A Letter from Our Founder, Col Needham," IMDb, October 17, 2010, http://www.imdb.com/features/anniversary/2010/letter; Alexa, "Top Sites in United States," accessed September 10, 2010, http://www.alexa.com/topsites/countries;1/US.

13. Other media was provided by CBS, Sony, and independent filmmakers according to Harrison Hoffman in "IMDb Now Serves Full Length Videos," *CNET News,* September 15, 2008, http://news.cnet.com/8301-13515_3-10042280-26.html.

14. Michael Cieply, "The Weekly Movie Scoreboard Motion Pictures Executives Debate the Value and Accuracy of Published Box Office Figures," October 5, 1987, 1. Cieply ties the shift in reporting to the computerization of statistics in the 1980s.

15. Others include Allmovie, Fandango and its subsidiary sites, movies.com, movieweb.com, and others. Fandango, which started out as a site collectively run by film exhibitors, was bought out by Comcast Interactive Media in 2007.

16. Chuck Tryon, *Reinventing Cinema: Movies in the Age of Media Convergence* (New Brunswick, NJ: Rutgers University Press, 2009).

17. Joshua Gamson, *Claims to Fame: Celebrity in Contemporary America* (Berkeley: University of California Press, 1994); P. David Marshall, *Celebrity and Power: Fame and Contemporary Culture* (Minneapolis, MN: University of Minnesota Press, 1997).

18. Less notable sites of the same ilk include blogs such as "Hollywood-Elsewhere." Some sites that attempt to emulate Knowles are Internet spinoffs of print publications. Deadline Hollywood began in this vein as a spinoff of a regular column in *LA Weekly*.

19. Lauren A. E. Schuker, "Site Brings Movies to Social Media," *Wall Street Journal*, December 3, 2009.

20. Movieclips, "About Movieclips," accessed April 4, 2011, http://movieclips.com/about/about_us.

21. Movieclips, "About Movieclips."

22. At the time of this writing, some of these sites include the following: Unexplained Cinema, home page, accessed April 21, 2011, http://unexplainedcinema.blogspot.com/; Cinema Styles: Music, Movies, Television, etc., home page, accessed April 21, 2011, http://cinemastyles.blogspot.com/; Obscure One Sheet, home page, accessed April 21, 2011, http://knifeinthehead.blogspot.com/; One Way Street, home page, accessed April 21, 2011, http://alanrode.xanga.com/; Anne Helen Petersen, Celebrity Gossip, Academic Style, accessed April 21, 2011, http://www.annehelenpetersen.com/; Glenn Kenny, Some Came Running: One of Those Foo Foo Film Sites, accessed April 21, 2011, http://somecamerunning.typepad.com/some_came_running; Tony Dayoub, Cinema Viewfinder, accessed April 21, 2011, http://www.cinemaviewfinder.com/; The Film Doctor: Notes on Cinema, home page, accessed April 21, 2011, http://filmdr.blogspot.com/; The Art of the Title Sequence, home page, accessed April 21, 2011, http://www.artofthetitle.com/; Erich Kuersten, Academic, accessed April 21, 2011, http://acidemic.blogspot.com/; One Day One Movie, home page, accessed April 21, 2011, http://movieoftheday.tumblr.com/; Movies in Frames, home page, accessed April 21, 2011, http://moviesinframes.tumblr.com/; Marya E. Gates, Cinema Fanatic, home page, accessed April 21, 2011, http://cinema-fanatic.com/; Pop Culture Ninja: Media on the Cutting Edge, home page, accessed April 21, 2011, http://popcultureninja.com/; Anatomy of a Classic: Frankly My Dears We Give a Damn, home page, accessed April 21, 2011, http://www.anatomyofaclassic.com/; Gore Girl's Dungeon: Hear Evil, See Evil, Speak Evil, home page, accessed April 21, 2011, http://goregirl.wordpress.com/; Octopus Cinema, home page, accessed April 21, 2011, http://octopuscinema.blogspot.com/; Stop the Planet of the Apes: I Want to Get Off, home page, accessed April 21, 2011, http://www.stopthepota.com/; A Life in Equinox: 5% Awesome, 95% Movies, 100% Random, home page, accessed April 21, 2011, http://univarn.blogspot.com/; and Pulp Truth, home page, accessed April 21, 2011, http://snobbyfilmguy.blogspot.com/.

Bibliography

Archival Sources

Academy of Motion Picture Arts and Sciences (AMPAS), Margaret Herrick Library,
   Special Collections
   AMPTP Collection
   Kuter Collection
   Mary Pickford Collection
AMPAS, Margaret Herrick Library, Biography Files
   Bart Lytton
   Mary Pickford
AMPAS, Margaret Herrick Library, General Subject Files
   American Cinematheque
   American Museum of the Moving Image
   Cinematheque Francaise
   George Eastman House
   Hollywood Entertainment Museum
   Hollywood Hall of Fame, 1956
   Hollywood Hall of Fame, 1976
   Hollywood Heritage, Inc.
   Hollywood Historic Trust
   Hollywood, Hollywood Hall of Fame
   Hollywood Memories Museum
   Hollywood Motion Picture and Television Museum
   Hollywood Museum
   Hollywood Museum, Le Bold
   Hollywood Studio Museum
   Hollywood Tours and Tourism
   Hollywood Wax Museum
   Lytton Center for the Visual Arts
   Max Factor Museum
   Motion Picture Exposition and Hall of Fame
   Movieland Wax Museum
   Museums and Collections, 1990
   Museum of Modern Art
   Museum of the Moving Image (MOMI)

Turner Entertainment

Universal Studios Tour

Museum of Modern Art (MoMA), New York

    Film Library Programs and Bulletins

    Film Library Scrapbooks, April 1935–April 1937

    Film Library, Special Collections

    Film Study Center, Special Collections

    Iris Barry Collection

    John Abbott Collection

    Museum of Modern Art Library

    Richard Griffith Collection, 1939–1950

Select Bibliography of Published Sources

Acland, Charles R. *Screen Traffic: Movies, Multiplexes, and Global Culture.* Durham, NC: Duke
University Press, 2003.

Adams, Bluford. *E Pluribus Barnum: The Great Showman and the Making of U.S. Popular
Culture.* Minneapolis: University of Minnesota Press, 1997.

Anderson, Christopher. *Hollywood TV: The Studio System in the Fifties.* Austin: University
of Texas Press, 1994.

Bennett, Tony. *The Birth of the Museum: History, Theory, Politics.* New York: Routledge,
1995.

Boddy, William. *New Media and Popular Imagination: Launching Radio, Television and Digital
Media in the United States.* New York: Oxford University Press, 2004.

Bommes, Michael, and Patrick Wright. "'Charms of Residence': The Public and the
Past." In *Making Histories: Studies in History Writing and Politics,* edited by Richard
Johnson, Gregor McLennan, Bill Schwarz, and David Sutton. London: Hutchinson,
1982.

Bordwell, David. *On the History of Film Style.* Cambridge, MA: Harvard University Press,
1997.

Bottomore, Stephen. "'The Collection of Rubbish.' Animatographs, Archives and
Arguments: London, 1896–97." *Film History* 7, no. 3 (Autumn 1995): 291–97.

Bourdieu, Pierre. *Distinction: A Social Critique of the Judgment of Taste.* Translated by
Richard Nice. Cambridge, MA: Harvard University Press, 1984.

Bourdieu, Pierre, and Alain Darbel. *The Love of Art: European Art Museums and Their Public.*
Translated by Caroline Beattie and Nick Merriman. Stanford, CA: Stanford
University Press, 1990.

Braudy, Leo. *The Hollywood Sign: Fantasy and Reality of an American Icon.* New Haven: Yale
University Press, 2011.

Clifford, James. *The Predicament of Culture: Twentieth-Century Ethnography, Literature and Art.*
Cambridge, MA: Harvard University Press, 1988.

Cooke, Lynn, and Peter Woolen, eds. *Visual Display: Culture beyond Appearances*. Seattle: Bay Press, 1995.

Davis, Mike. *City of Quartz: Excavating the Future in Los Angeles*. New York: Random House, 1992.

Decherney, Peter. *Hollywood and the Culture Elite: How the Movies Became American*. New York: Columbia University Press, 2005.

DeCordova, Richard. *Picture Personalities: The Emergence of the Star System in America*. Urbana: University of Illinois Press, 1990.

Duncan, Carol. *Civilizing Rituals: Inside Public Art Museums*. New York: Routledge, 1995.

Eckart, Charles. "The Carole Lombard in Macy's Window." *Quarterly Review of Film Studies* 3, no. 1 (Winter 1978): 1–21.

Eco, Umberto. *Travels in Hyperreality*. Translated by William Weaver. New York: Harcourt, 1983.

Elsaesser, Thomas. *European Cinema Face to Face with Hollywood*. Amsterdam: Amsterdam University Press, 2005.

———. *New German Cinema: A History*. New Brunswick, NJ: Rutgers University Press, 1989.

Ferreux, Hugette Marquand. *Musée du Cinéma Henri Langlois*. Paris: Maeght éditeur, 1991.

Feuer, Jane. "The Concept of Live Television: Ontology as Ideology." In *Regarding Television, Critical Approaches: An Anthology*, edited by E. Ann Kaplan. Los Angeles: American Film Institute, 1983.

Findlay, John M. *Magic Lands: Western Cityscapes and American Culture after 1940*. Berkeley: University of California Press, 1992.

Friedberg, Anne. *The Virtual Window: From Alberti to Microsoft*. Cambridge, MA: MIT Press, 2006.

Fuller, Kathryn. *At the Picture Show: Small-Town Audiences and the Creation of Movie Fan Culture*. Washington, DC: Smithsonian, 1996.

Gamson, Joshua. *Claims to Fame: Celebrity in Contemporary America*. Berkeley: University of California Press, 1994.

Goffman, Erving. *The Presentation of Self in Everyday Life*. Garden City, NY: Doubleday, 1959.

Goldfarb Marquis, Alice. *Alfred H. Barr: Missionary for the Modern*. Chicago: Contemporary Books, 1989.

Gomery, Douglas. *Shared Pleasures: A History of Movie Presentation in the United States*. Madison: University of Wisconsin Press, 1992.

Gottdiener, Mark. *The Theming of America: Dreams, Visions, and Commercial Spaces*. Boulder, CO: Westview, 1997.

Handler, Richard, and Eric Gable. *The New History in an Old Museum: Creating the Past at Colonial Williamsburg*. Durham, NC: Duke University Press, 1997.

Hannigan, John. *Fantasy City: Pleasure and Profit in the Postmodern Metropolis*. New York: Routledge, 1998.

Hansen, Miriam. *Babel and Babylon: Spectatorship in American Silent Film.* Cambridge, MA: Harvard University Press, 1991.

Hark, Ina Rae, ed. *Exhibition: The Film Reader.* New York: Routledge, 2002.

Harris, Neil. *Cultural Excursions: Marketing Appetites and Cultural Tastes in Modern America.* Chicago: University of Chicago Press, 1990.

———. "Museums, Merchandising and Popular Taste: The Struggle for Influence." In *Material Culture and the Study of American Life,* edited by Ian M. G. Quimby. New York: Norton, 1978.

Harvey, Sylvia. *May 1968 and Film Culture.* London: British Film Institute, 1978.

Herbert, Stephen, ed. "Film Museums." *Film History: An International Journal* 18, no. 3 (2006).

Herrnstein Smith, Barbara. *Contingencies of Value: Alternative Perspectives for Critical Theory.* Cambridge, MA: Harvard University Press, 1988.

Hiller, Jim, ed. *Cahiers du Cinéma: The 1950s: Neorealism, Hollywood, New Wave.* Cambridge, MA: Harvard University Press, 1985.

Horak, Chris. "The Hollywood History Business." In *The End of Cinema As We Know It: American Cinema in the Nineties,* edited by Jon Lewis. New York: New York University Press, 2001.

Horak, Jan-Christopher, ed. *Lovers of Cinema: The First American Film Avant-Garde, 1919–1945.* Madison: University of Wisconsin Press, 1995.

Houston, Penelope. *Keepers of the Frame: The Film Archives.* London: British Film Institute, 1994.

Huyssen, Andreas. *Twilight Memories: Marking Time in a Culture of Amnesia.* New York: Routledge, 1995.

James, David E. *The Most Typical Avant-Garde: History and Geography of Minor Cinemas in Los Angeles.* Berkeley: University of California Press, 2005.

Jones, Janna. *The Southern Movie Palace: Rise, Fall, and Resurrection.* Gainesville: University Press of Florida, 2003.

Judd, Dennis R., and Susan S. Fainstein. *The Tourist City.* New Haven, CT: Yale University Press, 1999.

Kapsis, Robert E. *Hitchcock: The Making of a Reputation.* Chicago: University of Chicago Press, 1992.

Karp, Ivan, and Steven D. Lavine. *Exhibiting Cultures: The Poetics and Politics of Museum Display.* Washington, DC: Smithsonian, 1991.

Klinger, Barbara. *Beyond the Multiplex: Cinema, New Technologies and the Home.* Berkeley: University of California Press, 2006.

———. "The Contemporary Cinephile: Film Collecting in the Post-Video Era." In *Hollywood Spectatorship: Changing Perceptions of Cinema Audiences,* edited by Melvyn Stokes and Richard Maltby. London: British Film Institute, 2001.

———. "The New Media Aristocrats: Home Theater and the Domestic Film Experience." *Velvet Light Trap* 42 (Fall 1998): 4–19.

Koszarski, Richard. *An Evening's Entertainment: The Age of the Silent Feature Picture, 1915–1928*. New York: Macmillan, 1990.

Leach, William. *Land of Desire: Merchants, Power, and the Rise of a New American Culture.* New York: Vintage, 1993.

Levine, Lawrence. *Highbrow/Lowbrow: The Emergence of Cultural Hierarchy in America.* Cambridge, MA: Harvard University Press, 1988.

Lewis, Jon. *The End of Cinema As We Know It: American Film in the Nineties.* New York: New York University Press, 2001.

Lindsay, Vachel. *The Art of the Moving Picture.* New York: Liveright, 1970.

Lowenthal, David. *The Past Is a Foreign Country.* Cambridge: Cambridge University Press, 1985.

Lumley, Robert, ed. *The Museum Time Machine: Putting Cultures on Display.* London: Routledge, 1988.

Lynes, Russell. *Good Old Modern: An Intimate Portrait of the Museum of Modern Art.* New York: Atheneum, 1973.

MacCannell, Dean. *The Tourist: A New Theory of the Leisure Class.* New York: Schocken, 1976.

Malraux, André. *The Voices of Silence.* Translated by Stuart Gilbert. Princeton, NJ: Princeton University Press, 1990.

Marchand, Roland. *Creating the Corporate Soul: The Rise of Public Relations and Corporate Imagery in American Big Business.* Berkeley: University of California Press, 1998.

Marshall, P. David. *Celebrity and Power: Fame and Contemporary Culture.* Minneapolis: University of Minnesota Press, 1997.

Marvin, Carolyn. *When Old Technologies Were New: Thinking About Electric Communication in the Late Nineteenth Century.* New York: Oxford University Press, 1988.

McCarthy, Anna. *Ambient Television: Visual Culture and Public Space.* Durham, NC: Duke University Press, 2001.

McGreevey, Tom, and Joanne L. Yeck. *Our Movie Heritage.* New Brunswick, NJ: Rutgers University Press, 1997.

McLuhan, Marshall. *Understanding Media: The Extensions of Man*, edited by Lewis H. Lapham. Cambridge, MA: MIT Press, 1994.

Meyrowitz, Joshua. *No Sense of Place: The Impact of Electronic Media on Social Behavior.* New York: Oxford University Press, 1985.

Miller, Toby, Nitin Govil, John McMurria, and Richard Maxwell. *Global Hollywood.* London: British Film Institute, 2001.

Miller, Toby, Nitin Govil, John McMurria, Richard Maxwell, and Ting Wang. *Global Hollywood 2*. London: British Film Institute, 2005.

Myrent, Glenn, and Georges P. Langlois. *Henri Langlois: First Citizen of the Cinema.* New York: Twayne, 1995.

Pesenti Campagnoni, Donata. "Tra Patrimonio Filmico e Patrimonio Cinematografico: Alcune tracce storiche sui musei del Cinema e dintorni." *Notizario Dell'Associazione Museo Nazionale Del Cinema* 49–50 (1997): 21–32.

Polan, Dana. *Scenes of Instruction: The Beginnings of the U.S. Study of Film*. Berkeley: University of California Press, 2007.

Powdermaker, Hortense. *Hollywood, the Dream Factory: An Anthropologist Looks at the Movie-Makers*. Boston: Little, Brown, 1950.

Prince, Stephen. *A New Pot of Gold: Hollywood under the Electronic Rainbow, 1980–1989*. New York: Scribner, 2000.

Robbins, Bruce, ed. *The Phantom Public Sphere*. Minneapolis: University of Minnesota Press, 1993.

Rotha, Paul. "A Museum for the Cinema." In *Rotha on Film: A Selection of Writings About Cinema*. Fairlawn, NJ: Essential Books, 1958.

Roud, Richard. *A Passion for Films: Henri Langlois and the Cinematheque Française*. New York: Viking, 1983.

Rubin, Joan Shelley. *The Making of Middlebrow Culture*. Chapel Hill: University of North Carolina Press, 1992.

Sherman, Daniel J., and Irit Rogoff, eds. *Museum Culture: Histories, Discourses, Spectacles*. Minneapolis: University of Minnesota Press, 1994.

Sklar, Robert. *Movie-Made America: A Cultural History of American Movies*. New York: Vintage, 1975.

Slide, Anthony. *Nitrate Won't Wait: Film Preservation in the United States*. Jefferson, NC: McFarland, 1992.

Sorkin, Michael, ed. *Variations on a Theme Park: The New American City and the End of Public Space*. New York: Hill & Wang, 1992.

Spigel, Lynn. "High Culture in Low Places: Television and Modern Art, 1950–1970." In *Disciplinarity and Dissent in Cultural Studies*, edited by Cary Nelson and Dilip Parameshwar Gaonkar. New York: Routledge, 1996.

———. *Make Room for TV: Television and the Family Ideal in Postwar America*. Chicago: University of Chicago Press, 1992.

———. "The Making of a TV Literate Elite." In *The Television Studies Book*, edited by Christine Geraghty and David Lusted. London: Edward Arnold, 1998.

———. *TV by Design: Modern Art and the Rise of Network Television*. Chicago: University of Chicago Press, 2008.

Stenger, Josh. "Consuming the Planet: Planet Hollywood, Stars, and the Global Consumer Culture." *Velvet Light Trap* 40 (Fall 1997): 42–55.

Sturken, Marita. *Tangled Memories*. Berkeley: University of California Press, 1997.

Susman, Warren. *Culture as History: The Transformation of American Society in the Twentieth Century*. New York: Pantheon, 1984.

Thompson, Kristin. *Exporting Entertainment: America in the World Film Market, 1907–1934*. London: British Film Institute, 1986.

Topelitz, Jerry. *Hollywood and After: The Changing Face of American Movies*. New York: Vintage, 1975.

Tryon, Chuck. *Reinventing Cinema: Movies in the Age of Media Convergence*. New Brunswick, NJ: Rutgers University Press, 2009.

Usai, Paolo Cherchi. *Burning Passions: An Introduction to the Study of Silent Film*. London: British Film Institute, 1994.

Vergo, Peter, ed. *The New Museology*. London: Reaktion Books, 1989.

Waller, Gregory. *Moviegoing in America: A Sourcebook in the History of Film Exhibition*. Malden, MA: Blackwell, 2002.

Waller, Gregory, and Charles Musser, eds. *Main Street Amusements: Movies and Commercial Entertainment in a Southern City*. Washington, DC: Smithsonian, 1995.

Wasko, Janet. *Hollywood in the Information Age: Beyond the Silver Screen*. Austin: University of Texas Press, 1995.

Wasser, Frederick. *Veni, Vidi, Video: The Hollywood Empire and the VCR*. Austin: University of Texas Press, 2001.

Wasson, Haidee. *Museum Movies: The Museum of Modern Art and the Birth of Art Cinema*. Berkeley: University of California Press, 2005.

Wilinsky, Barbara. *Sure Seaters: The Emergence of Art House Cinema*. Minneapolis: University of Minnesota Press, 2001.

Wreszin, Michael. *A Rebel in Defense of Tradition: The Life and Politics of Dwight MacDonald*. New York: Basic Books, 1994.

Young, Terence, and Robert Riley, eds. *Theme Park Landscapes: Antecedents and Variations*. Washington, DC: Dumbarton Oaks Research Library and Collection, 2002.

Zukin, Sharon. *Landscapes of Power: From Detroit to Disneyland*. Berkeley: University of California Press, 1991.

Index

Page numbers in *italics* refer to illustrations.